Young America's
COOK
BOOK

REVISED EDITION

Revised by DOROTHY CALLAHAN *and* ALMA SMITH PAYNE

CHARLES SCRIBNER'S SONS   *NEW YORK*

ACKNOWLEDGMENTS

Grateful acknowledgment is made to the following for their contributions to the preparation of this book and for help in the development of the new edition:

THE STAFF OF THE NEW YORK HERALD TRIBUNE HOME INSTITUTE where the original recipes were developed and tested and particularly to Esther Foley, B.S., Syracuse University, as head of the food testing laboratories

THE AMERICAN HOME ECONOMICS ASSOCIATION for permission to use materials from its publication *Handbook of Food Preparation,* prepared by the Terminology Committee of the Food and Nutrition Section

BETTY CROCKER of GENERAL MILLS, INC. for permission to use her Lemon Chiffon Cake recipe and for useful suggestions

NUTRITION SERVICE, STATE OF CALIFORNIA DEPARTMENT OF PUBLIC HEALTH, for permission to use material from its publication, *Is Potluck Lucky?*

MRS. FRANCES PROUT, former Home Economics Teacher, San Antonio, Texas Public Schools

THE UNIVERSITY OF CALIFORNIA DIVISION OF AGRICULTURAL SCIENCES, and particularly Hilda Faust, Ph.D., for assistance and materials on frozen desserts, preparing and freezing foods and home canning

UNITED STATES DEPARTMENT OF AGRICULTURE for assistance and materials on essential food groups, home freezing, home canning, dishwashing procedures and dehydrated foods

WESTINGHOUSE HOME ECONOMICS INSTITUTE for use of material from its bulletin, *Home Freezing Guide*

Through the courtesy of the following contributors, the photographs are reproduced in this new edition:

The Aluminum Cooking Utensil Co., Inc., 249; Alcoa Wrap, 289 bottom

American Meat Institute, page 12

Castleton China, Inc., 155 left

General Foods Kitchens, Swans Down Cake Flour, 155 right, 177

Rhoda Johnson, 51, 290, and the photographs listed below taken at Milton, Massachusetts

The Home Economics Department of the Milton Public Schools, Milton, Massachusetts, photos by Rhoda Johnson, 13, 43 top and bottom, 97, 107 top, 131, 144, 159, 208, 218, 219, 231, 235, 243, 254, 305. Equipment supplied by the Boston Edison Company, 44, 158, 261, 264

National Live Stock and Meat Board, 89 top and bottom

New York State College of Home Economics at Cornell University, 5, 137, 215

Pillsbury Mills, Inc., 43 middle

Poultry and Egg National Board, 39, 98

Reynolds Metals Company, 107 bottom

United Fresh Fruit and Vegetable Association, 117

United States Department of Agriculture, 11, 168, 289 top; Bureau of Home Nutrition and Home Economics, 89 middle

Aaron Weingarten, 7

Wheat Flour Institute, photographs by Fred G. Korth, 149, 273

Youngstown Kitchens, title page

PREFACE

IT IS with pleasure that we present this revision of *Young America's Cook Book*. The original edition contained a great deal of basic information much of which is as usable as when first published in 1938.

Since that time, however, food technology has brought about many changes in our eating and cooking habits. We have frozen, canned, dehydrated, instant and ready-mixes that combine easy preparation and good results. Speeded-up transportation and efficient packaging have made perishable and seasonal foods available the year round. Kitchen equipment and utensils assure uniform preparation with a minimum of effort.

A new desire has developed for food that is not only well and easily cooked but varied and imaginative. Herbs and spices are used for flavor subtlety. We are intrigued by the dishes of other countries and have adapted them to our basic American cuisine. Nowadays everyone in the family cooks—including the boys and Father. It's a social asset to know how to cook some specialty. Nutrition education has taught us that meals must be well balanced as well as good to eat.

Schools and colleges through their home economics courses are showing us that modern equipment and products help to make cooking simple and satisfying to all. Cooking as a creative outlet as well as a sound skill is the theme of our times.

Additions and changes along these lines have therefore been incorporated in this cook book by Dorothy Callahan and Alma Smith Payne, who have made this revision. You will find in the introductory sections standards of an adequate diet to assist you in meal planning; marketing tips; care of the kitchen; table setting and manners too. Canning and freezing procedures have been brought up-to-date. You'll pick up lots of ideas for barbecuing, picnicking, the one-dish meal, your lunch box, and parties of every kind—from the simple snack for the unexpected drop-ins to the complete dinner party to do on your own. Included are menus and recipes for many of your special interests—vacationing at beach or cottage, fishing and camping, festivities for all occasions.

PREFACE

This book is for you, the beginning cook, who wants to know some of the fundamentals of cookery, how to be proficient and have fun in the kitchen. We hope it will appeal to you and that the basic techniques and time-tested recipes will become a treasured collection for the years ahead.

The New York Herald Tribune
CLEMENTINE PADDLEFORD, *Food Editor*
ISABEL A. McGOVERN, *Home Economist*
EUGENIA SHEPPARD, *Women's Feature Editor*

CONTENTS

So You Are Going to Cook!

Knowing how to cook will give you a very agreeable sense of accomplishment and independence. Your sweet tooth, craving fudge, may start you off. Your initiation may be a stack of flapjacks one crisp morning at camp. But from the very beginning you will find it pleasant indeed to be able to turn out something good to eat—even if it is only a hamburger, grilled and seasoned just exactly right. Hiking, camping, your turn to entertain the crowd, emergencies at home, are all times when the competent cook comes into his own.

There is just enough suspense in cooking to keep you on tip-toe. Can you imagine how you will feel the first time you open an oven door, to find a pan of popovers light as ping-pong balls? Cooking is as fascinating a hobby as any you can name, and cooks collect recipes as stamp collectors do stamps.

It's Smart to Cook

Nowadays, it is smart to cook. Girls about to be married might have boasted once that all they could make was fudge and marguerites. But not any more! You don't hear so many men and boys say that they can't boil water. Men and women prominent in public affairs and society, home girls and career women, writers, athletes, princesses and opera stars are taking up cooking with enthusiasm and getting fun out of it. Smart hosts and hostesses are tying on aprons, for the kitchen is the new party room. By and by you will have your own specialties and be famous among your friends for them. Even good sandwiches make for easy hospitality. See illustration on *page 5*.

Know What to Cook and Why

If you are ambitious to know all about cooking, you will be interested in what you should cook and why. *The right food keeps you well.* More than anything else, it is the food you eat that keeps you straight and tall, and makes your teeth strong and beautiful, your hair shining with health, lips red and muscles fit. You need good food, and enough of it, to grow as you should, to see well, to study, to walk and dance and sing. You need it to sleep and rest. You cannot be happy without it. It affects your disposition.

As you cook ask yourself occasionally, "Am I giving enough thought to what I am selecting to cook?" Check up and see if you are choosing enough of the "protective" foods. They include:

Milk group: Some milk daily—
Children   3 to 4 cups
Teen-agers   4 or more cups
Adults   2 or more cups
Cheese and ice cream can replace part of the milk.

Meat group: 2 or more servings daily—
Beef, veal, pork, lamb, poultry, fish, eggs, with dry beans, dry peas and nuts as alternates.

Vegetable-fruit group: 4 or more servings daily, including—
A dark-green or deep-yellow vegetable important for Vitamin A—at least every other day.
A citrus fruit or other fruit or vegetable important for Vitamin C—daily.
Other fruits and vegetables including potatoes.

Bread-cereals group: 4 or more servings daily—
Whole grain, enriched, restored.

A girl who picks at her breakfast, or who skips it entirely, cannot make up at the other two meals for what she has missed. Bolting breakfast on the run will not give a boy the stamina that a game of football or tennis requires. Eating all the roast beef and skipping the carrots, gobbling a double dessert and ignoring the salad, is not playing fair with health. But choosing the right foods is not the whole story. Food must be prepared so that it retains its natural goodness and has eye and taste appeal.

The Kitchen Holds a Challenge

To know what to cook and why is an accomplishment, but to put this knowledge to work in the kitchen is a definite challenge. Meal planning, marketing, proper refrigeration and cooking methods all add to keeping the family better fed. Attractive service contributes to making mealtimes a gracious part of daily living.

Suggestions for the Beginning Cook. When you prepare whole meals the real joy in cooking begins. Think of pleasant combinations in foods and nutritional values. Plan to have contrasts in color, flavor and texture. Consider cost, time of preparation and method of service to be used. Plan meals which you can manage easily and smoothly, with no unnecessary labor in cooking, serving or clearing away.

Take stock of cooking space, available equipment and labor-saving devices so that they are used to best advantage. If the kitchen boasts electrical equipment such as beaters and mixers, a food blender, toaster, waffle iron and grill, coffee maker, French fryer or rotisserie, learn how to use and care for such equipment by studying the manufacturer's directions.

Make use of frozen, dehydrated and other prepared foods, mixes and labor-saving aids now available so that you can concentrate in the beginning on one or two well prepared dishes for each meal. Include hearty soups, casseroles or meat loaves which can be made ahead of use and reheated at time of serving.

Of course, you will want to keep in mind the family's likes and dislikes —introducing some new foods and serving some old favorites.

To Market, To Market. Plan your market order carefully to save both time and money. It is more practical to shop for three or four days supplies at one time, but the method is the same whether for one recipe, one meal or one week.

1. Obtain reliable recipes for each item on your menu.
2. List the kind and amount of supplies needed.
3. Check the list against your present stores.
4. Make a final list of the items to be purchased, grouping together the items to be purchased in the same store or section of the store.

Demand quality and shop around until you find it. Meat should be government inspected and graded. Vegetables should be garden fresh—wilted vegetables mean a loss in food value and flavor. Fruits should be firm without bruises—but should not be tested by squeezing or pinching. Brown and white eggs have the same food value and cooking qualities.

Be "penny-wise" when you shop. Cash and carry is the rule to stretch the food dollar. Watch for sales—five cents saved each day means $18.25 at the end of the year. Read labels on packaged and canned items, and check weights. The larger package or bottle may have a false bottom. Buy staples in large quantities whenever possible. Buy fresh produce in large quantities if you have adequate refrigeration and freezer space; otherwise, only in amounts for immediate use. Prepared mixes, puddings and the like are more costly than home-prepared products, but are real time-savers for special occasions. Space-savers, too, for camping stores.

Proper Refrigeration Is a Must. Efficient planning and marketing must be followed by efficient handling of the food in the home. Refrigerate all fresh foods briefly and prepare them just as close to eating time as possible. Food left sitting on the kitchen table represents not only loss in food value and flavor, but also, a definite health hazard. Meat should be unwrapped and placed immediately in the meat storage section of your refrigerator. Fresh vegetables and fruits (except tubers and bananas) should be washed and whisked into the food crisper. Dairy products require immediate refrigeration, too—eggs and butter away from foods with strong odors, such as cheese. Frozen foods require a storage temperature below freezing. Once defrosted, frozen products must be treated as fresh food. Never attempt to refreeze any thawed frozen food.

The versatile sandwich—for Ribbon Sandwiches (*page* 194) alternate slices of whole wheat and white bread.

Pinwheel Sandwiches (*page* 197) with bread sliced long way of loaf.

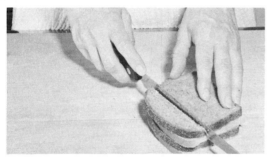

Remove crusts and spread with softened butter and filling.

Spread with cream cheese filling and roll tightly around olives.

Wrap and chill ½ hour.

Cut into thin ribbon slices and into triangles and thirds for dainty sandwiches.

Cut into ¼-inch slices just before serving.

Leftovers should be refrigerated promptly. Larger quantities of food (amounts that might raise the internal temperature of the refrigerator above 45° F.) should be cooled *quickly* to room temperature before refrigerating. With some foods, cooling can be hastened by spreading in a shallow container and stirring occasionally. Ready-to-serve food *kept longer than one hour* at room temperature may be contaminated with food poisoning bacteria. Creamed foods, cream-filled or custard-filled foods, sandwich and salad fillings (such as egg, chicken or fish) are high on the danger list. Prepare sandwich and salad fillings as near to serving time as possible, and then keep under refrigeration until used.

Give Thought, Even in the Simplest Meal, to Attractive Service. Suit your table setting to the occasion. Bare boards and paper plates are fine for the picnic or barbecue, and tray tables just right for the T.V. snack. But to enhance the enjoyment of the everyday meal, spotless linen or gay place mats, shining tableware, and sparkling glasses and dishes add glamor to even the simplest meal. A centerpiece—if just a pot of flowers or a bowl of fruit—adds much to the appearance of the table. This should be low so as not to obstruct the vision of those at the table. The table should be well-balanced, with the *covers* (a cover is the space and utensils used by one person at one meal) equal distances apart. Above all, avoid over-crowding the table.

Setting the Table. Except when using a lace tablecloth or table mats, use a table pad to protect the table and to help prevent noise. Lay the table-cloth with crease folding upwards, centered in the middle and running the length of the table. Lay the plate for each cover and then the silver in the order to be used. The silver used first is placed farthest from the plate. The knife, with the sharp edge towards the plate, and the spoons are placed to the right of the plate; the forks, with the tines pointing upwards, to the left of the plate. If no knife is used, the fork is placed to the right of the plate. The dessert silver is often served with the dessert. Place the glass at the tip of the knife and the bread and butter plate at the tip of the fork. Place the butter spreader either horizontally or vertically on the bread and butter plate. The napkin goes to the left of the fork, with the open corner at the lower right-hand corner. Place serving silver, salt and pepper shakers, sugar bowl and cream pitcher, following horizontal or lengthwise lines. Place chairs at each cover so that they can be used without too much moving in or out. Except on round tables, the lower edge of each cover should form a straight line, about one inch from the edge of the table. On round tables, the lower edge of each cover is a straight line, but is not parallel with the edge of the table.

Serving the Meal. The best-prepared meal and the most attractive table can be spoiled with hurried, careless serving. The dining room should be well-aired; the lighting neither too bright nor too dim.

An attractively-set table, as suggested in this place setting, goes hand in hand with careful planning and good preparations. (The salad knife, included in this setting, is correct though optional.)

There are several methods of serving the meal. In *formal style* service, a waiter or waitress serves each item of food to each guest. Today most of us do not have the help necessary for this type of service. In *buffet style* service, the utensils and food are placed on the table and the guests serve themselves, but are not actually seated at the table. This style is often used when entertaining large groups. *Family* or *English style* is most popular and is probably the type that we are most familiar with. The serving dishes of food are placed on the table and either served by the host and hostess, or passed to those at the table who serve themselves. (A hot pad is placed under the serving dish if there is no table pad to protect the table.)

There is no set rule for serving. Sometimes convenience dictates the method of service to be used. For T.V. or garden meals, informality will be the rule. But for general use, one accepted form is to pass and take away all foods from the left, beverages from the right, using the hand farthest away from the guest. Clear away leftover food and serving dishes first, and then used dishes. When necessary, the table is crumbed with a folded napkin and plate, and water glasses are refilled.

★   ★   ★   ★

As you select, prepare and serve an attractive meal and leave a clean kitchen you will be joining the many other young people, who, too, are learning the satisfaction of "turning out" a tasteful meal.

There Is No Guesswork in Our Kitchen

Cooking, nowadays, is an accurate job. Your grandmother may have blamed the weather if the cake failed to rise or the jelly did not jell, but the modern cook knows better. Guesswork has gone out of the kitchen. Learn how to follow a recipe.

Use Ingredients Called For. If the recipe calls for cake flour, you may not substitute all-purpose flour and expect the same cake that the recipe promises. *Unless otherwise stated, use all-purpose flour in all recipes which call for flour.* Your own good sense will tell you that you cannot expect success when the ingredients you use are different from those used when the recipe was developed. *However, margarine can be substituted for butter in all recipes.*

Measure Accurately. On *page* 11 you can see and study a picture of the most commonly used standard tools for measuring ingredients. Learn to use them properly. Use level measurements.

When you measure *flour*, sift it first, then pile it lightly into the cup and level off with your spatula. Level off *granulated sugar*, but press *brown sugar* down into the cup so that it holds the cup's shape when you turn it out. When you measure *liquids*, keep the cup flat on the table; you will then be sure of level measurement. When you measure *butter* or *other shortening* in amounts under one-fourth cup, use a tablespoon. Press shortening down into cup or spoon and scrape off level with the spatula.

9

How to measure shortening by the *water displacement method*, which many cooks prefer to do, we can best explain by an example. If you wish to measure one-half cup of shortening, put one-half cup of water into the measuring cup. Add just enough shortening to make the water reach the one-cup line. Pour off the water. You have left one-half cup shortening. To measure butter in the *print*, remember that one pound equals two cups, and that one stick, or one-fourth pound, equals one-half cup.

Baking powder and other ingredients used in small amounts are measured in the measuring spoons and leveled off accurately with the spatula.

Measure Heat and Time. A good cook must measure *heat* and *time*, as well as ingredients. Most modern ranges have oven thermometers and heat controls attached and they are a joy to work with. All you have to do is set them. (Some skillets and saucepans, too.) Other ranges have just the thermometers which register but do not control oven temperature. You must regulate the heat yourself.

Note when a dish goes into the oven or on the top of the range. See that it comes out or off at the right time. If you have an alarm clock, one attached to the range, perhaps, set it for the time a dish will finish. It will call you!

Some ranges come with time clocks attached which turn the heat off at the right time. Some, indeed, turn themselves on and off—so that you can slip a whole meal into the oven, set the heat control and time clock, be off, and come back to find the food cooked and waiting. But thermometers and heat controls cannot take over all the job. You must be alert. Attachments *can* get out of order. Have them repaired if necessary to insure good results.

Portable Thermometers. If your range has no oven attachments, you can still *measure* the heat and *control* it, too. Get a portable oven thermometer.

Prerequisites
for success:

Don't guess. Measure accurately. Use standard measuring cups and spoons. Sift flour before measuring. Make level measurements (see *page* 9).

The little spent on one will repay the cost over and over again in good food saved, and in the pleasure of food cooked exactly right. An oven thermometer will not control the heat of your oven—but it will tell you when you should turn the heat up or down.

Turn to *page* 13 and see the picture of an oven thermometer—and while you are at it, look at the thermometers to measure heat when you are deep fat frying, candy making, and roasting meats.

Work in an Orderly Way. Following a recipe takes *management*. Organize your worktable so that everything is out that needs to be out, everything within reach that should be, even the ingredients and equipment should be in convenient order.

You will notice that in many of the basic recipes given in this book the necessary utensils are listed, and the order of work given.

Take guesswork out of your kitchen. Don't be made to eat your mistakes! It's lots more fun to follow the parachute jumper's example and do it right the first time.

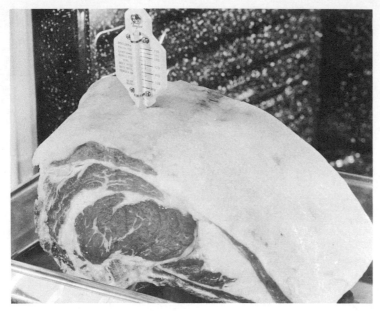

The meat thermometer—the surest and simplest way to determine when meat is done. Note clear markings indicating degrees F. and stage of doneness for each kind of meat.

Timing is important in all cooking, and especially when planning a meal. Plan for dishes that are to be eaten at the same time to finish at the same time. Be sure the jellied salad is chilled and set perfectly when you are ready to bring it on. Allow it plenty of time. Don't have a soufflé out of the oven and waiting for the vegetables to finish cooking, or for the table to be set. That soufflé will shrivel and wrinkle right up! When you are new at the game, and you have a whole meal to do, write down in black and white the time you estimate each dish will take to mix and cook. Follow your schedule and then—especially if you are having guests—half your mind will not be on the kitchen and you will be able to give full attention to your friends.

The Right Tools. The right tools for every job are in a well-ordered kitchen. That doesn't mean expensive tools, nor that the kitchen is cluttered with gadgets. One good sharp paring knife is better than two half-sharp ones. Better one good long knife that does several jobs well, than several that do no job well. And, incidentally, when knives are in plain view in a rack, they are more easily and safely reached and edges keep

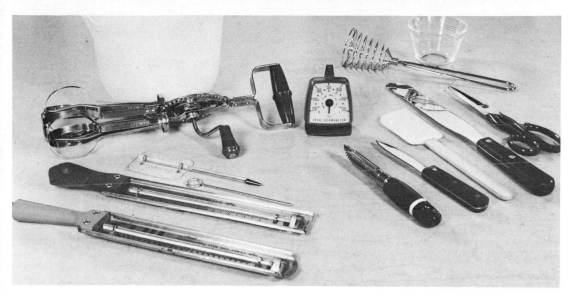

Good cooks have good tools—thermometers for accuracy, the right tools for efficiency.

sharper than when stored in a drawer with other tools. To protect blades, cut food on a board and use a sawing motion whenever possible.

Try to use food thermometers to take guesswork out of cooking. A meat thermometer will tell you when the meat is done to suit your family's taste—rare, medium or well done. A candy thermometer is an aid to creamy fudge and tasty frostings.

Best Tool for Each Job. It is fun to work out better and simpler ways to do things. The picture above will give you a few suggestions that clever cooks have figured out.

Use scissors for cutting up dates, for mincing parsley. Use them in preparing salads. They shred lettuce like magic. Cut up chicken with them; dice bacon, cut marshmallows—better dip the blades in water after each cut.

A good, sturdy beater saves time and energy. It does a better job than a cheaper one, and far outlasts it.

Whip cream in a deep, narrow conical bowl; the beater will work faster and there will not be much spattering. Try using a little egg beater and a very small bowl or cup when you have just one egg to beat. Suit the size of bowl to the number of eggs.

Use an apple corer to pare carrots ever so thin, if you don't want to scrape them. The slit in the corer does an excellent job.

We could go on indefinitely, for there is a knife, beater, spoon, bowl, kettle and pan for every task in the kitchen and a right and wrong way to use each. Good workmen have good tools.

Guideposts To Success

TERMS COMMONLY USED
TO DESCRIBE OVEN TEMPERATURES

Temperature degrees F.	*Term*
250 and 275	Very slow
300 and 325	Slow
350 and 375	Moderate
400 and 425	Hot
450 and 475	Very hot
500 and 525	Extremely hot

TEMPERATURES AND TIME USED IN BAKING

Type of Product	*Oven Temperature degrees F.*	*Baking Time minutes*
Breads, etc.		
Biscuits	425 to 450	10 to 15
Corn bread	400 to 425	30 to 40
Cream puffs	375	60
Muffins	400 to 425	20 to 25
Popovers	375	60

Type of Product	Oven Temperature degrees F.	Baking Time minutes
Quick loaf breads	350 to 375	60 to 75
Yeast bread	400	30 to 40
Yeast rolls, plain	400 to 425	15 to 25
sweet	375	20 to 30
Cakes with fat		
Cup	350 to 375	15 to 25
Layer	375	20 to 30
Loaf	350	45 to 60
Cakes without fat		
Angel food and sponge	350 to 375	30 to 45
Cookies		
Drop	350 to 400	8 to 15
Rolled	375	8 to 10
Egg, meat, milk and cheese dishes		
Cheese soufflé (baked in a pan of hot water)	350	30 to 60
Custard, plain, corn, etc. (baked in a pan of hot water)	350	30 to 60
Macaroni and cheese	350	25 to 30
Meat loaf	300	60 to 90
Meat pie	400	25 to 30
Rice pudding (raw rice)	300	120 to 180
Scalloped potatoes	350	60
Pastry		
One-crust pie (custard type), unbaked shell	400 to 425	30 to 40
Meringue on cooked filling in prebaked shell	350 or 425	12 to 15 4 to 4½

Type of Product	Oven Temperature degrees F.	Baking Time minutes
Shell only	450	10 to 12
Two-crust pies with un-cooked filling	400 to 425	45 to 55
Two-crust pies with cooked filling	425 to 450	30 to 45

APPROXIMATE MEASURES PER POUND OR UNIT OF FOOD MATERIALS MOST COMMONLY USED

Food	Measure	Food	Measure
Butter and other fats	2 cups	Orange juice	1 cup
Cheese, grated	4 cups	Grated rind	2 teaspoons
Chocolate, 1 ounce	1 square	Marshmallows, 1 oz.	4 pieces
Cocoa, 4 ounces	1 cup	Nuts, chopped	3⅔ cups
Coconut, shredded	5⅓ cups	Raisins, seedless 1	
Flour, sifted		pkge. (15 oz.)	2¾ cups
All-purpose	4 cups	Sugar	
Cake	4¾ cups	Brown, firmly	
Cornmeal	3 cups	packed	2¼ cups
Whole wheat, un-		Confectioners'	
sifted	3¾ cups	XXXX	3½ cups
Fruit, 1 medium to large		Fruit or very fine	2⅓ cups
Grapefruit juice	1 cup	Granulated	2¼ cups
Lemon juice	3 tablespoons	Powdered XX	2½ cups
Grated rind	1½ teaspoons		

COMMON MEASUREMENTS USED IN COOKERY

Dash	less than ⅛ teaspoon	½ cup	8 tablespoons or 1 gill
1 teaspoon	⅓ tablespoon	1 cup	16 tablespoons or ½ pint
1 tablespoon	3 teaspoons	1 pint	2 cups
¼ cup	4 tablespoons	1 quart	2 pints or 4 cups
⅓ cup	5⅓ tablespoons	1 gallon	4 quarts

CONTENTS OF COMMON CAN SIZES

No. 1 Picnic	1¼ cups	2 to 3 servings
No. 1 Tall	2 cups	4 servings
No. 2	2¼ cups	4 to 5 servings
No. 2½	3¼ cups	6 to 7 servings
No. 3	4 cups	8 servings
No. 5	6½ cups	12 to 13 servings
No. 10	12 cups	24 servings

TERMS USED IN MEAT AND VEGETABLE COOKERY

Barbecue—To roast meat on spit or rack over coals, or under a free flame or oven electric unit, usually basting with highly seasoned sauce.

Baste—To moisten meat or other foods while cooking to add flavor and to prevent drying of surface. The liquid is usually melted fat, meat drippings, fruit juice or sauce.

Blanch (precook)—To preheat in boiling water or steam. Used to inactivate enzymes and shrink food for canning, freezing and drying; and to aid in the removal of skins from nuts, fruits and some vegetables.

Boil—To cook in a liquid, usually water, at boiling temperature; bubbles rise continually and break on the surface. The boiling temperature of water at sea level is 212° F.

Braise—To cook slowly in a covered utensil in a small amount of liquid or in steam on top of range or in oven.

Broil—To cook directly under flame or red-hot heating unit, or over open fire, or grill.

Fricassee—To braise. Applied to poultry, game and some meats.

Fry—(1) To cook in small amount of fat, also called *sauté* or *pan-fry*; (2) to cook in a deep layer of fat, called *deep-fat frying*; (3) to cook in shallow layer of fat, 1 to 2 inches deep.

Garnish—Decorate.

Grill—See *broil*.

Julienne — To cut in match-like strips.

Marinate—To let stand in oil and vinegar or lemon juice to season.

Mince—To chop into very fine pieces.

Pan-broil—To cook uncovered, in hot frying pan, pouring off fat as it accumulates.

Parboil—To boil in water only until partly cooked.

Pare—To cut away outside covering.

Poach—To cook gently in hot liquid so that shape of food is retained. The temperature used varies with the food.

Process—The cooking period in all canning.

Roast—To cook by dry heat, usually uncovered, as in oven.

Sauté—To fry in small amount of fat.

Scald—To bring to temperature just below boiling point.

Sear—To brown surface of meat quickly at high heat (450°–550° F.).

Season—To add seasonings such as salt and pepper to taste.

Simmer—To cook in liquid below boiling point (about 185°–210° F.).

Stew—To cook slowly in a small amount of liquid for a long time.

Try out—To melt fat from connective tissues as in heating suet in a skillet.

TERMS USED IN BAKING

Beat—To make a mixture smooth or to introduce air by using a brisk, regular motion that lifts the mixture over and over.

Cream—To make soft, smooth and creamy by rubbing with back of spoon against side of bowl. To rub sugar and fat together to make creamy.

Fold—A down-across-up-and-over motion in batter with spoon or whip.

Knead—To work and press dough with the hands, at the same time folding and stretching.

Stir—To mix ingredients with a circular motion. (It may be said that when you stir you walk; when you beat you run.)

Whip—To beat rapidly to incorporate air—as in eggs, cream and gelatin mixtures.

Learn by Doing

In the beginning, there is a good deal to learn about cooking. It would not be much fun if there were not. However, every recipe in this book has been tested and retested and every one is outlined for you, step-by-step. Follow each recipe carefully but always confidently, taking one step at a time, and success will be yours.

It is wise to work with the less complicated dishes at first, of course. And in the very beginning it is a help to have someone who is interested in you within call—maybe your mother—to give a little nod of encouragement or word of advice should you need it.

If you don't know the meaning of a term or direction, *look it up on pages 17 to 18*. Presently it will all be so clear and so simple and you will be so proficient that nothing will please you more than having the kitchen all to yourself, and a brand new dish to tackle.

Getting to Work. Cleanliness is an absolute necessity in the kitchen. Wash your hands before starting to work, and rewash after any interruption in food preparation. Wear a clean, washable dress, smock or apron. Shoes should be comfortable.

Select your recipe. Read it through carefully. Collect ingredients, turn on oven (if it is to be used), and proceed with preparation. Work carefully in an orderly way and keep kitchen neat as you cook.

Safety in the Kitchen. Remember that the *kitchen can be the most dangerous room in the house*. Observe basic safety precautions by having sufficient light—preferably indirect and not glaring—to see what you are doing. Use a ladder-stool for high-shelf storage. Dip used matches in water. Turn utensil handles toward the rear of the range so that they will not catch sleeves or jewelry. Use pot holders for handling hot foods and use sharp knives only at work center. Give immediate care to kitchen accidents. Sweep up broken glass, don't try to pick it up with your hands. Gather last bits on a dampened cloth. Wrap all broken glass carefully so that no one will get hurt.

A little mopping up of water splashed on the floor will save a big mopping after feet have tracked it. Makes it safer, too. And of course, any other liquid, particularly grease, should be wiped up immediately with a cloth lightly dampened with warm suds and water. Clean "damaged" area, rinse and dry. And if the spot is stubborn, try steel wool No. o for easy riddance. (Apply a little wax after the floor is dry.)

A First Aid Kit in the kitchen, be it ever so small, can allay pain and panic. Each First Aid Kit holds a booklet of instructions, which you will find worth while to read should an emergency ever arise. Just for the record though—if you have a fire in your kitchen, smother it. Smother burning fat on floor or stove with flour or with a rug. Treat all burns and scalds as listed in your First Aid directions. (Cover with a paste of bicarbonate of soda and water if you have no special ointment.) *Keep the air out*. Put a disinfectant on all cuts. Bandage with sterile gauze and keep clean.

Clean Kitchen When Through. You can clean up the kitchen in jig time if you develop the habit of orderliness and learn quick and efficient ways to do the jobs at hand. No one likes to linger over clean-up if he must do it alone. But too many of us think of this as the bugaboo of kitchen work, which it isn't with modern know-how.

Heads and Hands Real Partners. Ever since the pioneering of Dr. Lillian Gilbreth and Mrs. Christine Frederick in time-and-motion-saving, homemakers of all ages have become increasingly aware that *careful advance planning* and *avoiding clutter* in food preparation will do much to speed clean-up. Actually, the modern way is to *clean as you go* and to have *order rather than disorder in the kitchen at all times.*

How to Be Efficient. Arrange and rearrange your work and supplies to simplify them. See that there is a place for everything, and everything in its place. Know how the equipment works—the range, refrigerator, sink (dishwasher and disposal) and small appliances—so that you get maximum efficiency with minimum effort.

Wash each dish and spoon as you go along. Put the bowls in which you have stirred eggs, batters, or doughs in cold water first, then into hot suds. On the other hand, dishes that have had large amounts of sugar or syrup in them should first be soaked in hot water. To clean grease-filled pans pour the melted fat into a bowl, if you wish to save it, or into the garbage— *never* down the sink. A greasy pan can be wiped out with a paper towel or piece of newspaper which can be burned or thrown into the garbage. Then plunge the pan into hot water combined with soap or detergent. Soak.

To loosen grease from oven, saturate a small piece of cloth with ammonia. Place the cloth in a large metal lid, such as the lid of a coffee can, and set in oven overnight. All you will have to do in the morning is to wipe down the sides of the oven and greasy area with the cloth; discard. Then with a second cloth or sponge, rinse oven and dry. Cheaper and easier to use than many of the commercial cleaners, too.

When you have had the bad luck to burn something in a crockery, agate enamel, or iron pan, soak it first in a solution of washing soda and water to loosen the scorched matter. Use two teaspoons of washing soda to one quart of water. With aluminium do not use washing soda, just soap or detergent and water and steel wool to make it shine.

Put whatever you are throwing away into the garbage pail immediately. Line the pail with paper, and scald it frequently. If the pail develops an odor or hard-to-get-rid-of dampness, use one of the commercial absorbent powders manufactured for this purpose. But frequent cleaning and drying should make this unnecessary.

Washing the Dishes. Here your head and hands can do a real team-up. Ask yourself what order of work will make for most efficient and speediest results? Have a plan before you begin; don't just begin with whatever dishes are handy. Perhaps a few suggestions will help you.

1. Wash all utensils used in food preparation before serving a meal, as outlined in the section on *How to Be Efficient.*

2. When the meal is finished, the first step is to get the dishes from the table to the sink. Here, cooperation can help. After a family dinner if each person will carry his own dishes and make one extra trip for table extras, it will save the dishwasher time and effort. When this is not possible, use a tray for step-saving.

3. Scrape, rinse, and stack each dish according to size and in the order to be washed—working from right to left if you are right-handed. This means that glassware will be nearest the washing area, then silverware, dishes, cutlery, and pots and pans.

4. Store and refrigerate leftover food in proper containers.

5. Empty garbage before you begin to wash dishes, being sure to drain off any moisture and to wrap securely.

6. Complete one operation at a time if you are working alone and for the average number of people. Usually this means that dishwashing will be completed before rinsing is done. This method is particularly successful if you have a spray attachment for rinsing.

7. Glassware, silverware and fragile pieces are generally towel-dried. Dishes that have been rinsed with scalding hot water are more sanitary if allowed to dry in dishrack.

Important Dishwashing Aids

Plenty of hot, soft water to dissolve soil.

Good cleaning agents to work with water, such as a mild soap, soap flakes or powder, or soapless detergent; an abrasive helper for sticky particles (but not for silverware); fine steel wool for scouring needs.

A scraper to remove food particles from dishes and pans.

For a single-bowl sink, one dishpan for rinsing; for table use, two dishpans for washing and rinsing. If you have a dishwasher you are lucky. All you have to do is to follow the manufacturer's directions.

A loosely-woven cloth or sponge; or dishmop or round brush, if you prefer to keep your hands out of water as much as possible.

A dishrack or drainer with "hooks" on the sides for glassware and a holder for silverware. This is a real timesaver and more sanitary, too. (Experiment with soapless detergents to see if you can find one that will leave glassware and silverware glistening and unstreaked if allowed to drain-dry.)

A rubber pad or shallow pan if drainboard does not slope or if dishwashing is to be done on table.

Linen or cotton dish towels for wiping fragile pieces.

Leave Kitchen Sparkling Clean. When you finish washing dishes, wash out dish towels unless they are to go into weekly wash.

Clean the sink.

Then check work areas, equipment, work surfaces and floor for any last jobs. Clean wooden, linoleum, vinyl, tile and steel counters with hot water combined with a small amount of mild soap or detergent. Use stiff brush on wooden surfaces, cleaning with grain of wood in long, straight strokes. Rinse and dry. Polish metal with clean, dry cloth.

Wipe enameled surfaces with a special commercial product made for this purpose, or use home-made soap jelly. To make jelly, save soap ends until you have one-fourth cup. Combine with one cup boiling water. Stir, and let cool. To use, dip a lightly dampened cloth or sponge into jelly and rub over soiled area—beginning at the bottom and working in long, slightly overlapping strokes. (Never work from top down, or round and round, if you want to avoid streaking.) Use a second cloth or sponge and clear water to rinse; dry. An application of light waxing is optional, but will help to preserve surface and to keep off soil.

Dry mop kitchen floor (unless spotted and not previously cleaned, in which case, use warm water combined with mild soap powder or detergent, rinse, and dry; wax).

Before you leave the kitchen, make a final check. Are the burners and oven turned off? Drawers and cupboard doors closed? Refrigerator door closed? Now clean-up is behind you.

A Good Breakfast
for a Good Start

For a really good start in the morning, you need a good breakfast. The experts say that breakfast should supply at least one third of your daily needs—and recommend that you include meat or egg and milk often.

Vary your breakfast fruit. Cool sticks of pineapple? Pineapple, cubed, a few strawberries tossed in with it, tastes very good. A bunch of cold grapes would be different and make breakfast seem not the same old thing every day. Have your daily glass of orange juice at lunch.

Vary your morning toast. Have you ever tried toasting pumpernickel? It has the chewy sweetness of a fresh-shelled nut. What about English muffins? And while we're going international, French toast? Try French toast with sprinkled sugar and lemon juice.

Don't forget hot breads. Try mixing the waffle batter after supper. Keep it in the refrigerator all night, then bright and early next morning bake it and have a real breakfast.

You have a dozen cereals to choose from. Why the same every morning? Try cooked ones with raisins; the ready-to-serve, with fruits—berries, dates and figs. You can have variety all through the menu, and every day in the week.

Service for Breakfast. Setting the table for breakfast is not so different from setting it for luncheon. Simplicity, of course, is the rule, although the linen and china are often very gay.

Silver, napkin, bread and butter plate, if used, and water glass are all arranged as in the picture on *page* 51. Note that the napkin edge, plate edge and silver handles are in line, about one inch from the edge of the table. Fork tines are up, and knife edge is toward the plate.

A medium-sized plate, ready set for the main course to come, is at each place, and if you are having fruit, the smaller plate holding it is placed on the larger one. If fruit juice is served, it is sometimes put on a coaster or small plate or saucer beside the water glass at the upper right of the plate. That simplifies service, as then the cereal in its bowl can be on the plate at each place.

Although the cereal may be served from the kitchen, the main course is usually served at the table. So is the beverage. The cups, saucers and beverage pot or jug are beside whoever pours it.

Re-read *The Kitchen Holds a Challenge* for more information on planning, marketing and serving.

FRUIT

APPLESAUCE

4 cooking apples (Baldwin, Spitzenburg, Winesap, or Rhode Island Greening) **½ cup water (about)**	Wash, pare and quarter apples. Remove cores and cut each in half, if desired. Add just enough water to steam fruit and keep from burning. Bring to a boil, cover and cook slowly for 20 to 30 minutes, or until soft.
¼ cup sugar *Makes about 4 portions.*	Add sugar and simmer just long enough to dissolve sugar. Serve hot or cold. Add 1 to 3 tablespoons lemon juice if apples are bland.

STRAINED APPLESAUCE

Follow recipe for Applesauce, only force cooked fruit through a sieve before adding sugar.

CINNAMON APPLESAUCE

Follow recipe for Applesauce, only cook 2 tablespoons cinnamon drops with apples.

BAKED APPLES

**4 large firm apples (Baldwin, Mc-
Intosh, or Spitzenburg)**
**8 tablespoons granulated or brown
sugar**
⅛ teaspoon cinnamon
2 teaspoons butter
¼ cup hot water (about)

Makes 4 portions.

Wash and core apples and place in baking dish. Mix sugar and cinnamon, then pile into cavities in apples and dot with butter. Add water only to cover bottom of pan.

Bake, covered, in 350° F. (moderate) oven for 30 to 40 minutes, or until just soft. Remove apples, boil syrup until thick and pour over apples. Serve hot or cold, plain or with cream.

BAKED STUFFED APPLES

Prepare apples for baking and fill each cavity with one of the following mixtures: 2 tablespoons granulated or brown sugar and ½ tablespoon chopped raisin, prunes, dates, figs or nuts; then dot each with ½ teaspoon butter. Bake as directed.

GLAZED BAKED APPLES

4 large firm apples
½ cup honey
4 tablespoons chopped nuts
2 teaspoons butter
¼ cup hot water (about)

For variety add:
1 tablespoon maraschino cherry liquid
to syrup

Wash, core, and pare apples about 1 inch down from stem end. Place in shallow baking dish. Fill each cavity with honey, nuts and butter. Add water only to cover bottom.

Bake, covered, in 350° F. (moderate) oven about 30 minutes, or until just soft. Baste well with syrup in pan. Place under broiler to glaze tops.

CITRUS FRUIT JUICES

1 lemon
1 grapefruit
3 small oranges

Makes about 2¾ cups or 4 small glasses.

Squeeze juice from washed fruits, using a juice extractor which removes seeds and membrane but permits pulp to pass through. Chill thoroughly.

GRAPEFRUIT OR ORANGE HALVES

2 grapefruit, or 4 medium-sized oranges
2 tablespoons sugar, or 4 tablespoons honey, if desired

Makes 4 portions.

Cut washed fruit in halves crosswise and remove seeds. Loosen flesh in each section by cutting along membranes and skin of each. Cut out centers with scissors. Chill and serve plain or sprinkle with sugar or honey and garnish as desired.

BROILED GRAPEFRUIT HALVES

Follow recipe for Grapefruit Halves, only dot ½ teaspoon butter over each half. Place on rack in preheated broiler (3 to 4 inches below heating unit) and cook for 10 to 15 minutes, or until delicately browned. Serve hot. *Makes 4 portions.*

GRAPEFRUIT OR ORANGE SECTIONS

Cut off rind and all skin from washed fruit as in paring an apple, holding fruit over bowl to catch juice. Cut along membranes of each sector, then lift out section and remove seeds, if present. Squeeze juice from remaining membrane and pour over sections. Chill and serve plain or sweetened with sugar, honey or syrup for breakfast or dessert; or serve in fruit cup or salad. One grapefruit has about 12 sections; one orange, from 8 to 10 sections.

BANANAS

Use ripe, firm bananas; the yellow banana is well speckled with brown when ripe. Serve whole, or sliced with sugar and cream, or with a wedge of lemon. To prevent discoloration sprinkle with lemon juice or rub with a tart fruit.

BAKED BANANAS

Bake large bananas in 350° F. (moderate) oven about 20 minutes, or until skins split open. Serve in skins, cutting off tops, or remove fruit. Sprinkle with sugar and lemon or pineapple juice.

BERRIES

Remove soft or imperfect fruit and wash in colander to remove sand or grit. Drain, then stem or hull. Sprinkle with fine granulated (berry) sugar and let stand ½ to 1 hour before serving. If stored overnight, remove imperfect berries but do not wash and hull. Eight to 12 large perfect strawberries may be served, unhulled, around a mound of confectioners' sugar. *One quart makes 4 to 6 portions.*

FRESH PINEAPPLE

Pineapples are ripe when spines pull out easily from crown. Wash, dry and cut around crown, or twist top leaves until crown comes off. Stand upright on board and with sharp, long-bladed knife, cut downward to remove rind. Remove "eyes" with small pointed knife. Shred, cut in wedges or cubes. Sprinkle with sugar and chill in refrigerator. *One medium-sized pineapple makes 5 or 6 portions.*

SHREDDED PINEAPPLE

Stand pared pineapple upright on board, stick large fork into top and hold firmly with left hand. Shred with a sharp-tined, strong fork to hard core.

PINEAPPLE WEDGES OR CUBES

Lay pared pineapple on its side on board and cut in slices, ¼ to ½ inch thick. Remove core. Cut in wedges or cubes.

PINEAPPLE SPEARS OR STICKS

Stand pared pineapple upright on board. Cut downward in half, then in quarters. Remove core from each piece, then cut in ½- to ¾-inch strips or wedges and divide each in half.

PINEAPPLE CONES

Stand unpared, washed pineapple upright on board. Hold firmly by crown and with sharp knife cut around each "eye" to the core, making a pointed piece, then pull out wedge. Arrange 6 to 8 cones around a mound of confectioners' sugar.

PINEAPPLE BOATS

Lay unpared, washed pineapple on its side on board and cut through crown into quarters or sixths. Remove core and run knife along rind of each piece, then cut down to rind in ¼-inch slices, leaving fruit in place. Chill and serve with a fork. Sprinkle lightly with sugar, if desired.

DRIED FRUITS

Modern processing of dried fruit has eliminated the need of long soaking periods. Just wash fruit quickly in several waters and it is ready to cook. The length of cooking time varies with the degree of softness desired. Fruit may be cooked with or without sugar, depending upon your preference—but the addition of sugar makes a thicker and more attractive syrup.

STEWED PRUNES

Wash prunes, cover with water and simmer about 30 minutes. Sugar to taste (¼ to ½ cup per pound of fruit) may be added during last 5 minutes of cooking. For extra flavor, a slice of orange or lemon, or cinnamon stick, may be cooked with prunes. One pound contains 30 to 60 prunes, according to size. *Allow 4 to 6 prunes per portion.*

STEWED APRICOTS

Wash apricots, cover with water and simmer about 35 minutes. Sugar to taste (½ to 1 cup per pound of fruit) may be added during last 5 minutes of cooking. One pound contains about 80 halves. *Allow 4 to 6 halves per portion.*

CEREALS

COOKED CEREALS

Cereals are cooked to improve flavor, texture and digestibility. Both regular and quick-cooking types are available. With either, it is important to use sufficient water, and to add cereal gradually to rapidly boiling water so that boiling does not stop.

SERVICE SUGGESTIONS FOR COOKED CEREALS

Allow ½ to ⅔ cup cooked cereal for each person. Cereals may be varied in any one of the following ways:

Dried fruits, such as raisins or plumped currants, sliced apricots, dates, figs or prunes, may be stirred into cereal just before serving. Use ¼ to ½ cup fruit for 2 cups cereal.

Fresh or canned fruits, such as berries, sliced apricots, bananas, or peaches, may be sprinkled over serving.

Ready-to-serve cereals such as flaked cereals, crispies, grape-nuts or bran flakes, may be sprinkled over serving.

Creamy cereals may be chilled in individual molds; to serve, unmold and serve with canned fruit, or fresh fruit and cream.

FARINA

2½ cups water
¾ teaspoon salt
½ cup farina or other finely ground cereals such as Cream of Wheat or Rye, Wheatena or Ralston

1 cup cream or rich milk
granulated or brown sugar

Makes about 2 cups cooked cereal, or enough for 4.

Measure water and salt into top part of double boiler. Heat to boiling over direct heat. Gradually sprinkle cereal into water so that boiling does not stop, stirring to keep it from lumping. Boil 5 minutes, then place over boiling water. Cover and cook about 20 minutes.

Serve in warm cereal bowls, allowing ½ cup per portion. Serve with cream and sugar.

QUICK-COOKING CEREALS

Many finely ground and flaked cereals can be cooked in a very short time over direct heat. For method, follow directions on package.

ROLLED OATS

Follow recipe for Farina, only substitute 1 cup rolled oats for farina and use 2 cups water (about) and 1 teaspoon salt. Other flaked cereals such as flaked wheat or Pettijohn's may be used instead of rolled oats. Add ½ to 1 cup more water if cereal is too stiff. *Makes 2 to 3 cups cooked cereal, or enough for 4 to 6,* (See recipe, *page* 30.)

CORNMEAL MUSH

Follow recipe for Farina, only substitute cornmeal for farina and use 3 cups water (about) and 1 teaspoon salt. *Makes about 3 cups cooked cereal, or enough for 4 to 6.* (See recipe, *page* 30.)

LEFT-OVER CEREALS

To reheat left-over cereal, place in double boiler, add small amount of milk or water and stir until cereal is smooth, then heat.

FRIED MUSH

Cooked cereal must be thick to mold. Pack cereal such as cornmeal, rolled oats or Wheatena in straight-sided loaf pan which has been rinsed with cold water. Cover to keep crust from forming. When cold and firm, cut in ¼- to ⅓-inch slices. Sauté in bacon fat or butter over medium heat for 10 to 15 minutes, or until browned on both sides. Serve hot with butter and syrup, honey or jelly, or with crisp bacon or small sausages. *Two cups mush, fried, will serve about 4.*

READY-TO-SERVE CEREALS

Allow ⅔ to 1 cup, or 1 unit per portion. These cereals should be served fresh and crisp. If left exposed for some time and in prolonged damp weather, crisp and freshen by heating in 350° F. (moderate) oven about 5 minutes. Serve with light cream or rich milk and sugar. Fresh or stewed fruit may be served with cereal.

TOAST

PLAIN TOAST

Use bread slices, ¼ to ½ inch thick stale bread if you have it. Brown quickly for soft toast and slowly for dry, crisp toast. To toast in broiler, lay slices on rack in broiling pan. Place under flame or heat unit and toast on both sides, turning several times to brown evenly and keep slices from curling. Place on hot plate and serve hot with butter.

BUTTERED TOAST

Spread hot toast with softened butter and serve hot.

CINNAMON TOAST

Cut slices of hot thin toast in strips or triangles and spread with softened butter. Sprinkle generously with mixture of sugar and cinnamon, using ½ teaspoon cinnamon to ¼ cup sugar. Place in hot broiler to melt sugar. Serve hot for breakfast or afternoon tea.

TOASTED ENGLISH MUFFINS

Split English muffins and toast quickly in broiler or on toaster, browning on one or both sides, as desired. Spread generously with softened butter and serve hot with marmalade, jelly or jam, or cover with a creamed meat, fish or vegetable.

MILK TOAST

Allow ½ cup milk for each slice of bread. Scald in double boiler and keep covered. Toast bread, spread generously with softened butter and sprinkle lightly with salt. Place in hot cereal bowl or soup plate and pour hot milk over top, or serve milk in hot pitcher.

FRENCH TOAST

2 eggs, slightly beaten
¼ teaspoon salt
1 cup milk
6 slices bread
3 tablespoons fat (about)

Makes 4 to 6 portions.

Mix together eggs, salt and milk in deep plate. Dip bread into mixture. Sauté slowly in butter, bacon drippings or other fat, in heavy frying pan, turning to brown both sides. Add more fat if necessary to keep slices from sticking. Place on hot plate and serve with butter, jelly or syrup.

FLUFFY FRENCH TOAST

Follow recipe for French Toast. Separate eggs. Add ¼ teaspoon cream of tartar to egg whites. Beat until stiff but not dry. Beat egg yolks slightly and add salt and milk. Fold egg whites into egg yolk mixture and then proceed as directed.

BEVERAGES

HOW TO MAKE GOOD COFFEE

To make good coffee, use coffee that has been freshly ground for your type of coffee maker. Buy coffee in small quantities and store in an airtight container. The pot must be scrupulously clean and the water freshly drawn. Serve immediately after brewing.

DRIP COFFEE

Use finely ground or drip-grind coffee, allowing 2 level tablespoons for each cup of water. Heat lower part of coffee pot by filling with hot water. Just before making coffee, empty and adjust upper part containing measured coffee. Pour freshly boiling water over coffee. Place pot on asbestos mat over low heat to keep hot. The water should drip through in about 5 minutes; then remove container with grounds and keep coffee hot. Do not let it boil. For *Vacuum Drip Coffee*, follow directions given with pot.

PERCOLATED COFFEE

Use medium or finely ground coffee, allowing 2 level tablespoons for each cup of water. Measure cold water into pot. Put basket with coffee in pot and heat. When water begins to percolate, reduce heat and continue percolating 8 to 12 minutes, or until coffee is clear and amber colored. Remove basket with grounds and keep coffee hot. Do not let it boil.

DEMI-TASSE

Use 3 to 4 level tablespoons coffee for each cup of water and prepare by any method. Serve hot in small cups. After-dinner coffee or demi-tasse is always strong and usually served black.

ICED COFFEE

Prepare strong coffee. Pour hot coffee over cracked ice in tall glasses. Serve with plain or whipped cream.

CAFÉ AU LAIT

Prepare strong or double strength coffee. Scald an equal quantity of milk and pour into hot pot. When ready to serve, pour coffee and milk simultaneously in equal amounts into heated cups. Top with whipped cream.

PICNIC COFFEE

Use medium-grind coffee; 1 pound measures 5 to 5½ cups and makes 40 to 50 cups of coffee. Put coffee in bag made of muslin or several thicknesses of cheesecloth, allowing space for coffee to double in bulk. Tie securely and drop into large kettle or boiler containing 2 gallons of freshly boiling water. Cover tightly and let stand over low heat or in warm place 6 to 10 minutes. Remove bag, cover tightly and keep hot. Make just before serving.

CAMP COFFEE FOR FOUR

Follow directions for Picnic Coffee, using ½ cup coffee and 4 cups freshly boiling water.

INSTANT COFFEE

Use 1 teaspoonful instant coffee for each cup of water. Place coffee in cup or pot, add boiling water, stir and serve.

TEA

Use about 1 teaspoon tea leaves to each cup of freshly boiling water. Use tea leaves or prepared tea bags. Heat earthenware, china, or glass teapot or pitcher, by filling with hot water. Drain pot and place tea in it. Add freshly boiling water, cover and steep in warm place 3 minutes. Serve with pot of hot water.

TEA ACCOMPANIMENTS

Tea accompaniments may be simple or more elaborate. Serve one or several of the following: granulated sugar or sugar cubes; cream or milk; wedges of lemon, lime or orange, or thin slices of any, plain or with several whole cloves inserted in each; lemon, lime or orange juice; sprigs of fresh mint; candied ginger, cherries, pineapple or citrus fruit rinds.

SPICED TEA

Follow directions for Tea, only double the amount of tea leaves and steep with spices, allowing 3 whole cloves and small piece of stick cinnamon to each cup of boiling water. Serve with pot of freshly boiling water, and strained lemon juice and sugar. To serve iced, pour hot tea over cracked ice in tall glasses.

ICED TEA

Follow directions for Tea, only double the amount of tea leaves used. Pour hot tea over cracked ice in tall glasses. Serve with slice or wedge of lemon, lime, or orange, and sugar. For clear, sparkling tea, cool tea quickly rather than slowly.

ICED TEA FOR TWENTY

Follow directions for Tea, using ½ cup tea to 2 quarts freshly boiling water. Pour hot tea over block of ice in large pitcher.

HOT COCOA

2½ to 3½ tablespoons sugar
4 tablespoons cocoa
dash of salt
½ cup water
3½ cups milk
¼ cup heavy cream, whipped, or 8
marshmallows

Makes 1 quart or enough for 4.

Mix sugar, cocoa and salt in saucepan. Stir in water and boil and stir 2 minutes.

Stir in milk and heat slowly until scalded —just below the boiling point. Cover and keep hot over boiling water. Just before serving beat with rotary beater until frothy. Serve plain or with whipped cream or marshmallows. Cinnamon may be sprinkled over cream, if desired.

HOT CHOCOLATE

Follow recipe for Hot Cocoa (above) only substitute 1 to 1½ squares chocolate for cocoa and boil chocolate, sugar, salt and water for 4 minutes. A dash of cinnamon or cloves may be cooked with it, if desired.

EGGS

COOKED EGGS

To cook eggs use a deep saucepan with cover, small or large, depending on number to be cooked. Use enough water to cover eggs. Pour boiling water over eggs or slip them into the boiling water by means of a tablespoon or ladle. Cover and simmer (below boiling point) for 3 to 20 minutes.

Soft-Cooked Eggs

Simmer 3 to 5 minutes.

Medium-Hard-Cooked Eggs

Simmer 5 to 8 minutes.

Hard-Cooked Eggs

Simmer 15 to 20 minutes. Then drain quickly and cover with cold water to prevent the formation of, or reduce the amount of, dark ring likely to form between the yolk and white.

CODDLED EGGS

Use enough water to cover eggs. Bring water to a boil and remove from heat. Slip eggs carefully into water. Cover and let stand 4 to 8 minutes.

POACHED EGG

To keep egg round, poach one at a time. Use a small saucepan and boiling salted water, allowing 1 teaspoon salt for 2 cups water. Stir water until it is in circular motion, then slip egg from saucer into the vortex. Reduce heat and baste egg with hot water in pan until white is set and the yolk covered with a white film. It will take from 3 to 5 minutes. Remove egg with perforated pancake turner and place on slice of buttered hot toast. Season.

To poach several eggs at a time, use a frying pan, shallow pan or patented poacher. Slip eggs, one at a time, into boiling salted water. Reduce heat, cover and cook for 3 to 5 minutes.

FRIED EGGS

Heat butter or bacon fat in frying pan over slow heat, using about 1 tablespoon for 2 eggs. Slip eggs into pan, one at a time, from saucer. Baste with fat in pan to cook the tops. Cook until set, or for 3 to 5 minutes. To fry on both sides, omit basting and turn with broad spatula or pancake turner when white is partially set. Sprinkle with salt and pepper before serving. Eggs fried at high heat or too long become leathery and tough.

BAKED OR SHIRRED EGGS

Put buttered, shallow, individual ramekins on baking sheet. Place 1 tablespoon light cream and 1 egg in each. Sprinkle with salt and pepper and 1 tablespoon buttered dry crumbs. Bake in 350° F. (moderate) oven for 15 to 20 minutes, or until eggs are set. Serve in ramekins. Sprinkle grated cheese or sweet basil over buttered crumbs just before baking, if desired.

BAKED TOMATO AND EGG

Use one medium tomato for each egg. Wash and cut off stem end, and scoop out center. Sprinkle inside with salt. Break egg into center. Season substituting thyme for sweet basil and sprinkle with buttered crumbs. Bake as for Baked Eggs.

SCRAMBLED EGGS

4 teaspoons butter
4 eggs
½ teaspoon salt
⅛ teaspoon pepper
¼ cup rich milk or light cream

Makes 4 small portions.

Melt butter in double boiler. Keep water in bottom pan boiling gently. Beat eggs until whites and yolks are well mixed. Add salt and pepper, stir in milk and pour into double boiler. With spatula or large spoon scrape cooked portion slowly from bottom and sides, forming large soft flakes. Serve on hot platter with broiled bacon, ham, sausages or mushrooms, or with toast, and garnish with parsley.

SCRAMBLED EGGS WITH TOMATO

Follow recipe for Scrambled Eggs, only substitute ½ cup canned tomatoes for milk, and add ½ teaspoon sugar and a dash of scraped onion. *Makes 4 portions.*

SCRAMBLED EGGS AND MEAT

Follow recipe for Scrambled Eggs, only add 2 tablespoons chopped meat, dried beef, boiled ham, broiled bacon or fried sausage to uncooked egg and milk mixture. *Makes 4 portions.*

SCRAMBLED EGGS (in frying pan)

Follow recipe for Scrambled Eggs, only melt butter in a frying pan over a slow fire. Add beaten egg mixture and cook until thickened, stirring constantly and scraping from bottom and sides of pan.

OMELET

2 tablespoons butter
4 eggs
½ teaspoon salt
dash of pepper
¼ cup milk

Melt butter in frying pan over low heat. Beat eggs slightly with fork. Add salt, pepper and milk.

Pour egg mixture into frying pan. As omelet cooks, lift edges with spatula to permit uncooked part to run to the bottom. When the omelet is of creamy consistency, and the bottom is lightly browned, fold the omelet over and serve on hot platter.

Makes 4 portions.

FLUFFY OMELET

A good fluffy omelet is very light, about once and a half as high as the unbaked omelet. The top is delicately browned, dry and set, springing back when touched with finger. The bottom is evenly browned and glossy. The finished omelet is folded in half with bottom side out. The inside is porous and spongy and the many air cells are set throughout. Moist and tender it falls slightly on standing.

Utensils Needed

Medium-sized (9-inch) frying pan; measuring cup and spoon, tablespoon; large deep bowl, small bowl, rotary beater; spatula, rubber scraper.
Makes 1 medium-sized omelet and serves about 4.

Order of Work

1. Assemble utensils and ingredients.
2. Light oven or turn on heat and adjust for 350° F. (moderate) oven.
3. Prepare omelet mixture. Cook and bake.
4. Fold over and place on hot platter, garnish and serve at once.

RECIPE

1 tablespoon butter
4 eggs, separated
½ teaspoon salt
dash of pepper
¼ cup milk
parsley for garnish

Heat butter in frying pan over low heat. Beat egg whites until stiff but not dry. Beat egg yolks until thick and light colored. Stir in seasonings and milk, then fold into egg whites. Turn into hot frying pan using scraper. Cook slowly for 3 to 5 minutes, or until omelet puffs up and is browned on bottom. Test by lifting up edge of bottom with spatula.

Place in 350° F. (moderate) oven for 10 to 15 minutes, or until top springs back when pressed with finger and is browned.

Omelet Variations:

Spread one of the following over one-half of omelet before folding:

½ cup tart jelly
¾ cup sautéed, sliced mushrooms
½ cup grated cheese

Remove from oven. Fold in half by cutting 1-inch incisions at opposite ends, then creasing along center from cut to cut, and folding in half. With spatula slip omelet on hot platter. Serve at once.

Tempting fare for breakfast or brunch—bacon fried in small pieces to be added to eggs for Scrambled Eggs and Bacon (*pages* 37–38).

BROILED BACON

Lay thin slices of bacon or Irish or Canadian bacon on rack. Place in dripping pan and bake in 350° F. (moderate) oven, turning once to brown and crisp both sides. Or place rack with bacon in broiling pan and broil until crisp and brown, turning once. *Allow 1 to 3 slices per portion.*

FRIED BACON

Lay bacon slices in frying pan. Place over slow heat and cook about 10 minutes, or until brown and crisp, turning frequently to keep slices straight. Pour off fat if much accumulates. Remove crisp slices, one by one. Drain.

FRIED HAM

Rub moderately hot, heavy frying pan with ham fat, or grease slightly. Lay ham in pan and cook slowly, turning to brown both sides. For ¼-inch slice, allow about 10 minutes; for ⅜- to ½-inch slice, allow 15 to 20 minutes. Browned ham may be covered and cooked slowly, turning several times.

FRIED SAUSAGES

Separate link sausages. Fry over low heat turning to cook and brown all sides. Pour off fat as it accumulates. Drain sausages on absorbent paper and serve hot with fried or scrambled eggs, or griddlecakes. *One pound serves 4 to 6.*

FRIED SAUSAGE CAKES

Shape sausage meat into flat cakes. Fry over low heat, turning to cook and brown both sides. Drain on absorbent or unglazed paper and serve hot. *One pound makes about 10 small cakes.*

GRIDDLECAKES

Good griddlecakes, pancakes or flapjacks may be small, medium or large; thin and moist, or thick and less moist. They are round, golden brown on both sides, porous and tender.

Utensils Needed	*Order of Work*
Griddle or heavy frying pan; mixing bowl, small bowl; flour sifter, measuring cup and spoons;	1. Assemble utensils and ingredients. 2. Place griddle over medium heat; if new rub lightly with fat before baking first

rotary beater; tablespoon or narrow-mouthed pitcher; pancake turner or broad spatula

cakes. It is hot if cold water sputters or boils when dropped on surface.

3. Mix batter, drop from spoon or pitcher on hot griddle, bake.
4. Stack on hot plate; serve hot.
5. Left-over batter may be covered tightly and kept in refrigerator several days.

RECIPE

2 cups sifted flour
3 teaspoons double-action baking powder
1 teaspoon salt
1 tablespoon sugar
1 to 2 eggs, well beaten
1½ cup milk (scant)★
2 tablespoons fat, melted

Sift flour, measure 2 cups into sifter. Add baking powder, salt and sugar, then mix and sift. Beat eggs until light, then stir in milk. Add to flour mixture and beat or stir until smooth. Stir in fat.

Drop medium-thin batter from tip of tablespoon or pitcher on ungreased griddle to make round cake. Griddle will hold 3 to 4 cakes. Turn cakes when full of bubbles and tops are set but not dry, turning each only once.

Makes about 24 small to medium (3- to 4-inch) cakes.

★ For thick cakes use:
1 to 1⅓ cups of milk

Stack about 4 on hot plate and serve with butter and syrup, jelly, or sugar. Or butter cakes, sprinkle each with sugar, or spread with jam. Stack 6 to 8 cakes, cut in wedges and put one on each hot plate.

MODIFICATIONS OF GRIDDLECAKES

Rolled Jelly Pancakes

Follow recipe for Griddlecakes, only make them 4 to 6 inches large. Spread each with butter and a tart jelly or jam and roll tightly. Serve 3 or 4 on a hot plate. *Makes about 16 cakes.*

Sour Milk Griddlecakes

Follow recipe for Griddlecakes, only substitute ¾ teaspoon baking soda for baking powder, and sour milk or buttermilk for sweet milk. Add ¼ to ½ cup more sour milk, if necessary, to make a medium-thin batter. *Makes about 24 cakes.*

WAFFLES

Good waffles are well browned on both sides, light and porous, crisp and tender, not soft and limp, bready or tough. Plain waffles are not sweet. Dessert waffles are delicate in flavor, richer and sweeter than plain waffles.

Utensils Needed	*Order of Work*
Plain cast iron or aluminum waffle iron or an electric waffle iron; mixing bowl, small bowl; flour sifter, measuring cup and spoons; rotary beater, tablespoon; pitcher, fork.	1. Assemble utensils and ingredients. 2. Heat waffle iron; if not heat-controlled, test with drop of cold water. It will sputter and boil when hot enough. It is usually not necessary to grease iron. 3. Mix batter, pour into pitcher, drop on hot iron and bake. 4. Serve on hot plate, whole or part. 5. Left-over batter may be covered tightly and kept in refrigerator several days.

Makes about 6 waffles.

RECIPE

2 cups sifted flour
2½ teaspoons double-action baking powder
1 teaspoon salt
2 to 3 eggs, separated
1½ cups milk
¼ cup shortening, melted

Sift flour, measure 2 cups into sifter. Add baking powder and salt, mix, then sift into bowl.

Beat egg whites until stiff but not dry. Beat egg yolks until thick and stir in milk. Add to flour mixture and beat until smooth. Stir in shortening and fold in egg whites.

Drop batter from pitcher into center of hot iron, partially filling each compartment. Close iron tightly and bake until steam no longer escapes, or about 3 minutes. Open iron and lift out with fork. Place on hot plate. Serve with syrup, sugar or jelly.

Nut Waffles, add:
¼ to ½ cup chopped nuts to batter

All American breakfast specials.

Serve French Toast (*page* 32) with sugar, jelly or syrup.

Golden griddlecakes (*page* 40)—know how to make them well. Be sure to wait until the bubbles come and multiply before you turn the pancakes, and turn just once. Serve hot off the griddle with syrup, jelly or sugar.

Accompany your breakfast specials with hot fried sausages (*page* 40).

HAM OR BACON WAFFLES

Follow recipe for Waffles, only sprinkle 2 tablespoons finely chopped cooked ham or crisp bacon over batter of each waffle before closing iron. *Makes about 6 waffles.*

CHEESE WAFFLES

Follow recipe for Waffles, only add ½ to 1 cup grated cheese to batter before folding in egg whites. *Makes 7 to 8 waffles.*

There's no rush at brunch time. An inviting table, good food, all the time in the world to eat, make this buffet Ham and Waffle Brunch a friendly meal. (See *page 46, Order of Work for Preparing Ham and Waffle Brunch*.)

Brunch

for Special Days

"Brunch" is the inspired name for an inspired meal, for it is that combination of breakfast and luncheon which fits into a holiday schedule so perfectly. It is not so simple as breakfast, not so elaborate as luncheon. "Brunch" saves time and labor in the kitchen, for it reduces the number of meals for the day to two. Those who live by the clock all week welcome this informal meal, eaten when the spirit moves, alone or with the family or friends.

Young people don't very often have the opportunity to eat away from home at breakfast time, so why not introduce "brunch" to your crowd, and watch how pleased everybody will be.

"Brunch" service will be determined by whether it is "sit-down" or self-service.

A "brunch" table is arranged exactly as for breakfast or luncheon. Because it is a festive or holiday meal, however, the linen and china are usually a bit more gay. Flowers, of course, are always effective.

For a help-yourself "brunch" note the arrangement in the picture *opposite*. There you see the plates piled at one end of the table near the waffle baker. The syrup and marmalade are convenient. Cups and saucers —with the spoons on the saucers—are handy to the coffee at the other end of the table. Cream and sugar are nearby. Between waffle baker and coffee are the other foods arranged so that the guest can go from one to another and help himself comfortably. Silver and napkins are there for

45

each to take. Individual trays make the carrying of food to tables on the porch or elsewhere a simple matter.

BRUNCH MENU SUGGESTIONS

Help Yourself Brunch

(Together or Separately)

Cantaloupe with Lemon
Ready-to-serve Cereal with
Bananas and Cream
Marmalade Grill with Sausages, 48
Butterscotch Slices, 187
Cocoa, 35 with Marshmallows

★

Tomato Juice
Griddlecakes, 40   Butter
Syrup   Lemon Juice and Sugar
Crisp Bacon, 40
Crackers   with   Cream   Cheese   and
Conserve
Milk   Coffee, 33   Cream

"Sit-down" Brunch

(All Together)

Grapefruit Halves, 27
Poached Eggs with Mushrooms, 47
Toast   Butter   Jam
Doughnuts, 187
Chocolate, 35 with Whipped Cream
Coffee, 33   Cream

★

Whole Strawberries with Sugar
Chicken-Cornbread Shortcake, 283
Cornbread, 65   Butter   Peach Jam
Drop Cookies, 183
Iced Chocolate, 203
Coffee, 33   Cream

Order of Work for Preparing Ham and Waffle Brunch

1. Prepare the following and place in refrigerator until ready to serve; then place on table as indicated: Tomato   and   sauerkraut   juices poured into pitcher for serving. Washed and dried fruit arranged in bowl for serving. Butter rolls or squares arranged on plate for serving. Cream   poured   into   pitcher   for serving.

2. Set table, arranging linen, silver, glasses, cups and saucers, trays, electric waffle iron, sugar bowl on small tray, marmalade jar on small tray.

3. Heat plates, platter, syrup pitcher and jug for milk in warming oven or with hot water.

4. Prepare waffle batter (*page* 42), turn into pitcher and place on table.

5. Start frying of ham (*page* 40); when browned, cover and cook slowly. Just before serving, place on hot platter and cut in strips.

6. While cooking ham, start heating waffle iron.

7. Start coffee (*page* 33) on table or in kitchen. Place prepared coffee on tray on table.

8. Scald milk in double boiler. Serve in hot pot near coffee (*page* 34).

9. Heat maple syrup. Serve in hot pitcher on tray with marmalade.

10. Bake waffles; serve whole, half or quarter on hot plate.

POACHED EGG WITH MUSHROOMS

¼ **cup sliced mushrooms**
1 tablespoon butter
½ **cup top milk or rich milk**

Sauté mushrooms slowly in butter in small frying pan for 5 minutes, turning frequently. Add top milk and heat to boiling, then reduce heat.

1 slice hot toast, buttered, 1 egg
salt and pepper

Slip egg from saucer into mushroom mixture and cook slowly for 3 to 5 minutes, basting with liquid in pan. With skimmer, remove egg to buttered hot toast and put mushroom mixture around egg. Season with salt and pepper, and serve at once.

Makes 1 *portion*

POACHED EGG IN TOMATO

½ **cup canned tomatoes (pulp and juice)**
1 tablespoon butter

Break up tomatoes, if whole, in small frying pan. Add butter and heat to boiling, then reduce heat.

1 egg
1 slice hot toast, buttered
salt and pepper

Slip egg from saucer and cook slowly for 3 to 5 minutes, basting with tomatoes in pan. With skimmer remove egg to buttered hot toast and put mixture around egg. Season with salt and pepper, and serve at once.

Makes 1 *portion*

MARMALADE GRILL WITH SAUSAGES

1 pound small sausages

Fry sausages over low heat until brown on all sides. Drain on absorbent paper and keep hot.

8 slices bread
6 tablespoons butter
4 tablespoons orange marmalade

Make sandwiches, spreading lightly with butter and not too generously with marmalade. Spread outside of sandwiches with butter. Toast both sides in sandwich grill or frying pan. Serve on hot plates, topping each with about 3 sausages.

Makes 4 portions.

Good Luncheon Dishes —
Good Suppers, too

You will find in this chapter luncheon and supper dishes which will be your standbys as long as you cook. Some will be familiar, many will be new; but old or new, they are the makings of day after day luncheons and suppers for every season in the year.

Specialize in quick breads. Look upon creamed soups, chowders, casseroles and creamed dishes, as main courses. Add a dessert or sweet salad, a hot bread, to make a meal. Two or three courses are enough.

Table service for luncheon and supper is simple. Attractive plain or embroidered linens, or lacy luncheon cloths may be used, or your most colorful and unusual runners or mats. Napkins lie at the left of each place, at the left of the forks with the open corner at the lower right-hand corner. Candles are not used in daylight, but at evening supper-time they are inviting and charming for special occasions. Flowers, a small plant or an ornamental dish in the table center is always the rule.

Silver for luncheon or supper is set according to the usual plan. Forks to the left, in the order used, the last used next to the plate. Knives and spoons are at the right, knife next to the plate, and the spoons are arranged in the order used, beginning from the outside, and working toward plate. When no knife is to be used, the forks may be placed at the right.

Bread and butter plates are above the fork at the left, and the water glass above the tip of the knife at the right. The picture on *page 51* shows you a well-set place at a luncheon table, arranged for a soup or casserole main course.

The Kitchen Holds a Challenge gives other hints on planning, marketing and serving. See special chapters for salad and dessert suggestions and recipes.

SUGGESTIONS FOR LUNCHEON OR SUPPER MENUS

Simple—Family

Meal-in-a-Sandwich, 202
Baked Apple, 26   Cream
Beverage

★

Corn-Pepper Custard, 63
Cheese Muffins, 65
Cabbage and Pineapple Salad, 144
Frosted Cup Cakes, 179
Beverage

★

Minches, 63   Mashed Potatoes, 123
Popovers, 66   Conserve
Sliced Tomato Salad
Fresh Fruit
Beverage

★

Leek and Potato Soup, 52
Cheese Biscuit, 67   Butter
Orange Marmalade, 219
Danish Apple Cake, 154
Beverage

More Elaborate—Company

Veal Salad, 147
Toasted English Muffins, 32
Strawberry Shortcake, 225
Whipped Cream
Beverage

★

Cheese-Chive Soufflé, 61
Potato Chips   Sautéed Tomatoes
Nut Bread, 69   Butter
Sunny-Side-Up Mold, 153
Iced or Hot Beverage

★

Chicken Croquettes, 58 Creamed Peas
Parker House Rolls, 71   Butter
Avocado-Grapefruit Salad, 146
Tumble Torte, 154   Beverage

★

Manhattan Clam Chowder, 53
Pretzels   Butterscotch Rolls, 68
Cucumber Salad
Deep-Dish Apple Pie, 168
Beverage

SOUPS AND CHOWDERS

CREAM SOUPS

2 cups Thin White Sauce
  (*page* 109)
1 to 1½ cups seasoned, prepared vegetable and liquid, or chicken and stock

Make white sauce, cover and keep hot over boiling water.

Prepare cooked vegetable or chicken as directed below. Add to white sauce and

Make something special out of a two course lunch with soup, salad and a hot bread—
fresh fruit for dessert.

**garnish with: paprika, nutmeg,
minced parsley or chives,
whipped cream, croutons, or
popped corn**

Makes 4 (¾ to 1 cup) portions.

heat thoroughly. Add additional seasoning
to taste.

When ready to serve, beat with spoon or
rotary beater. Serve in heated bowls or
large cups and garnish as desired.

CREAM OF CELERY SOUP

Use outer stalks of celery. Cook 1 ½ cups finely sliced celery and
1 slice onion in ⅔ cup salted water about 15 minutes. Remove onion and add
celery and liquid to thin white sauce. Season with celery salt. Garnish with
croutons, minced parsley or chives.

CREAM OF CHICKEN SOUP

Add 1 cup minced chicken and ½ cup chicken stock to thin white
sauce. Season to taste and garnish as desired.

CREAM OF CORN SOUP

Heat 2 cups or 1 can (No. 303) canned cream corn and 1 slice
onion in 1 cup milk in double boiler about 10 minutes. Remove onion and force
corn through sieve. Add pulp and liquid to thin white sauce. Garnish with
popped corn, paprika or whipped cream.

CREAM OF PEA SOUP

Heat 1 ½ cups or ⅔ can (No. 2) cooked or canned peas, ½ of liquor from can or ½ cup cooking water, dash of scraped onion and ½ teaspoon sugar about 10 minutes. Force through sieve and add with ½ cup rich milk to thin white sauce. Garnish as desired. *Makes about 4 portions.*

CREAM OF SPINACH SOUP

Use 1 cup cooked spinach and liquid (about 1 pound fresh spinach). Heat and force through sieve. Add pulp and liquid, dash of scraped onion and ½ cup rich milk to thin white sauce. Garnish with a dash of nutmeg. *Makes about 4 portions.*

CREAM OF TOMATO SOUP

Cook 2 cups or 1 can (No. 303) canned tomatoes and 1 small slice onion about 10 minutes. Force through sieve and reheat. Just before serving, stir hot tomato pulp and juice gradually into hot thin white sauce. Season to taste and serve at once. Garnish as desired. If soup curdles, beat with rotary beater until smooth. *Makes about 4 portions.*

LEEK AND POTATO SOUP

1 quart beef stock, or 1 quart
    water and 4 bouillon cubes
4 medium-sized potatoes
1 bunch leeks
½ teaspoon salt
⅛ teaspoon pepper
3 tablespoons butter

Measure stock into large saucepan. Pare and cut potatoes in pieces and add to stock. Wash leeks, cut off green leaves from blanched stems or bulbous roots, and add these with seasonings to soup kettle. Bring to a boil, then cook, covered, about 20 minutes, or until potatoes are soft. Force all through coarse sieve. Keep hot.

Cut remaining white part of leeks in thin slices crosswise and sauté slowly in butter about 10 minutes, or until light golden brown, stirring constantly. Add to hot soup, rinsing pan with stock mixture. Season to taste and dilute with water or stock if thick.

Makes 4 large portions.

MANHATTAN CLAM CHOWDER

2 white onions, minced
½ clove garlic, minced
¼ cup chopped celery
2 tablespoons minced green
  pepper
3 tablespoons butter
2 cups diced potatoes
3 cups boiling water
2 teaspoons salt
1 stick (2-inch) cinnamon
3 whole cloves
1 bay leaf
1 can (No. 1) or 1½ cups minced
  clams
1½ cups tomato juice
dash of cayenne
dash of allspice
4 pilot or crisp crackers

Makes 4 large portions.

Prepare onion, garlic, celery and green pepper, and sauté slowly in butter in large saucepan about 4 minutes, stirring constantly. Add potatoes, hot water, salt and spices tied in cheesecloth bag. Boil, covered, about 15 minutes, or until potatoes are just soft.

Then add clams and tomato juice to soup mixture and bring to a boil. Remove spice bag and add cayenne and allspice.

Pour into heated tureen or bowls over plain or crumbled crackers.

NEW ENGLAND CLAM CHOWDER

⅓ pound salt pork, diced
2 small onions, minced
2 cups diced potatoes
2 cups boiling water
2 teaspoons salt
⅛ teaspoon pepper
2 cups milk
1 can (No. 1) or 1½ cups minced
  clams
4 pilot or crisp crackers, plain or
  crumbled

Makes 4 large portions.

Chop or dice salt pork. Try out or fry slowly in large saucepan. Add onions and sauté 5 minutes, stirring to brown evenly. Then add potatoes, hot water and seasonings. Boil, covered, about 15 minutes, or until potatoes are just soft.

Add milk and clams, and bring to a boil. If fresh clams are used, chop or grind 1 pint and cook in liquor 5 minutes; then add to soup mixture.

Pour into heated bowls over crackers.

OYSTER STEW

1 quart milk

1 pint (20 to 28) oysters
4 tablespoons butter
½ teaspoon salt
dash of pepper
¼ teaspoon Worcestershire sauce
paprika
crackers or oysterettes

Makes 4 portions.

Scald milk in double boiler. Keep hot.

Pick over oysters, removing bits of shell. Drain and reserve liquor. Cook oysters in butter over low heat until edges begin to curl, or about 5 minutes. Season and add with liquor to hot milk.

Pour at once into heated bowls. Sprinkle with paprika and serve with crackers.

RICE DISHES

Modern processing, with the development of *converted* rice, has changed cooking methods. Cleaning, washing and sometimes most of the cooking has been completed before the rice leaves the factory. Washing of converted rice before cooking is unnecessary and is wasteful of flavor and food value. However, old-process rice, which requires washing under running water to remove loose starch, is still available, so you will need to check your package of rice for washing directions.

Rinsing after cooking has been eliminated. Instead, just enough liquid is used to cook rice to desired degree of softness and to be completely absorbed during the cooking process.

Brown or white rice may be used interchangeably in the following recipes. Allow about 20 minutes extra for cooking brown rice, and additional water may need to be added if rice becomes too dry. One teaspoon butter, margarine or salad oil may be added to the cooking water.

STEAMED RICE

Follow package directions for washing. Use 3 cups water or milk, 1 teaspoon salt and 1 cup rice. Bring water and salt to rapid boil in top part of double boiler. Add rice slowly so that boiling does not stop. Boil 2 minutes. Cover and cook over boiling water about 40 minutes, or until just soft. *Makes about 3 cups rice, or 4 to 6 portions.*

BOILED RICE

Follow package directions for washing. Use 1 ¾ cups water, 1 teaspoon salt and 1 cup rice. Bring water and salt to a rapid boil in saucepan. Add rice slowly so that boiling does not stop. Cover and cook over low heat from 20 to 30 minutes, or until just soft. Add more water during cooking if rice becomes too dry. Uncover for last 5 minutes of cooking, shaking pot occasionally or stirring with fork to separate grains and make rice fluffy. *Makes about 3 cups rice.*

PRE-COOKED RICE

Do not wash rice. Combine 1 ½ cups boiling water, 1 teaspoon salt and 1 ⅓ cups pre-cooked rice in saucepan. Mix just enough to moisten all rice Cover and remove from heat. Let stand 13 minutes. *Makes about 3 cups.*

RICE-RING

1 recipe Boiled Rice (above) **or
   3 cups cooked rice**
2 eggs, beaten
½ cup milk or light cream

Boil or steam rice. Beat eggs until foamy, then stir in milk. Add to boiled rice, stirring gently to mix well.

Turn into well-greased, 8-inch ring mold and set in pan of hot water. Bake in 350° F. (moderate) oven about 30 minutes, or until set.

Unmold on heated chop plate and fill with well-seasoned creamed chicken, fish or mushrooms, as desired.

Makes 4 to 6 portions.

CHICKEN OR VEAL CASSEROLE

3 cups cooked rice

6 medium-sized onions
1 cup sliced celery
3 tablespoons butter
1 bay leaf
¼ teaspoon thyme
¼ teaspoon sage
**2 cups cubed, cooked chicken or
   veal**
¼ cup heavy cream

Makes 4 to 6 portions.

Boil or steam rice. Keep hot.

Cut onion and celery in thin slices. Sauté slowly in butter about 10 minutes, stirring to brown evenly. Add seasonings and simmer, covered, 5 minutes. Stir in chicken and heat thoroughly. Add to hot cooked rice, tossing lightly with fork until mixed. Turn into greased large casserole. Pour cream over top and bake in 400° F. (hot) oven 15 minutes, or until browned.

SHRIMP AND RICE CASSEROLE

2 cups cooked rice (*page* 54)
2 cups Thin White Sauce (*page* 109)
⅓ pound sharp cheese
dash of cayenne
1½ cups or cans (No. 1) cooked shrimps, or 1 pound fresh shrimps, cooked (*page* 106)
3 tablespoons butter, melted
⅔ cup dry bread crumbs

Makes about 4 portions.

Cook rice, using ⅔ cup rice. Keep hot. Make white sauce and keep hot. Grind cheese or chop fine, add to sauce and stir until melted. Add cayenne.

Prepare canned or fresh shrimps as directed. Pour half of sauce into greased 1½-quart casserole. Place half of rice over sauce. Arrange shrimps on top and cover with remaining rice. Pour remaining sauce over all and top with buttered crumbs.

Bake in 350° F. (moderate) oven about 25 minutes, or until browned. Serve hot.

PASTE SPECIALTIES

BOILED MACARONI

Use about 1½ quarts rapidly boiling water and 2 teaspoons salt to 1 cup (1- to 2-inch pieces) broken or elbow macaroni, shells or small shapes. Add slowly to water so that boiling does not stop. Boil 9 to 12 minutes, or until tender. Drain in colander and add 2 tablespoons butter or margarine. Reheat in sauce or in covered colander placed over hot water. Macaroni, spaghetti and noodles about double in bulk on cooking. Allow 1 to 1⅓ ounces uncooked macaroni per portion.

BOILED SPAGHETTI

Use 4 to 5 quarts water to 1 package (8 to 9 oz.) spaghetti. Place ends in boiling salted water and coil down as they soften, being sure that boiling does not stop during addition. Drain, butter and reheat as above.

BOILED NOODLES

Follow directions for Boiled Macaroni.

BAKED MACARONI AND CHEESE

2 to 3 cups **Medium White Sauce**
(*page* 109)
½ **package (9 oz. pkge.) macaroni,**
boiled
1½ **to 2 cups grated cheese**
2 **tablespoons butter**
½ **cup dry bread crumbs**

Makes 4 to 6 portions.

Make white sauce and keep hot. Cook macaroni and arrange in layers with sauce and cheese, using about ⅓ of each for separate layers. Cover with buttered crumbs.

Bake in 350° F. (moderate) oven for 25 to 30 minutes, or until browned.

SPAGHETTI MÉLANGE

1 **large onion, chopped**
¼ **cup chopped green pepper**
4 **tablespoons olive oil or bacon fat**
1 **pound beef chuck, ground**
3½ **cups or 1 can (No. 2½) toma-**
toes
½ **package (9 oz. pkge.) spaghetti,**
boiled (*page* 56)

Makes about 4 portions.

Sauté onion and pepper in oil slowly for 5 minutes. Add beef and continue browning for 15 minutes, stirring frequently. Add tomatoes and let simmer 10 minutes. Boil spaghetti. Drain and add to meat-tomato mixture, stirring enough to mix.

SPAGHETTI WITH MARINARA SAUCE

1 **recipe Marinara Sauce** (*page* 111)
1 **package (9 oz.) spaghetti, boiled**
(*page* 56)

Makes 4 to 6 generous portions.

Make Marinara Sauce and keep hot. Pour over spaghetti, served on heated plates.

HELPS IN DEEP-FAT FRYING

Use a deep kettle or saucepan (about 2 quarts) with straight sides; a frying basket or large strainer to hold food and to make easy the lowering of food into hot fat, and removing of food when it has finished frying; a fat thermometer with clip to hook over side of kettle for accurate testing of temperature of fat; a fat which can be heated to a high temperature without smoking, using about 2½ pounds, or enough to half-fill kettle and immerse food.

Procedure: Heat fat to the desired temperature and regulate heat to keep it constant. Adjust thermometer so that bulb is covered but does not touch bottom. If a thermometer is not available, drop a 1-inch cube of bread into hot fat and note time for browning. If it browns in 60 seconds, the fat is right for doughnuts; in 40 seconds, it is right for croquettes; in 20 seconds, it is right for French fried potatoes. This method is only approximate. The thermometer method indicates exact temperatures called for in recipes. Do not heat fat until it smokes. Do not fry too much food at one time; that cools the fat too fast and food is likely to be fat soaked. After using, strain fat through cheesecloth or fine strainer; store in covered container.

CROQUETTES

Croquettes are made of meat, chicken, fish, eggs, cheese, vegetables, cereals, or nuts—often left-overs. They may be shaped as cones, cylinders, balls or cutlets. Each is covered with a golden brown, crisp crust, and the inside is moist and savory, not dry nor greasy.

Utensils Needed

A flat-bottomed, straight-sided, deep kettle; wire basket or egg whip for lowering food into or lifting it out of fat; special fat thermometer for testing temperature of fat; shallow pan lined with absorbent paper; double boiler, measuring cup and set of spoons; tablespoon, spatula, saucer.

Order of Work

1. Assemble utensils and ingredients.
2. Prepare croquette mixture; chill.
3. Fill kettle about ⅔ full with lard, hydrogenated fat, corn oil or cottonseed oil. Heat slowly to 375°–385° F.
4. Shape croquettes.
5. Roll in crumbs, egg, then crumbs. Place in frying basket.
6. Fry 2 to 5 minutes.
7. Drain on absorbent paper. Serve hot.
8. Strain fat through several thicknesses of cheesecloth into container.

RECIPE

1 cup Thick White Sauce (*page* 109)

2 cups ground or diced, cooked meat, chicken or fish

1 teaspoon grated onion or Worcestershire sauce

1 cup fine bread crumbs

1 egg, slightly beaten

1 tablespoon milk or water

any savory sauce

Makes about 12 small croquettes, or 4 to 6 portions.

Make white sauce. Stir in meat, chicken or fish and seasoning. Chill several hours. When cold, shape into cylinder, cone or ball shapes, using about 1 heaping tablespoon for each.

Place crumbs on 2 flat plates, and egg mixed with milk in shallow bowl. Roll shapes in crumbs, then dip in egg mixture and roll again in crumbs.

Fry in hot deep fat (375°–385° F.) for 2 to 5 minutes, or until browned. Drain. Serve hot with a sauce.

EGG CROQUETTES

Follow recipe for Croquettes, only substitute 2 cups chopped hard-cooked eggs (*page* 36) for meat.

SWEET POTATO-ALMOND CROQUETTES

4 medium-sized sweet potatoes, cooked

2 tablespoons butter

1 teaspoon salt

¼ teaspoon pepper

2 tablespoons brown sugar

½ cup chopped, blanched almonds

1 cup crushed cornflakes

1 egg, slightly beaten

1 tablespoon water

Makes 12 patties or 6 portions.

Boil or bake sweet potatoes (*pages* 119–122). Mash or put through ricer. Add butter, seasonings and nuts, and beat until fluffy. Chill.

Shape into patties or cylinders, using about 1 heaping tablespoon for each.
Roll in crumbs, dip in egg-water mixture and roll again in crumbs.

Fry in hot deep fat (375° F.) for 3 to 4 minutes, or until golden brown. Drain and serve hot.

SOUFFLÉS

CHEESE SOUFFLÉ

A good soufflé is light and puffy, about once and a half as high as the unbaked dish. It shrinks slightly on standing. It is topped with a browned crust, often uneven and cracked, which springs back when touched. The inside is spongy and the air cells are set. It is moist, tender, with a rich cheesy flavor.

Utensils Needed

1½-quart casserole, pan to hold casserole or water-jacketed casserole; saucepan; measuring cup and spoons, tablespoon; deep bowl, small bowl, rotary beater; grater; rubber scraper.

Makes 1 large casserole and serves 4 to 6.

Order of Work

1. Assemble utensils and ingredients.
2. Grease casserole very well.
3. Light oven, or turn on heat and adjust for 350° F. (moderate) oven.
4. Mix soufflé mixture and bake.
5. Serve at once with a creamy sauce.

RECIPE

3 tablespoons butter
3 tablespoons flour
1 cup milk
1 cup (¼ lb.) grated American cheese
½ teaspoon salt
⅛ teaspoon paprika
3 eggs, separated

Melt butter, stir in flour. Stir in milk and cook 5 minutes, stirring until thickened. Add cheese and seasonings to sauce, stirring until cheese is melted. Remove from heat.

Beat egg whites until stiff. Beat egg yolks until thick; then stir into cheese sauce. Fold in egg whites gently but thoroughly with flecks of white showing.

Turn into greased casserole using scraper. Set in shallow pan of hot water.

Bake in 350° F. (moderate) oven for 30 to 60 minutes, or until delicately browned and firm to touch. Garnish as desired.

CHEESE-CHIVE SOUFFLÉ

1 recipe Cheese Soufflé
½ teaspoon minced chives or
   onion
1 teaspoon minced parsley

Serves 4 to 6.

Follow recipe for Cheese Soufflé, only stir chives and parsley into cheese mixture before folding in egg whites.

TOMATO-CHEESE SOUFFLÉ

1 cup strained tomato juice
3 tablespoons quick-cooking
   tapioca
1 cup grated American cheese
½ teaspoon salt
dash of cayenne
3 eggs, separated
parsley

Serves 4 to 6.

Boil tomato juice and tapioca 1 minute, stirring constantly. Add cheese and seasonings, and stir until cheese is melted. Remove from heat.

Beat egg whites until stiff. Beat egg yolks until thick; then stir into cheese sauce. Fold in egg whites.

Turn into greased large casserole and set it in pan of hot water.

Bake in 350° F. (moderate) oven for 30 to 60 minutes. Garnish with parsley and serve at once.

CHICKEN SOUFFLÉ

Follow recipe for Tomato-Cheese Soufflé, only substitute 1 cup milk for tomato juice and 1 cup minced chicken for cheese. For variety add ½ teaspoon minced chives or onion, 1 teaspoon minced parsley or 2 tablespoons minced pimiento to the cheese-egg yolk mixture before folding in egg whites. If desired, turn into greased individual casseroles, set in pan of hot water and bake in 350° F. (moderate) oven about 30 minutes. Serve with a sauce or creamed vegetable. *Makes 6 individual casseroles.*

RICE AND CHEESE SOUFFLÉ

1 cup **Boiled Rice** (*page* 55)
1 cup **Medium White Sauce**
  (*page* 109)
1 cup **grated American cheese**
2 tablespoons **chopped green pep-**
  per
½ teaspoon **scraped onion**
¼ teaspoon **paprika**
2 **eggs, separated**

Makes about 4 portions.

Boil rice. Make sauce; add cheese, green pepper, onion and paprika, stirring until cheese is melted. Stir in rice and remove from heat.

Beat egg whites until stiff. Beat egg yolks until thick; stir into rice-cheese mixture. Fold in egg whites. Turn into greased casserole and set in shallow pan of hot water.

Bake in 350° F. (moderate) oven for 30 to 60 minutes, or until browned and firm to touch. Serve at once.

MISCELLANEOUS

WELSH RABBIT

1 cup **Thin White Sauce**
  (*page* 109)
1 teaspoon **dry mustard**
2 cups (½ lb.) **grated American**
  cheese
4 slices **buttered hot toast**

Makes 4 portions.

Make white sauce, only stir in mustard with flour. Keep hot over boiling water. Add cheese to sauce, stirring until melted.

Serve on hot toast.

TOMATO RABBIT

1 can **condensed tomato soup**
2 cups (½ lb.) **grated American**
  cheese
1 **egg, slightly beaten**
¼ teaspoon **dry mustard**
6 slices **hot toast, buttered and cut**
  in halves

Makes 4 portions.

Heat soup and cheese over hot water, stirring until cheese is melted.

Beat egg until foamy. Then stir in mustard and a small amount of cheese sauce. Stir this slowly into remaining hot cheese sauce.

CORN-PEPPER CUSTARD

3 eggs, beaten
2 cups milk
2 cups canned corn
¼ cup chopped green pepper
1 teaspoon salt
¼ teaspoon pepper
1 tablespoon sugar
2 tablespoons butter, melted

Makes 4 to 6 portions.

Beat eggs until foamy in deep bowl. Add remaining ingredients and stir very well. Turn into greased 1½-quart casserole.

Place in pan of hot water and bake in 350° F. (moderate) oven about 45 minutes, or until knife comes out clean when inserted into center. Serve hot.

CORN-HAM CUSTARD

Follow recipe for Corn-Pepper Custard, only substitute ½ cup minced cooked ham for green pepper. *Serves 4.*

SCOTTISH "MINCHES"

1 pound beef, ground
2 cups water
4 medium-sized onions, peeled
1 teaspoon salt
⅛ teaspoon pepper

Use chuck, flank, neck, brisket or heel of round. Wipe and grind coarsely, or have butcher do it. Add water, stirring with fork until mass is smooth. Add peeled onions and seasonings, and bring to a boil. Then simmer, covered, for 30 minutes, or until onions are soft when pricked.

½ cup water
2 tablespoons flour
3 cups Mashed Potatoes (*page* 123)
paprika

Makes about 4 portions.

Stir water gradually into flour to make a smooth paste. Add to meat mixture and cook about 5 minutes, stirring constantly. Arrange on hot platter with border of hot, mashed potatoes, sprinkled with paprika.

QUICK BREADS

PLAIN MUFFINS

Good muffins are light, about twice as large as the unbaked muffins. They have rough, high and rounded, but not peaked, tops which are covered with well-browned, tender crusts. Good muffins have a moist, tender crumb, which is medium-fine grained and free from large holes and tunnels. They are delicate in flavor and not too sweet.

Utensils Needed

Medium-sized muffin pans; mixing bowl, small bowl and saucepan; flour sifter, measuring cup and set of spoons, spatula; rotary beater and rubber scraper

Order of Work

1. Assemble utensils and ingredients.
2. Grease the muffin tins.
3. Light oven or turn on heat and adjust for 400° F. (hot) oven.
4. Mix dough, fill pans and bake.
5. Serve very hot.

RECIPE

2 cups sifted flour
2½ teaspoons double-action baking powder
1 teaspoon salt
3 tablespoons sugar
1 egg, beaten
1 cup milk
3 tablespoons shortening, melted

Makes about 12 medium-sized muffins and serves 4 to 6.

Sift flour, measure 2 cups into sifter. Add baking powder, salt and sugar. Mix well, then sift into mixing bowl.

Beat egg until foamy, then stir in milk and melted shortening. Add to flour mixture, stirring only until mixed—not smooth.

With spoon, dip batter into greased cups or muffin pans, using a rubber scraper to empty spoon. Fill ⅔ full.

Bake in 400° F. (hot) oven about 25 minutes, or until firm to touch.

NUT, CURRANT OR DATE MUFFINS

Follow recipe for Plain Muffins, only stir ½ cup washed, dried fruit or ½ cup chopped nuts into flour mixture. Dried fruits such as raisins, figs, apricots or prunes may be used. *Makes about 12 medium-sized muffins.*

BACON MUFFINS

Follow recipe for Plain Muffins, only add ⅓ cup chopped, crisp bacon to flour mixture. *Makes about 12 medium-sized muffins.*

BLUEBERRY MUFFINS

Follow recipe for Plain Muffins (*page 64*), only stir 1 cup blueberries or huckleberries into flour mixture. *Makes about 14 medium-sized muffins.*

CHEESE MUFFINS

Follow recipe for Plain Muffins (*page 64*), only stir ½ cup cheese and ¼ teaspoon paprika into flour mixture. Sprinkle cheese over the tops of the filled muffin pans. *Makes about 12 medium-sized muffins.*

WHOLE WHEAT MUFFINS

Use recipe for Plain Muffins (*page 64*), only substitute 1 cup unsifted whole wheat flour for 1 cup sifted all-purpose flour. Stir whole wheat flour into sifted flour, baking powder, salt and sugar mixture. *Makes about 12 medium-sized muffins.*

CORNBREAD

1 cup sifted all-purpose flour
1 cup yellow cornmeal
3 teaspoons double-action baking powder
1 teaspoon salt
2 teaspoons sugar
1 egg, beaten
1 cup milk
3 tablespoons shortening, melted

Makes 6 (4-inch) squares.

Sift flour, measure 1 cup into sifter. Add cornmeal, baking powder, salt and sugar. Mix well, then sift into mixing bowl.

Beat egg until foamy, then stir in milk and melted shortening. Add to flour mixture, stirring until well mixed.

Turn batter into greased shallow pan, 8 × 12 inches. Bake in 400° F. (hot) oven for 30 to 40 minutes. Serve hot. Split and toast left-over bread.

CORNBREAD WITH BACON

Follow recipe for Cornbread, only sprinkle 1 to 4 slices bacon, diced, over top of batter in pan and bake as directed. When baked place under broiler for 1 minute to crisp bacon. Serve hot. *Makes 6 (4-inch) squares.*

CHEDDAR CORN MUFFINS

Follow recipe for Cornbread, only bake in greased small muffin pans, or corn or bread-stick pans for 20 minutes. Then sprinkle 1 cup grated American cheese over tops and continue baking about 5 minutes, or until a bubbly brown crust is formed. Serve hot. *Makes about* 12 *small muffins, or* 9 *corn sticks.*

POPOVERS

(All ingredients at room temperature)

1 cup sifted flour
½ teaspoon salt
2 eggs, beaten
1 cup milk (scant)
1 tablespoon shortening, melted

Bacon Popovers, add:
1 teaspoon chopped, crisp bacon to each cup

Makes about 8 *popovers.*

Sift flour, measure 1 cup into sifter. Add salt and sift into bowl.

Beat eggs until foamy and stir in milk and shortening. Add to flour and beat until smooth (1 minute with mixer; 2 minutes by hand). Do not overbeat.

Fill cold custard cups or muffin tins ⅓ full and bake in 375° F. (moderate) oven about 60 minutes, or until popovers are firm.

BAKING POWDER BISCUITS

Good biscuits are very light, about twice as large as the unbaked biscuits. They are fairly regular in shape with straight sides and flat tops covered with well-browned, tender crusts. Good biscuits have a creamy white crumb, which is fine, even-grained and flaky, and which pulls apart in layers or sheets.

Utensils Needed	*Order of Work*
Small baking sheet or pan; mixing bowl; flour sifter, measuring cup and set of spoons; spatula, knife or pastry blender; metal spoon and biscuit cutter; rolling pin and board	1. Assemble utensils and ingredients; the baking sheet need not be greased. 2. Light oven or turn on heat, and adjust for 450° F. (very hot) oven. 3. Mix dough. Knead, roll, cut and bake. 4. Serve very hot.

RECIPE

2 cups sifted flour
2½ teaspoons double-action baking powder
1 teaspoon salt
4 tablespoons shortening ★

¾ cup milk (about) ★

Makes about 14 medium-sized biscuits and serves 4 to 6.

★ For richer biscuits use:
  ⅓ cup shortening
  ⅔ cup milk (about)

Sift flour, measure 2 cups into sifter. Add baking powder and salt. Mix well, then sift into mixing bowl.

Cut in shortening until mixture is uniform, like coarse meal.

Stir in milk quickly to form a soft, but not sticky, dough. If not soft enough, add 1 to 2 tablespoons more milk; or, if too soft, add less milk the next time.

Turn dough out on lightly floured board and knead just enough to shape into smooth ball. Roll or pat lightly, ½ inch thick. Cut with floured biscuit cutter. Place rounds on ungreased baking sheet, ½ inch apart for crusty biscuits, and close together for soft ones.

Bake in 450° F. (very hot) oven for 10 to 15 minutes, or until well browned.

CHEESE OR NUT BISCUITS

Follow recipe for Baking Powder Biscuits (above), only stir ⅓ to ½ cup grated American cheese or chopped nuts into flour and shortening mixture before adding milk. *Makes about 24 small (1½-inch) biscuits.*

SCONE BISCUITS

Follow recipe for Baking Powder Biscuits (above), only cut rolled dough with knife to make triangles. Brush with cream or milk and sprinkle with sugar before baking.

DROP BISCUITS

These are often made when time is short. Follow recipe for Baking Powder Biscuits (above), only increase milk to about 1 cup. Drop from teaspoon on ungreased baking sheet, about ½ inch apart. Bake in 450° F. (very hot) oven for 10 to 15 minutes. *Makes about 16 biscuits.*

BUTTERSCOTCH ROLLS

1 recipe Baking Powder Biscuits
  (*page* 66)

Prepare dough for biscuits and roll into an oblong, ¼ inch thick.

4 tablespoons butter
⅓ cup firmly packed brown sugar

Cream together butter and sugar. Spread over rolled dough. Roll as for jelly roll and cut in 1-inch slices. Place slices, cutside down, in greased muffin pans, or close together in greased pan.

Makes about 10 rolls.

Bake in 400° F. (hot) oven for 15 to 20 minutes. Remove at once from pan.

NUT CARAMEL ROLLS

3 tablespoons butter
4 tablespoons brown sugar
½ cup chopped nuts

Melt butter in 8-inch square pan. Stir in sugar to mix well, then sprinkle nuts over top. Remove pan from heat.

1 recipe Butterscotch Rolls
  (*above*)

Make butterscotch rolls, placing slices in pan on top of butter, sugar and nuts.

Bake in 400° F. (hot) oven for 15 to 20 minutes. Invert on heated plate.

STEAMED BROWN BREAD

½ cup sifted rye flour or
  all-purpose flour
½ cup cornmeal
¾ teaspoon baking soda
½ teaspoon salt
½ cup whole wheat flour
½ cup seedless raisins
6 tablespoons dark molasses
1 cup thick sour milk or buttermilk

Sift rye or all-purpose flour, measure ½ cup into sifter. Add cornmeal, soda and salt. Mix well, then sift into mixing bowl. Stir in unsifted whole wheat flour and washed and dried raisins.

Mix molasses and sour milk, then stir into flour mixture. Turn into well-greased top part (quart-size) of double boiler, filling it only ⅔ full. Cover tightly.

Cook 3 hours over gently boiling water, adding boiling water as needed. Remove cover and place top part in 350° F. (moderate) oven about 15 minutes to dry top.

Makes 1 large loaf.

Remove bread and cool on rack. Wrap in waxed paper.

NUT BREAD

3 cups sifted flour
3¾ teaspoons double-action baking powder
1 teaspoon salt
½ cup sugar
1 cup chopped nuts
1 egg, beaten
1 cup milk
4 tablespoons shortening, melted

Sift flour, measure 3 cups into sifter. Add baking powder, salt and sugar. Mix well, then sift into mixing bowl. Stir in nuts.

Beat egg until foamy, then stir in milk. Add to flour mixture, stirring only until mixed. Stir in shortening.

Turn into greased loaf pan and bake in 350° F. (moderate) oven about 1 hour, or until crust is brown on top and bread shrinks slightly from sides.

Remove from pan and cool on rack. Then store in covered container. Bread should be 24 hours old to cut in thin slices.

Makes 1 loaf, 9 × 5 × 3 inches.

DATE-NUT BREAD

Follow recipe for Nut Bread, only substitute ½ cup firmly packed brown sugar for granulated sugar, reduce nuts to ½ cup, and add 1 cup finely sliced dates. Stir brown sugar, nuts and dates into sifted flour mixture. Seedless raisins, currants or sliced dried apricots may be used instead of dates.

WHOLE WHEAT NUT BREAD

Follow recipe for Date-Nut Bread, only substitute 1½ cups unsifted whole wheat flour for 1½ cups all-purpose flour, and black walnuts for nuts.

ORANGE BREAD

Follow recipe for Nut Bread, only substitute ½ to 1 cup finely chopped candied orange peel for 1 cup nuts; or use ½ cup each chopped candied orange peel and nuts.

INDIVIDUAL COFFEE RINGS

2 cups sifted flour
2½ teaspoons double-action baking powder
1 teaspoon salt
2 tablespoons sugar
⅓ cup shortening
1 egg, beaten
⅓ cup milk
2 tablespoons butter, melted

⅓ cup flour
2 tablespoons sugar
dash of salt
½ teaspoon cinnamon
2 tablespoons butter

Makes about 12 individual cakes.

Sift flour, measure 2 cups into sifter. Add baking powder, salt and sugar, mix well, then sift into mixing bowl. Cut in shortening until well mixed.

Beat egg until foamy, then stir in milk. Add to flour-shortening mixture, stirring quickly to form a stiff dough. Turn dough out on lightly floured board and knead just enough to shape into smooth ball. Roll ⅓ inch thick and cut with floured large doughnut cutter. Place on ungreased baking sheet and brush tops with melted butter.

For topping, mix and sift flour, sugar, salt and cinnamon. Cut in butter. Top each ring with mixture. Bake in 450° F. (very hot) oven for 12 minutes.

QUICK COFFEE CAKE

Follow recipe for Individual Coffee Rings, with the following changes: Prepare soft biscuit dough, increasing milk to ⅔ cup, then spread dough in greased 8-inch square pan. Brush top with melted butter and sprinkle topping mixture evenly over surface. Bake in 400° F. (hot) oven about 30 minutes. *Makes 8-inch coffee cake.*

POINTS ON MAKING YEAST BREAD AND ROLLS

Yeast—Either active dry yeast or compressed yeast cake may be used interchangeably in the same amount in all recipes (1 package equals 1 cake). Active dry yeast is dissolved in warm water (115° F.); compressed yeast cake is dissolved in lukewarm water (95° F.) before use.

Kneading—Turn stiff dough out on lightly floured board. Cover with a bowl and let stand 10 minutes to tighten up. To knead, place hands on dough, raise and move it forward with fingers, then press it down and away from you with heels of hands, using a rolling motion. Turn dough slightly and repeat kneading motion until dough is smooth and elastic, and the bubbles or blisters are distributed evenly. Sprinkle flour on board as necessary to keep dough from sticking. Hands may be greased lightly or floured to make handling easier. It will take about 5 minutes to knead the dough.

Rising—Return kneaded dough to mixing bowl which has been scraped clean and greased. Brush lightly with melted fat and cover with clean cloth and loosely fitting lid. Set pan in warm place away from draught or in a large pan of lukewarm water (110° F.), keeping the temperature of water constant. It will take from 2 to 4 hours for dough to double in bulk. A second rising is not necessary for good rolls.

Shaping—When dough is light and has doubled in bulk, knead lightly in bowl for ½ to 1 minute to distribute the gas bubbles; then mold as desired. Brush tops with melted butter, cover and let rise in warm place until doubled in bulk (about 1 hour).

For bread, flatten dough and fold lengthwise (stretch and pull to lengthen). Bring the 2 ends to center and overlap together tightly. Place in greased bread pan with seamside down.

For biscuits or buns, cut off small pieces of dough and fold sides under repeatedly until top is smooth and dough is round. Place in greased pan, about 1 inch apart.

For cloverleaf rolls, shape very small pieces into round balls, dip in melted butter and place 3 in each section of greased muffin pan.

For Parker House rolls, roll dough ¼ inch thick and cut with floured biscuit cutter. Make crease across center of each round and spread with melted butter. Fold each over and press lightly on fold and along edges. Place rolls 1 inch apart on greased sheet.

Baking—Bake in a preheated 400° F. (hot) oven for bread; 400° to 425° F. (hot) oven for rolls. When done, bread will shrink from the side of the pan and will sound hollow when removed from pan and tapped on the bottom of the loaf. Remove bread and rolls from pan and cool on rack. For shiny top, brush lightly with melted butter.

STANDARD BREAD OR ROLLS

(Points on Making Yeast Bread and Rolls, *page 70*)

Utensils Needed

Large mixing bowl with cover, pan large enough to hold bowl; flour sifter, measuring cup and spoon. Wooden spoon, rolling board and pin (rolls); knife, biscuit cutter; clean cloth; bread pans, baking sheet, or muffin pans.

Order of Work

1. Assemble utensils and ingredients.
2. Mix dough, knead, and let rise in warm place until doubled (2 to 4 hours).
3. Shape into bread or rolls. Let rise until doubled (about 1 hour).
4. About 15 minutes before baking, light oven or turn on heat and adjust for 400° F. (hot) oven for bread; 400° to 425° F. (hot) oven for rolls.
5. Bake bread 30 to 40 minutes; bake rolls 15 to 25 minutes.
6. To reheat cold rolls, place in paper bag, sprinkle with water and heat in 400° F. (hot) oven for 5 minutes.

RECIPE

1 cake compressed yeast or 1 package active dry yeast
¼ cup milk
¾ cup milk, scalded
¾ teaspoon salt
2 tablespoons sugar
3 tablespoons shortening
3 to 3½ cups sifted flour melted butter or other fat

Makes 1 loaf of bread or 18 rolls.

Crumble compressed yeast in ¼ cup lukewarm milk; or sprinkle active dry yeast over ¼ cup warm milk. Stir until dissolved.

Pour hot milk into large bowl. Add salt, sugar and shortening. Cool until bottom of bowl feels slightly warm (85° F.). Add dissolved yeast. Add 1 cup flour and beat thoroughly. Stir in remaining flour gradually, adding just enough to make a dough that leaves the sides of bowl.

Knead until smooth and elastic. Brush with melted butter. Cover, let rise in warm place until doubled.

Knead, and shape into bread or rolls. Place in greased pans. Brush with melted butter, cover and let rise in warm place until doubled.

Bake bread in 400° F. (hot) oven for 30 to 40 minutes; bake rolls in 400° to 425° F. (hot) oven for 15 to 25 minutes.

REFRIGERATOR ROLLS

Follow recipe for Standard Rolls (*page 72*). When dough is light, knead it about 5 minutes to permit escape of gas, then place in greased bowl. Brush top with melted butter, cover tightly and place in refrigerator until ready to use. About 1 ½ hours before baking, remove desired quantity of dough, shape, as desired, and proceed as for rolls. Dough can be kept for several days in refrigerator, and quantities baked as needed. *Makes about 2 dozen rolls.*

SWEET YEAST ROLLS

Follow Standard Bread or Rolls recipe (*page 72*). Increase sugar to ¼ cup and shortening to ⅓ cup. Add 1 egg, well beaten, to soft dough. Bake in 375° F. (moderate) oven for 20 to 30 minutes.

COFFEE BREAD

1 cake compressed yeast or 1 package active dry yeast
¼ cup milk
½ cup milk, scalded
½ teaspoon salt
⅓ cup sugar
6 tablespoons shortening
3 cups flour (about)
1 egg, well beaten

¼ cup sugar
⅓ cup flour
¼ cup chopped nuts
4 tablespoons butter

Makes 1 (9-inch) square coffee cake.

Note: To reheat bread, sprinkle top with water and place in 400° F. (hot) oven about 5 minutes.

Combine ingredients as directed for Standard Bread or Rolls recipe (*page 72*), only add well-beaten egg to sponge mixture before adding last half of flour. Add flour to make a stiff dough which can be beaten but which is too soft to knead.

Cover dough and let rise in warm place until spongy and doubled in bulk. Then cut down or beat thoroughly and spread evenly in greased 9-inch square pan.

Mix together sugar and flour. Stir in nuts and butter to make a crumbly mass. Sprinkle over dough in pan. Cover and let rise in warm place until doubled in bulk (1 to 2 hours).

Bake in 375° F. (moderate) oven for 20 to 30 minutes. Serve warm.

A Well-Served Dinner
Is an Achievement

A dinner is the test of a cook's ability. All cooking experience leads to the well-served dinner. See *The Kitchen Holds a Challenge* for hints on planning, marketing and serving. In this chapter you will find recipes for appetizers, soups, meats, sauces and vegetables served at dinner. (See special chapters for salad and dessert suggestions and recipes.) There are also suggested menus. Some of the recipes are what is known as basic and the menus should be looked upon as patterns. When you master the recipes and use the menus, try to look upon them as foundations upon which to build your own cooking accomplishment. As you acquire skill and new tastes in food, there will be little changes in many dishes that you will think of yourself. Personality counts in cooking, too. However, in all dinner planning there are things constantly to keep in mind.

Planning the Dinner. For a family dinner which you are managing by yourself attempt only one new dish. For guests, never attempt *any* recipe that you don't know thoroughly. If you are anxious to have something new and special for special guests, have a dress rehearsal for the family, first. As many cooks have become famous for simple dinners made up of simple foods, like meat pies and corned beef and cabbage, as have for ethereal soufflés and complicated desserts.

Suit the Meal to the Weather. A hot, filling meal on a stifling day is a sorry failure. On the other hand, a cold meal on a summer evening turned unexpectedly cool or rainy—as it has a way of doing, especially at

74

seashore and mountains—is far from cheery. There is always a way to turn ingredients for the hot meal into something cool and appetizing; and vice versa, with the ingredients for the cold dinner. The chicken and vegetables which you intended to use in a pie can, with a little gelatin, be made into a chilled jellied chicken loaf. On the other hand, chicken, ham, tongue or cooked vegetables, planned for a salad, can, with White Sauce (*page* 109), be turned into a hot, appetizing dish.

Food Preparation. Meat makes the dinner. Know how to prepare a good steak and roast, how to broil and fry poultry and fish to the proverbial turn. Then when you can take the less expensive and less tender cuts, and by patient attention and artful seasoning, turn them into savory Swiss steaks, pot roasts, fragrant brown stews or tasty casseroles, you will have won your spurs. Taste each dish before it is taken to the table to see that it is well seasoned. Experiment with new seasonings. Learn to use herbs, garlic, and condiments to develop food flavor.

Try Planking. A most interesting way of presenting food at dinner is on a plank. Many meats and fish, and a few vegetables can be cooked, from beginning to end, on the plank. Besides decidedly making the most of food, planking helps a cook in managing her kitchen. Cooking utensils can be washed and put away while the plank is in the oven.

Dinner Service. Colorful cloths, mats or T.V. trays may be used at dinner, except for the most formal affairs, when white damask is the perfect spread.

The rules for setting the family dinner table are practically the same as for the family luncheon. The picture of a place setting for an informal dinner (*page* 7) will give you a very good idea of an attractively and correctly set place. The silver is arranged very much as for luncheon, except that there is more of it, because there are more courses at dinner.

A bowl of fresh flowers, a small flowering or ornamental plant, a bowl of colorful fruit or vegetables, or even a piece of bright china, pottery or glass makes an attractive centerpiece at dinner.

SUGGESTED FAMILY DINNER MENUS

Warm Weather Dinners

Veal Aspic, 263   Horseradish
Asparagus Hollandaise, 119
Potato Chips, 123
Hot Cornbread, 65
Melon-Mint Cup, 77
Iced Tea, 35

★

Tomato Juice
Boiled Halibut, 105 Green Sauce, 111
Green Peas, 118
Cucumber-Radish Salad, 140
Lemon Ice Cream, 160
Rolls   Butter
Beverage

★

Sliced Corned Beef   Mustard
Sautéed Zucchini, 121
Broiled Tomatoes, 126
Hot Biscuits, 66 Strawberry Jam, 218
Fruit Gelatin, 152   Whipped Cream
Beverage

★

Baked Dinners

Vegetable Cocktail, 78
Baked Stuffed Pork Chops, 93
Baked Sweet Potatoes, 122
Coleslaw, 140
Rye Crisp   Baked Custard, 151
Beverage

Cold Weather Dinners

Vegetable Soup, 81
Minute Steak, 82
Baked Sweet Potatoes, 122
Cauliflower au Gratin, 121
Celery   Radishes   Bread   Butter
Date Custard Pie, 169
Beverage

★

Pot Roast, 90   Brown Gravy, 86
Franconia Potatoes, 122
Broccoli, 118   Boiled Carrots, 118
Green Salad, 139   Biscuits, 66
Gingersnap Cheese Cake, 154
Beverage

★

Ham Loaf, 88 Cucumber Sauce, 113
Corn Fritters, 121 with Lemon Juice
and Sugar
Baked Squash, 125   Rye Crisp
Mixed Fruit Salad, 146
Rice Meringue Pudding, 254
Beverage

★

Sunday Dinners

Grape Juice-Ginger Ale Cup, 77
Fried Chicken, 99
Chicken Gravy, 86
Mashed Potatoes, 123   Spinach, 124
Tomato Salad

Biscuits, 66   Plum Jelly, 223
Vanilla Ice Cream, 159
Drop Cookies, 183

Emergency Dinners

Canned Mushroom Soup
Cheese Soufflé, 60   Crisp Bacon
Asparagus Salad   Rolls   Butter
Mixed fruit   Beverage

★

Antipasto, 78
Baked Mackerel, Essex Style, 105
Baked Potatoes, 122
Cabbage au Gratin, 121
Jelly   Muffins, 64
Candy Apple Pie, 269

★

Creamed Frizzled Beef, 283
Baked Potato, 119 Frozen Vegetable
Crisp Salad, French dressing 134
Fruit   Cookies   Beverage

APPETIZERS

GRAPE JUICE-GINGER ALE CUP

⅔ **cup chilled grape juice**
⅔ **cup chilled ginger ale**
1 teaspoon lemon or lime juice

Makes about 4 portions.

Combine ingredients. Serve in chilled cocktail glasses, allowing ⅓ cup for each.

FROSTED LIME-GRAPEFRUIT COCKTAIL

2 tablespoons honey
1½ tablespoons lime juice
1 cup grapefruit juice
2 tablespoons lemon juice
¼ cup sugar

Makes about 4 portions.

Mix honey and fruit juices. Chill.

Frost chilled cocktail glasses, dipping rims in lemon juice, then in sugar. Fill with juice. Serve at once.

MELON-MINT CUP

3 tablespoons lemon juice
1 cup diced watermelon
1 cup diced cantaloupe
mint jelly, diced

Makes about 4 portions.

Sprinkle lemon juice over melons. Toss lightly with fork. Chill.
Pile in glasses, top with jelly. Serve.

VEGETABLE COCKTAIL

3 tomatoes, diced
1 small cucumber, diced
½ cup diced celery
½ green pepper, finely sliced
2 teaspoons scraped onion
3 tablespoons lemon juice

Makes about 4 portions.

Prepare vegetables, cutting tomatoes in larger cubes and slicing pepper very thin. Add onion and lemon juice. Chill. Pile in sherbet glasses. Serve.

ANTIPASTO

4 small tomatoes, in wedges
12 scallions
2 cooked beets, sliced
1 sweet red pepper, sliced
12 thin slices salami
1 small can anchovies
8 ripe olives
olive oil and vinegar

Makes 4 portions.

Prepare, then arrange vegetables, salami, anchovies and olives attractively on 4 plates. Chill. Serve with olive oil and vinegar.

SEAFOOD COCKTAILS

1 tablespoon lemon juice
¼ cup tomato ketchup
2 teaspoons horseradish
2 drops tabasco sauce, or 3 drops Worcestershire sauce
½ teaspoon salt
1 cup prepared seafood
lemon or lime wedges

Makes about 4 portions.

For sauce, combine lemon juice, ketchup, horseradish, tabasco or Worcestershire sauce, and salt. Chill.

Prepare seafood as directed below. Place in cocktail glasses, add sauce. Garnish with lemon or lime wedges. If desired, serve cocktail glass in bowl of shaved ice.

LOBSTER COCKTAIL

Use Boiled Fresh Lobster (*page* 106) or canned lobster. Break in pieces; chill. Serve with sauce.

SHRIMP COCKTAIL

Use Boiled Fresh Shrimp (*page* 106), removing black vein in back under running water. Dry, dice; chill. Serve with sauce.

CRABMEAT COCKTAIL

Use boiled fresh crabmeat (*page* 108) or canned crabmeat. Flake meat from bony tissue; chill. Serve with sauce.

OYSTER OR CLAM COCKTAIL

Use small or medium-sized oysters; cherrystone or little neck hard-shelled clams, allowing 5 or 6 to each portion. Remove all bits of shell; chill. Serve with sauce.

SOUPS

SOUP STOCK

Stock is a basic soup, and may be made of meat, fish, poultry or vegetables. Vegetables are added to meat stock to contribute flavor and, at end of cooking, are strained out.

Stock may be served plain or used as the foundation of many clear soups. Jellied soups are made with stock; and creamed soups can be made with stock substituted for part of the milk. When vegetables are added to stock for vegetable soup, they are allowed to cook in it only long enough to become tender, and not until they are mushy or strong.

To remove fat from stock, strain through sieve or cheesecloth and allow to become cold quickly. Remove solid fat which forms on top.

To clarify stock, combine egg white and the crushed shell of 1 egg with 2 tablespoons cold water. Add to cold stock. Heat slowly to boiling, stirring constantly. Remove from fire, add ¼ cup cold water and let settle. Strain through 2 thicknesses of cheesecloth.

BROWN SOUP STOCK (BOUILLON)

**4 pounds soup bone from hind or
  fore shank, cracked open**
marrow or 2 tablespoons fat
2½ quarts cold water

¼ cup diced carrot
¼ cup chopped celery leaves
¼ cup diced onion
2 sprigs parsley
2 teaspoons salt

Makes 2 quarts stock or bouillon.

Wipe and cut lean beef in small cubes. Brown ½ of meat in marrow or fat. Add to water with remaining meat. Heat slowly to boiling and boil 10 minutes. Skim thoroughly, cover and simmer 3 hours, removing scum as it forms.

Add vegetables, seasoning. Cook 1 hour.

Strain through fine sieve or several thicknesses of cheesecloth. Cool. When cold, remove fat. Use as stock or bouillon.

WHITE STOCK

Follow recipe for Brown Soup Stock, only substitute for beef shin 4 pounds knuckle of veal, veal scraps, or fowl (largely bones), or a combination of both.

CONSOMMÉ

Follow recipe for Brown Soup Stock, only substitute for the beef shin the following: 2 pounds lean beef, cut in 1-inch cubes; 1 pound marrow bone, cracked; 2 pounds knuckle of veal, cut in pieces. Sauté vegetables in 1 tablespoon butter until lightly browned before adding to stock. Chicken stock or bones may be added to the soup kettle.

GARNISHES FOR SOUPS

Finely minced parsley, cooked, julienne carrots, okra slices, thin slices of mushrooms, alphabet macaroni, rice, barley, tapioca and thin slivers of lemon, may be used in small amounts as soup garnishes.

JELLIED BOUILLON OR CONSOMMÉ

2 to 3 teaspoons gelatin
2 tablespoons cold water
**2 cups boiling Brown Stock
  (above) or Consommé**
salt and pepper
lemon wedges

Makes about 4 portions.

Soak gelatin in water 5 minutes. Add hot stock to softened gelatin. Stir until dissolved, and season highly. Chill until firm. Pile into cups. Garnish with lemon wedges.

FAMILY VEGETABLE SOUP

⅓ cup chopped leeks or onion
½ cup diced carrot
½ cup diced celery
½ cup shelled green peas
½ cup thinly sliced string beans
2 tablespoons chopped parsley
1¼ quarts Brown Stock (*above*)
1 cup canned tomatoes
salt and pepper

Makes about 1½ quarts soup, or 4 to 6 generous portions.

Prepare fresh vegetables and add to stock. Bring to boil. Cover, and simmer about 20 minutes, or until vegetables are done.

Add canned tomatoes and season to taste. Reheat 5 minutes and serve in heated tureen or bowls.

MEATS

BROILED MEATS

Well-broiled tender steaks and chops, 1 to 2 inches thick, are cooked on outside to brown the fat and meat fiber, and to develop the flavor and aroma of the meat. The inside of each steak or chop is juicy, retaining much of the natural juices and extractives. The color of the fiber and juices changes with each degree of doneness and varies with each kind of meat.

All tender cuts of meat with small amount of connective tissue, except veal and fresh pork, can be broiled successfully in an oven broiler or grill, over live coals, or in a heavy frying pan. Spareribs and other pork can be broiled over live coals. Meats are broiled at moderate temperature, turning when half done. Time of broiling varies with thickness of meat and degree of doneness desired. See specific recipes for approximate time for broiling.

Oven-Broiled Meats—Remove broiler pan. Preheat broiler about 10 minutes with broiler door closed. (Some broilers do not require preheating. Follow directions for your oven.) Trim off excess fat and wipe meat with a cloth. Lay on rack in broiler pan. (Cold rack need not be greased.) Adjust broiler rack so that top of meat is approximately 2 inches below heat for ¾ to 1 inch cuts, 3 inches for thicker cuts. Broiler door is left ajar during broiling in some ovens. Follow directions for your oven. When half done, season and turn meat with vegetable tongs or long fork, being careful not to pierce meat. Then continue broiling until cooked to the desired degree of doneness (*pages 82 83*).

Pan-Broiled Meats—Heat a heavy frying pan and rub it with piece of suet or fat from meat. Trim and wipe meat with cloth, sear on both sides, turning with tongs or fork, being careful not to pierce meat. Reduce heat and cook over low heat until half done. Season and turn. Continue cooking to the desired degree of doneness (*pages 82–83*). If fat accumulates, pour it off to avoid frying meat.

Allow ½ to ¾ pound uncooked steak, or 1 to 2 chops per portion.

BROILED STEAK

(Oven or Pan-Broiled, *page* 81)

Allow ½ to ¾ pound per portion. Select any tender steak such as club or Delmonico, porterhouse or T-bone, sirloin, or beef tenderloin fillets; or less tender cut such as round, chuck, or cubed steaks from *choice young animals. Oven-broil or pan-broil* according to thickness of cut, to rare, medium-rare or well-done stage. Spread broiled meat with butter or baste with drippings in pan. Sprinkle with salt and pepper, and place on hot platter. Garnish, as desired, and serve at once.

For porterhouse, 1½ inches thick, allow: rare, 16 minutes; medium-rare, 20 minutes; well-done, 26 minutes.

For cubed steak, ¼ to ½ inch thick, allow: rare, 2 to 3 minutes; medium-rare, 3 to 4 minutes; well-done, 4 to 5 minutes.

For tender round steak, ¾ to 1 inch thick, allow: rare, 10 minutes; medium-rare, 14 minutes; well-done, 18 minutes.

MINUTE STEAKS FOR FOUR

4 small individual steaks, ¼- to ½-inch thick
butter
salt and pepper
parsley

Allow ½ to ¾ pound for each steak.

Any small, thin and tender cut from chuck, rib or loin is called a minute steak. Pan-broil quickly, allowing 3 to 4 minutes for entire cooking. Spread with butter, sprinkle with salt and pepper, garnish with parsley and serve at once.

BROILED FROZEN STEAK OR CHOPS

(Oven or Pan-Broiled, *page* 81)

Frozen steaks or chops may be broiled, frozen or just thawed. Directions for broiling are included with packaged meats and should be followed. If frozen, allow slightly longer time for total broiling. If not cooked at once, allow meat to thaw out slowly in refrigerator before broiling, then broil to rare, medium-rare or well-done stage as desired. Allow about ½ pound for each portion or serving.

BROILED LAMB OR MUTTON CHOPS

(Oven or Pan-Broiled, *page* 81)

Allow 1 to 2 chops per portion (⅓ to ⅔ pound). Select chops from lamb, or choice mutton (aged for 2 to 5 weeks), such as loin, rib, shoulder, or hip (loin-end of leg). Remove fell, or thin, parchment-like skin, from chops. Oven-broil or pan-broil according to thickness of cut, to medium-rare or well-done stage. Season, place on hot platter, garnish and serve at once.

For rib or loin chops ¾ inch thick, allow: medium-rare, 12 minutes; well-done, 14 minutes.

For rib or loin chops (double) 1½ to 2 inches thick, allow: medium-rare, 18 to 25 minutes; well-done, 25 to 32 minutes.

GRILLED SAVORY HAMBURG

(See Broiled Steak, *page* 82)

1 pound beef ground
½ teaspoon salt
¼ teaspoon celery salt
½ teaspoon minced onion
1 tablespoon ketchup
⅓ teaspoon Worcestershire sauce
butter

Makes about 4 portions.

Mix beef with seasonings. Shape into large cutlet, about 1 inch thick, on a greased, long-handled, fine-meshed, wire broiler.

Place on rack in preheated broiler and broil to rare, medium or well-done stage. Place on hot platter, spread with butter.

FRIED MEAT CAKES

½ small onion, chopped
1 tablespoon butter or margarine
¾ pound beef, ground
¼ pound pork, ground
¾ teaspoon salt
dash of pepper
⅓ cup soft bread crumbs
½ cup milk or stock
flour
2 tablespoons fat

Makes 8 cakes or 4 portions.

Sauté onion in butter about 2 minutes, then add to meat in mixing bowl. Add seasonings, crumbs and milk, and beat thoroughly.

Shape into flat cakes, about 1 inch thick, using 1 heaping tablespoon for each. Roll in flour and sauté in fat about 15 minutes, turning to brown both sides. Remove cakes to hot platter and keep hot. Prepare gravy (*page* 86). Serve in small bowl.

ROASTED MEATS

The larger the tender cut of meat, the more juicy and economical the roast. A well or ideally roasted tender piece of meat is browned on outside, enough to improve the appearance, flavor and aroma of fat and meat fiber. Inside, it is tender, juicy and moist with natural juices and extractives which vary in color and amount with kind of meat and with each degree of doneness—rare, medium-rare, or well-done—to which it has been roasted.

All tender meats (with bone left in or boned and rolled) including beef, veal, lamb, mutton, pork and large game, as well as poultry and small game, can be roasted or baked, uncovered, by dry heat in an oven or on a spit over an open fire. Meats may be roasted successfully in a 325° F. (slow) oven to the desired degree of doneness. Add no water and basting is unnecessary.

Approximate Minutes per Pound—The most generally used method for testing for doneness of meat is to roast it an approximate number of minutes per pound for each degree of doneness desired for inside of meat. With experience one does learn to gauge time with some degree of accuracy. For poultry and small game this method of testing is used very largely.

The Meat Thermometer—The surest and simplest way to determine when meat is done is to use a meat thermometer with the degrees Fahrenheit or the stages of doneness for each kind of meat (see *page* 12) definitely marked. With a skewer make an incision into the fleshy part of the meat, then insert the thermometer so that the bulb is in the thickest part of the lean meat and does not rest against bone or in fat. When the thermometer reaches the desired temperature, push the thermometer down slightly. If the temperature drops, continue cooking to correct temperature.

OVEN-ROASTED MEATS

Wipe meat with damp cloth and rub with salt and pepper, allowing ½ teaspoon salt per pound. It may or may not be sprinkled with flour. Place meat, fat side up, on rack in baking pan. (Rack may not be necessary when roasting meat with bone.) If meat is very lean, lay strips of fat pork or bacon on top. Insert thermometer into center of big muscle. Place pan with meat in oven so that thermometer can be read easily. Roast, uncovered, in 325° F. (slow) oven until thermometer registers the desired degree of doneness for inside of meat; or allow the number of minutes per pound suggested in the specific recipes (*pages 85 to 87*).

CARVING ROASTS

Practice is essential to master the art of carving. A large fork to hold the meat securely with left hand and a large, sharp knife for slicing, are essential tools for carving. When possible, cut meat across the grain in slices, ⅛- to ¼-inch thick. Place roast conveniently on a platter large enough to hold slices or cuts; do not *cover* platter with vegetables or garnish. A *standing rib* or *rolled roast* or *thick slice of meat* is placed with cut surface on platter and the meat is cut in slices, horizontally, across grain. A *whole ham* or *leg of lamb* is placed, fat side up, on platter, with bone end to right or left of carver, according to whether it is right or left leg. Slice down to bone, commencing from the choice center section and slicing outwards. A *loin* of *lamb* or *pork* is placed, fat side up, on platter; the individual chops are separated readily by cutting downward. A *crown* of *lamb* or *pork* is separated, also, into the individual chops.

BEEF ROAST

(For method, see Oven-Roasted Meats, above)

Allow ½ to ¾ pound of meat (meat and bone) per portion. Select a tender cut, small or large, according to the number to be served. Allow for some left-over meat. For small roast, choose: 1 rib (3½ to 4 lb.), standing, or boned and rolled; or top sirloin, or boned and rolled chuck (4 to 5 lb.) from choice young beef. For large roast, choose: 2 ribs (6½ to 7½ lb.), standing, or boned and rolled, or choice top sirloin or rolled chuck (6 to 7 lb.). Place standing rib roast on bone ends with fat side up; place thick rolled roast on side with fat side up; or place thick slice of meat on one of cut surfaces. Season and insert thermometer as directed (*page* 84). Roast, uncovered, in 325° F. (slow) oven to the desired degree of doneness for inside of meat. Degrees below are for inside of meat.

For rare beef (140° F.)*:* allow about 20 to 30 minutes per pound. The center of roast is a bright rose red, shading to a lighter pink toward outside; the meat is very juicy.

For medium-rare (160° F.)*:* allow about 30 to 40 minutes per pound. The center of roast is light pink, shading to a brownish-gray toward outside; the meat is slightly less juicy.

For well-done (170° F.)*:* allow about 35 to 45 minutes per pound. The entire roast is brownish-gray, moist with a scant amount of light-colored juice.

BROWN GRAVY

¼ cup drippings (fat and juice) from any roast
¼ cup flour

2 cups liquid (drippings and water, or stock), or half stock and half milk
salt and pepper

Makes about 2 cups gravy.

Skim the excess fat from drippings in roaster and pour drippings into bowl. Then measure ¼ cup and return to roaster and heat slowly. Add flour, stirring until flour is well browned.

Add liquid gradually, stirring constantly until thickened, then cook 3 minutes longer. Season to taste. Part milk may be used. Sour cream may be added for flavor.

CHICKEN GRAVY

Follow recipe for Brown Gravy; use butter or drippings from roast or fried chicken; brown flour lightly; use 2 cups chicken stock, or half stock and half milk, or light cream. *Makes about 2 cups.* For **Giblet Gravy,** add finely chopped, cooked or baked giblets.

LAMB OR MUTTON ROAST

Allow ½ to ¾ pound of lamb or mutton (meat and bone) per portion. For small roast, choose: loin, rib or boned shoulder, or half leg of lamb (4 to 6 lb.). For large roast, choose: leg of lamb (6 to 8 lb.), or leg of mutton, aged for 5 weeks (10 to 12 lb.). Do not remove fell or parchment membrane from leg. It protects the meat and shortens roasting time. Place leg, skin side down, in open roaster. Season and insert thermometer as directed (*page* 84). Roast, uncovered, in 325° F. (slow) oven to the desired degree of doneness for inside of meat. Method on page 85.

For well-done lamb or mutton (180° *F.*): allow 30 to 35 minutes per pound for large roasts; 40 to 50 minutes per pound for small roasts. Temperature is for inside of meat. The entire roast is grayish-brown and the flavor of mutton less pronounced.

MINT-FLAVORED GLAZED ROAST LAMB

Roast lamb as directed, basting meat frequently the last hour with mixture of ½ cup apple jelly dissolved in ½ cup hot water and 1 bunch mint, finely chopped. Serve on hot platter with gravy made by thickening liquor in pan with paste made of 1 tablespoon flour and ¼ cup water.

VEAL ROAST

Allow ½ to ¾ pound of veal (meat and bone) per portion. Use loin, rib, shoulder (boned), or round. Season and insert thermometer, as directed (*page* 84). Place strips of fat salt pork or bacon across top. Roast, uncovered, in 325° F. (slow) oven until meat is well done. (For method, see Oven-Roasted Meats, *page* 85.)

For well-done veal (170° *F.*): allow 45 to 60 minutes per pound for shoulders; 25 to 35 minutes per pound for leg or loin. The entire roast is light in color—almost a white—with a browned surface; it is fairly moist, not dry. Temperature given is for inside of meat.

PORK ROAST

Allow ⅓ to ½ pound pork (meat and bone) per portion. Select cut from loin, rib, ham, or boned and rolled shoulder or butt. Wipe with damp cloth, season and insert thermometer, as directed (*page* 84). Roast, uncovered, in 325° F. (slow) oven until meat is well done and outside is browned and crisp. (For method, see Oven-Roasted Meats, *page* 85.)

For well-done pork (185° *F.*): allow for small roasts, and boned and rolled roasts, 40 to 50 minutes per pound; allow for large roasts (ham), 25 to 30 minutes per pound. Temperature given is for inside of meat.

MEAT LOAF

1 clove garlic, chopped
1 small onion, chopped
4 tablespoons chopped suet
1½ pounds lean beef, ground
1 teaspoon salt
⅛ teaspoonful pepper
1 cup soft bread crumbs
1 egg, beaten
⅔ cup milk

Makes about 6 portions.

Sauté garlic and onion slowly in suet for 5 minutes. Add to ground meat in large bowl. Sprinkle with salt and pepper, and mix well. Stir in crumbs, egg and milk. Shape into loaf. Place in greased pan.

Bake in 300° F. (slow) oven for 60 to 90 minutes, or until browned. Remove to hot platter and serve hot with Brown Gravy (*page* 86) or sauce.

VEAL LOAF

Follow recipe for Meat Loaf with the following changes: omit garlic; substitute veal for beef; add ¼ pound salt pork, ground, and 2 tablespoons lemon juice; place 3 slices bacon over top of loaf.

HAM LOAF

Follow recipe for Meat Loaf with the following changes: omit garlic, onion, suet and salt; substitute for beef, 1¼ pounds lean smoked ham, ground, and ½ pound lean fresh pork, ground.

BRAISED MEATS

A well-braised piece of meat is browned on outside to develop flavor; uniform in color throughout; slightly moist on inside with a colorless juice; tender with a tendency for muscle fibers to fall apart.

Less tender and tougher cuts of meat (in large or small pieces), including beef, veal, lamb, mutton, pork and large game, as well as poultry and small game, are braised—browned on all sides in fat, if desired, then cooked, covered, on top of stove or in 325° F. (slow) oven for a long time, in meat juices or small amount of liquid.

Meat makes the dinner.

A rolled rump roast makes a tender pot roast (*page* 90), served with brown gravy made from pan drippings.

A young turkey roasted to perfection (*page* 100) and attractively garnished with cranberry-filled orange halves.

A baked ham studded with cloves and basted with cider (*page* 94), surrounded with sprigs of kumquats.

POT ROAST

Allow about ½ pound meat per portion. Choose a compact piece of meat, weighing not less than 3 pounds, solid or boned and rolled, from round, rump or chuck. Wipe meat with damp cloth and rub with mixture of ¼ cup flour, 1½ teaspoons salt and ⅛ teaspoon pepper. Brown meat over moderate heat in ¼ cup chopped suet in heavy kettle or Dutch oven, turning with tongs to brown all sides. It will take 15 to 30 minutes. Slip a rack under meat so it will not stick to pan. Add ½ cup water or tomato juice. Cover tightly and cook over low heat for 3 to 3½ hours, or until tender. One-half hour before meat is done, place 4 or 6 medium-sized potatoes, boiled for 15 minutes, around meat, turning them once. Place roast on hot platter and arrange potatoes around it. Serve with Brown Gravy (*page* 86) made from drippings.

SWISS STEAK

1½ pounds round or chuck steak,
**   1 to 1½ inches thick**
⅓ cup flour
¾ teaspoon salt
⅛ teaspoon pepper
2 tablespoons chopped suet or fat
1 small onion, sliced

1 bay leaf
½ cup water
1½ cups canned tomatoes

Makes about 4 portions.

Wipe meat. Mix flour, salt and pepper. Sprinkle ½ on steak, then pound in thoroughly with wooden potato masher or edge of heavy saucer. Turn meat over and repeat process with remaining flour.

Sauté meat in suet in heavy frying pan or Dutch oven about 15 minutes, or until browned. Add onion the last 5 minutes.

Add bay leaf, hot water and tomatoes, bring to a boil, cover and simmer 1 hour, or until very tender, turning meat occasionally. Serve steak with sauce over it.

BEEF STEW

2 pounds shin of beef, or chuck, cut
**   in 1½-inch cubes**
¼ cup flour
1 teaspoon salt
⅛ teaspoon pepper
3 tablespoons chopped suet
1¼ cups water

Roll meat in mixture of flour, salt and pepper. Sauté in suet until well browned. Transfer meat to casserole. Add water to drippings in pan, bring to a boil and pour over meat.
Bake, covered, in 325° F. (slow) oven for 2½ to 3 hours.

4 small onions, sliced
4 small carrots, diced
3 tablespoons butter

Makes about 4 portions.

Sauté onions and carrots in butter slowly about 10 minutes, stirring to brown evenly. Add to meat and continue baking ½ hour. Or cook stew slowly in tightly covered kettle on top of stove.

NEW ENGLAND BOILED DINNER

4 pounds corned beef: brisket, navel, flank or neck
water
8 small onions
1 medium-sized rutabaga, pared, quartered, and cut in wedges
8 parsnips, pared and cut in halves, lengthwise
8 medium-sized carrots, scraped
8 medium-sized potatoes, pared
1 medium-sized cabbage, quartered, cored, then cut in eighths

Makes about 8 portions.

Be sure that meat is tied securely. Ask your butcher if meat needs soaking to keep from being too salty. If so, soak, and discard water.

Place meat in large kettle and cover with boiling water. Cover and simmer 3 hours. Remove scum if necessary.

Skim excess fat on liquid, then bring meat to a boil. Add whole onions, prepared rutabaga, parsnips, carrots and potatoes, and boil gently, uncovered, 20 minutes. Add cabbage and boil 10 to 15 minutes longer, or until vegetables are just tender.

Place meat on hot large platter and arrange vegetables around it.

CORNED BEEF AND CABBAGE

Follow recipe for New England Boiled Dinner, only omit all vegetables but cabbage, and use one large head. Add cabbage 10 to 15 minutes before meat is done. Place meat on hot platter. Drain cabbage, arrange it around meat and sprinkle with salt and paprika. *Makes about 8 portions.*

BREADED VEAL CUTLETS

1 pound round of veal, ½ inch thick
salt and pepper   flour
1 egg, slightly beaten
1 tablespoon water
½ cup fine bread crumbs
¼ cup fat

Makes about 4 portions.

Wipe meat with damp cloth, cut in 4 pieces. Sprinkle with salt and pepper. Roll in flour, egg mixed with water, then crumbs.

Sauté slowly in fat until well browned, allowing about 15 minutes for each side.

BRAISED VEAL CHOPS OR CUTLETS

**4 rib or loin chops, or 1 pound
round of veal, ½ inch thick and
cut in 4 pieces**
¼ cup flour
½ teaspoon salt
⅛ teaspoon pepper
4 tablespoons bacon fat
⅓ cup hot water
⅔ cup sour heavy cream
paprika

Makes 4 portions.

Wipe meat with damp cloth. Roll in mixture of flour, salt and pepper.

Brown quickly in fat on both sides. Add hot water, cover and simmer ½ hour, turning occasionally. Then add sour cream, sprinkle with paprika and simmer 15 minutes. Serve with pan gravy poured over meat.

SCHNITZEL

Follow recipe for Braised Veal Chops, using round of veal, only substitute ⅓ cup canned tomatoes or 1 large tomato, peeled and cut in sections, for hot water. Add ¼ cup chopped mushrooms and 4 tablespoons parmesan cheese with sour cream. *Makes 4 portions.*

BRAISED PORK CHOPS

Use rib, loin or shoulder chops, ¾ to 1 inch thick. Wipe with damp cloth. Brown chops in hot, heavy frying pan which has been rubbed with fat. Then sprinkle with salt and pepper, cover and cook slowly about 50 to 60 minutes, or until tender, turning once. Serve with Brown Gravy (*page 86*). *Allow 1 chop per portion.*

PORK TENDERLOIN PATTIES

Use 2 small or 1½ large pork tenderloins (1 to 1½ lb.); one tenderloin makes 4 to 6 patties. Roll in well-seasoned flour and sauté in ¼ cup butter until browned on both sides. Add ½ to ¾ cup light cream, cover and simmer about ½ hour, or until tender. *Serves 4 to 6.*

BAKED STUFFED PORK CHOPS

4 double rib pork chops
1½ cups **Bread Stuffing** (*page* 102)
salt and pepper
2 tablespoons fat
4 strips bacon or salt pork

Makes 4 portions.

Wipe chops, slit each between the bones to make pocket for stuffing.

Make stuffing and pile into chop pockets; season. Sauté chops in fat on both sides. Place in roasting pan with a strip of bacon over each. Bake, uncovered, in 350° F. (moderate) oven for 1 hour, or until done.

PORK AND APPLE PIE

2 tablespoons finely chopped salt pork or bacon
1 pound pork shoulder, cut in pieces
1 tablespoon flour
½ teaspoon salt
½ teaspoon sage
2 tablespoons water
2 cooking apples, pared and sliced
½ recipe **Baking Powder Biscuits** (*page* 66)

Makes about 4 portions.

Try out salt pork or bacon in heavy frying pan. Add pork, sprinkle with mixture of flour, salt and sage, and sauté slowly until browned, stirring frequently. Turn into small (1 quart) baking dish. Add water to frying pan, bring to a boil and pour over meat. Cover with apple slices.

Make dough. Roll to fit dish. Place on top and slash to permit escape of steam. Bake in 400° F. (hot) oven for 30 to 40 minutes.

HAM

Modern processed hams and picnic hams, that are precooked and ready-to-serve, can be purchased. Flavor is improved, though, if they are baked in a 325° F. (slow) oven for a short time. Follow directions on the package.

SMOTHERED HAM (SMOKED)

1 slice smoked ham, 1 inch thick
4 tablespoons brown sugar
1 teaspoon dry mustard
2 cups rich milk

Makes 4 to 6 portions.

Place ham in large casserole. Sprinkle mixture of brown sugar and mustard over top, and cover with milk.

Bake, covered, in 350° F. (moderate) oven for 1 hour, removing cover 15 minutes before ham is done. Serve on hot platter with liquid in pan poured over it.

BOILED HAM (SMOKED)

Scrub and rinse ham; if strong-cured, soak several hours or overnight. Place, rind side up, in large kettle. Cover with boiling water and simmer, covered, until tender. Water should not boil. If thermometer is inserted (*page* 84), place ham in kettle so that thermometer extends over water and can be read. When inside of ham registers 160° F., ham is cooked. To serve cold, cool in stock until lukewarm; then peel off rind. Serve hot or cold with Fluffy Cucumber (*page* 113) or Raisin Sauce (*page* 112).

For whole ham (8–12 lb.): allow 15 to 20 minutes per pound, or about 4 hours for 16-pound ham.

For half ham: allow 30 minutes per pound.

For picnic butts or shank ends: allow 40 to 50 minutes per pound.

BAKED HAM (SMOKED)

1 **Boiled Smoked Ham, 8–10 pounds** (above) ½ **to 1 cup firmly packed brown sugar** 2 **teaspoons dry mustard** ¼ **cup whole cloves, long stemmed** ½ **cup cider or vinegar** *Makes 25 to 30 portions.*	Boil ham. Remove rind, and place in roaster or pan. Rub surface with mixture of brown sugar and mustard. Stud with cloves and pour cider over all. Bake, uncovered, in 325° F. (slow) oven about ½ hour.

MEAT SPECIALTIES

BROILED CALF'S LIVER

1 **pound calf's liver,** ½ **inch thick** **melted butter** **salt and pepper** **Lemon Butter** (*page* 113) *Makes about 4 portions.*	Remove skin and veins. Wipe with damp cloth. Brush with butter. Broil about 12 minutes, turning once. Spread with Lemon Butter. Serve hot.

BROILED BEEF LIVER

Follow recipe for Broiled Calf's Liver, only marinate slices in French dressing for 1 hour before broiling.

LIVER AND BACON

4 to 8 slices bacon
1 pound liver
3 tablespoons flour
½ teaspoon salt
dash of pepper
butter

Makes about 4 portions.

Fry bacon slowly in frying pan until crisp. Remove, drain and keep hot for serving. Prepare liver. Roll in seasoned flour and sauté in bacon fat for 10 to 12 minutes, turning once. Spread with butter. Serve with crisp bacon.

BOILED SWEETBREADS

Allow ½ to 1 pair per portion. They spoil quickly and should be cooked at once. Wash and drop into boiling, salted, acidulated water (1 teaspoon salt and 1 tablespoon vinegar to each quart of water). Simmer, covered, 20 minutes. Drain and cover with cold water. When cool enough to handle, remove membrane and tubes. Then broil, sauté, cream or prepare, as desired.

POULTRY

PREPARATION OF POULTRY FOR COOKING

All fresh undrawn poultry, whether freshly killed, solidly frozen and held in storage for several weeks or months and sold in frozen state, should have a clean, clear, unblemished, unbroken and moist skin. Young birds have the following characteristics: fine, smooth, pliable and tender skin with some pin feathers but few long hairs; soft and elastic flesh; soft breastbone, easily bent at end. Quick-frozen poultry comes clean and drawn, ready for cooking. Keep poultry frozen until ready to use, but do not roast until completely thawed. Defrost frozen poultry in the refrigerator before cooking—24 hours for a small to medium bird, or 48 hours for a large one. Thawing may be hastened by placing wrapped poultry under running cold water for 2 to 6 hours. Take bird out of refrigerator at least 2 hours before time to roast so that it will be at room temperature.

DRESSING OF POULTRY

Singe by holding bird over direct flame, turning to expose all surfaces. *Remove pin feathers* with small pointed knife or tweezers.

Draw bird, if not dressed at market, as follows: Cut off head, then feet at leg joints. Cut around vent, then make small slit under breastbone. Insert first 2 fingers, loosen organs from back and sides and pull out lungs, heart, liver, gizzard and entrails. Separate gizzard, heart and liver. Carefully cut away gall bladder (green bag) from liver. Cut down through thickest muscle of gizzard to tough lining, open, then pull out sac. Remove any lung tissue and kidneys from back, and cut away oil sac at tip of tail. Slit

skin down the back of neck and leave enough to tack over and back. Cut muscle of neck near body, then twist off neck. Push neck skin forward, then remove crop.

Wash bird thoroughly, inside and outside, but do not let it stand in water. Wipe dry with clean cloth or absorbent paper. Wash giblets and neck.

CUTTING UP POULTRY FOR COOKING

To cut up bird to broil (when drawn and cleaned), cut through ribs and breastbone, then through backbone, using poultry or strong shears, or a sharp knife. If undrawn, cut off head and feet, then cut through backbone, from neck to tail. Lay open and remove entrails and giblets, and proceed as for drawn bird. Wash and dry thoroughly. For small squabs, split down back but not through breast; for large birds, cut in half, then again in half.

To cut up bird to fry or fricassee, see picture on *page* 97. Use poultry or strong shears and sharp knife. Remove leg, cutting through skin between leg and body, pull back leg and separate at hip joint; sever thigh from drumstick. Cut through skin around wing, pull back and disjoint. Repeat on other side. Separate breast from back; cut through breastbone lengthwise and split back in half.

STUFFING AND TRUSSING FOR ROASTING

Stuffing—Choice of dressing depends on the type of poultry or game. For chicken or turkey, use any well-seasoned dressing. For duck or goose, use a dry dressing, with fruit, or sharp seasonings; or use sweetened, cored and quartered apples; or use celery tops or onions for flavor only. Rub inside with salt. Pile stuffing lightly into body and neck cavities, allowing: 2 to 3 cups for chicken; 4 to 5 cups for capons; 6 to 8 cups for turkey; 3 cups

for duck; 4 cups for goose. Sew large cavity together; draw skin back over neck and fasten to back with skewer. Stuff half turkey; cover cut side with parchment paper and tie securely with heavy string.

Trussing—With chicken and turkey, fold wing tips under and against back. Press thighs close to body—run skewer through thighs and body, if large turkey. Tie ends of legs together,

Cutting up chicken for cooking.

1. Remove the whole leg with a sharp knife.

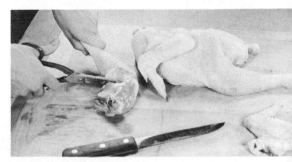

2. Sever the second joint with scissors.

3. Snip up the back and breast, after you've cut off the wings.

4. Cut the breast and back apart at either side.

Then fry or fricassee as directed in recipes (*pages* 99, 100).

using middle of long string, and bring string down and fasten around tailpiece. Turn bird over on breast. Cross string and bring each end forward around skewers and over front and tip of wings, or ends of skewer at neck. Tie strings securely in middle of upper back. No strings should cross over breast. Duck or goose need not be trussed.

A plump tender chicken, broad-breasted and short-legged, trussed with skewers and string (*page* 96) and ready for roasting (*page* 100).

CARVING AND SERVING ROASTED POULTRY

Place roasted bird on platter, with legs to the right, in front of the host. A sharp carving knife and serving spoon are at the right and a large fork at the left. To carve, put fork through breastbone to hold firmly when slicing.

For chicken and turkey, pull leg away from body and sever at thigh joint. Separate thigh and leg at joint end. If large, each may be cut in half parallel with bone. Pull wing away from body and sever at joint close to body. Cut breast in thin slices, on a slant and against the grain. Serve both light and dark meat with stuffing on each hot plate. Carve other half as indicated.

For duck and goose, poultry or strong shears are a great convenience. Joints are set toward back and are sometimes difficult to sever. Proceed much as for chicken. Or cut lengthwise with shears through breastbone, then backbone. Cut each half in two or three pieces and serve one piece to each guest.

COOKED GIBLETS

To clean giblets (heart, gizzard and liver), see *page* 96. Cover gizzard, heart (neck and tips of wings may be added) with cold water. Bring to a boil, cover and simmer for ½ to 1 hour, adding liver and ½ teaspoon salt the last 20 minutes of cooking. Chop, add to gravy or dressing. Use stock for gravy.

BROILED CHICKEN OR YOUNG TURKEY

Allow about ¾ pound per portion, or 1 small squab broiler, ½ medium-sized broiler, or ¼ large broiler or young turkey. Squab broilers weigh ¾ to 1¼ pounds, dressed; broilers, 1½ to 2½ pounds, dressed; and young turkeys, 3 to 4 pounds, dressed. (Oven or Pan-Broiled Meats, *page* 81.)

Prepare for broiling. Wash and dry thoroughly. Rub with butter or oil and sprinkle with salt and pepper. Lay, skin side down, on greased rack in broiling pan, or in greased, hot frying pan. Oven-broil or pan-broil at 350° F. or at moderate heat until done, turning to brown both sides.

For broiling at moderate heat (350° F.)*:* allow about 20 to 40 minutes according to age and size of bird.

Quick-Frozen Broilers may be thawed, then broiled; or thawed just enough to separate halves, then broiled. Follow directions on package when given.

FRIED CHICKEN

1 chicken fryer (2½ lb.), cut in
  pieces (*page* 96)
½ cup flour
1½ teaspoons salt
⅛ teaspoon pepper
¼ cup butter
¼ cup bacon fat
Chicken Gravy (*page* 86)

Makes about 4 portions.

Prepare chicken. Put chicken and seasoned flour into paper bag. Shake vigorously to "coat" chicken. Sauté in butter and bacon fat in heavy frying pan about 15 minutes, or until well browned. Cover and cook slowly until tender, turning occasionally. Allow about ½ hour for broilers; ¾ hour for small fryers; 1 hour for large fryers.

SMOTHERED CHICKEN

Follow recipe for Fried Chicken with following changes: add ½ to 1 cup light cream to well-browned chicken; transfer to casserole, cover and bake in 325° F. (slow) oven for about 45 minutes; or simmer browned chicken in cream, covered, on top of stove.

CHICKEN FRICASSEE

Allow about ¾ pound chicken per portion. Choose fowl weighing about 4 pounds. Clean and cut in pieces for cooking (*page* 95). Place in large kettle, add boiling water to almost cover. Simmer, covered, about 2 hours, or until tender, adding 1 teaspoon salt when half done.

Roll pieces in well-seasoned flour and sauté slowly in ⅓ cup butter about 15 minutes to brown lightly. Remove chicken to hot platter and keep hot. Make Chicken Gravy (*page* 86) with chicken stock and cream. Pour over chicken.

ROAST CHICKEN OR TURKEY

If possible, get one of the new style chickens or turkeys, broad-breasted and short-legged. When buying ready-to-cook fresh or frozen poultry, allow ¾ to 1 pound chicken or turkey per portion. Select a young tender bird weighing, dressed, as follows: roasting chicken, 3½ to 4 pounds; capon, 6 to 9 pounds; turkey, 8 to 24 pounds, or half turkey split down center back and breast. If not eviscerated, singe, clean, wash and dry. Rub inside with salt. Stuff lightly, just before cooking, with any desired Stuffing (*page* 102), then truss (*page* 96). Place bird, breast side up, in shallow pan without water. Rub with olive oil or butter and sprinkle with salt and pepper. Place half turkey, paper side down, on rack. Cover with a piece of cheesecloth dipped in olive oil or fat, or wrap tightly in aluminum foil. Roast, uncovered, in 325° F. (slow) oven. Test at the end of 45 minutes. If bird is cooking too fast, reduce temperature to 300° F. (slow). (And if you are a Western cook, you may want to reduce temperature and cooking time.) As the cheesecloth dries, dip in drippings in pan and re-cover bird. Remove cloth or aluminum foil last 30 minutes for richer browning. When done the flesh on drumstick and thigh is soft and the legs can be moved from the body. A thermometer, with bulb inserted in center of inner thigh muscle, should register 195° F. The center of the stuffing should be 165° F. Remove to hot platter. Garnish as desired. Prepare gravy from drippings in pan (*page* 86), using stock from giblets and adding chopped giblets, if desired. Serve in bowl.

Roast Duck or Goose—Allow ¾ to 1½ pounds duck or goose per portion. Follow recipe for Roast Chicken or Turkey (above), except for goose, omit rubbing with olive oil or butter, and prick skin well with sharp fork if fat. For duck and goose, increase the heat to 425° F. (hot) oven near the end of roasting to add color and crispness to skin.

Note—For all poultry, the smaller the bird the longer the time per pound.

For roasting chicken: allow 25 to 30 minutes per pound.

For roasting turkey: allow 25 to 45 minutes per pound for birds up to 12 pounds; 22 to 25 minutes per pound for birds up to 24 pounds; 25 to 40 minutes per pound for halves and quarters.

For roasting duck: allow 35 to 50 minutes per pound.

For roasting goose: allow 20 to 25 minutes per pound.

GLAZED ROAST FOWL OR OLD TOM

Cook or steam whole fowl about 2 hours and old tom 3 hours, or until almost tender. Then stuff, truss, rub with olive oil and sprinkle with salt and pepper. (See Roast Chicken.) Wrap tightly in aluminum foil.

Roast, uncovered, in 325° F. (slow) oven in shallow pan without water, until tender and well browned, or 10 to 15 minutes per pound. One-half hour before bird is done, remove foil and spread surface with ½ cup tart jelly, then baste frequently with jelly mixture in pan. Allow ¾ pound for each.

CHICKEN POT PIE

1 fowl (4 lb.), cut in pieces
1 onion, sliced
¾ cup celery leaves
2 sprigs parsley
½ pound mushrooms, sliced
¼ cup butter
3 tablespoons flour
salt and pepper
Baking Powder Biscuits (*page 66*)

Makes 6 to 8 portions.

Cook fowl as for fricassee (*page 100*). Remove chicken. Simmer onion, celery and parsley in stock ½ hour. Strain and use for gravy. Separate meat from bone.

Sauté mushrooms in butter 5 minutes, stirring frequently. Stir in flour and brown lightly. Add 2 cups stock gradually, stirring until thickened. Add chicken, season to taste and turn into greased large casserole.

Make biscuit dough, roll and cut in rounds. Place on top of chicken mixture. Bake in 400° F. (hot) oven for 25 to 30 minutes.

BREAD STUFFING

¼ cup chopped onion
3 tablespoons chopped celery
⅓ cup butter, melted

3 cups cubed, soft bread crumbs
½ teaspoon salt
⅛ teaspoon pepper
¼ teaspoon poultry seasoning, or thyme or marjoram; or 1 tablespoon sage

Makes about 3 cups stuffing, or enough for 1 bird (5 lb.) or large fish.

Sauté onion and celery in butter in heavy saucepan over low heat until slightly yellow, stirring constantly. Remove from heat.

Add bread crumbs and seasonings, tossing lightly with a fork to mix well.

Use as stuffing for meat, poultry or fish.

APPLE-RAISIN STUFFING

Follow recipe for Bread Stuffing, only add 1 cup chopped apple and ½ cup seedless raisins to stuffing. *Makes about 4 cups stuffing.*

NUT-PRUNE STUFFING

Follow recipe for Bread Stuffing, only omit onion and poultry seasoning, and add ¼ cup chopped walnuts, ¾ cup chopped stewed prunes and 1 tablespoon chopped parsley. One egg, slightly beaten, may be added, if desired. *Makes about 4 cups stuffing.*

SAUSAGE-BREAD STUFFING

½ pound sausage meat
¼ cup chopped onion
3 tablespoons chopped celery
4 cups cubed, soft bread
½ teaspoon salt
⅛ teaspoon pepper

Makes about 5 cups stuffing.

Fry sausage, onion and celery until lightly browned, stirring constantly. Remove from heat and pour off excess fat.

Add bread, salt and pepper, mixing lightly with a fork.

Use as stuffing for poultry.

FISH AND FISH COOKERY

Salt and fresh-water fish and shellfish are included in the term "fish." Fish can be purchased fresh, canned, pickled, dried and salted, and smoked.

Fresh fish can be had fresh from the water or solidly frozen, whole or in steaks and fillets; quick-frozen, ready for the pan; alive in tanks or on ice.

Selection and Storage—All fresh fish are perishable and cannot be held for any length of time unless packed in ice or solidly frozen. Fresh fish are free from slime, or foreign odor; the scales adhere and the flesh is firm. To keep in refrigerator, wrap securely or put in covered container and place in coldest part of box.

Preparation of Fish for Cooking—Fish are usually cleaned at the market; however, all must be looked over and cleaned if necessary. For directions for scaling, skinning and boning fish, see *Fishing and Hunting* (*page* 295). Quick-frozen fish are ready for cooking and can be used, without pre-thawing, thawed, or thawed just enough to separate pieces. Thaw fish in the refrigerator.

HOW TO COOK AND SERVE FISH

Well-cooked fish is firm and shapely, the flesh is juicy and moist, and the color and flavor maintained or enhanced. The vinegar or lemon juice used in boiling fish preserves the color and keeps the flesh firm. Fish are never tough and all can be cooked by *dry heat* (broiling, frying and baking), or by *moist heat* (boiling or steaming and braising), under proper conditions. Fish vary in amount of fat they contain, and those best suited for each method of cooking are given with specific recipes. Fish requires a short cooking period. The time varies with the shape and size of the fish or piece, and the cooking temperature. Allow from 8 to 15 minutes to broil steaks or fillets in ½ to 1 pound pieces; 40 to 60 minutes in a 350° F. (moderate) oven for a dressed fish weighing 3 to 4 pounds. Allow extra time for frozen or thawing fish, and cook at slightly higher temperature (400° F.). Fish is done when the flesh loosens slightly from the bone and separates easily into flakes.

Sauces and garnishes are chosen to supply needed color, flavor, to add richness to lean fish, and to modify the flavor of fat fish. Sliced cucumbers, tomatoes and radishes, lemon or lime slices or wedges, plain, or dipped in minced parsley, sprigs of parsley and watercress, cut hard-cooked eggs, all make attractive and palatable garnishes. Sauces and relishes such as lemon butter, Hollandaise and tartar sauces, tomato and dill sauces, egg and cheese sauces, chili sauce or pickle relish should be chosen to complement or contrast with the flavor of the fish.

Vegetables, in like manner, can help to point up the flavor of fish and to supply color and texture. Asparagus, peas, spinach, broccoli and string beans, carrots and sweet potatoes, broiled and baked tomatoes and Harvard beets, lima beans, onions and cauliflower with a sprinkling of browned buttered crumbs, potatoes in any form, all can be served with fish dishes.

BROILED FISH

Choose one of the following: bass, bluefish, haddock, halibut, mackerel, perch, salmon, smelts, sole, swordfish or trout. Small or whole fish are split down the back, large fish are cut in 1-inch slices or made into fillets. Place whole fish, skin side down, on well-greased broiler rack. Place slices on rack. Brush lean fish with melted butter or olive oil. Sprinkle with salt, pepper and lemon juice.

Place in preheated broiler, about 2 inches from heating unit, and broil until fish is browned. Do not turn as fish is apt to break. Thin slice will be done when brown. Lower rack and continue cooking thicker slices. Allow 10 to 15 minutes for total broiling. Place on hot platter and garnish as desired, and serve with a rich, tart sauce. *Allow ½ pound whole fish or ⅓ pound sliced fish per portion.*

FRIED FISH

(Helps in Deep-Fat Frying, *page* 57)

1½ pounds fat for frying
1½ pounds fillet of haddock, cut in pieces
¼ cup flour
1 teaspoon salt
⅛ teaspoon pepper
1 egg, slightly beaten
1 tablespoon water
¼ cup fine bread crumbs

Makes about 4 portions.

Fill kettle for frying about ½ full with fat. Attach thermometer. Heat to 375° F. Roll fish in seasoned flour, dip in egg mixed with water, and roll in crumbs. Put in frying basket.

Lower basket into hot fat and fry 1 to 4 minutes.

PAN-FRIED FISH

Choose one of the following: bass, bluefish, cod, flounder, haddock, perch, pike, sole, swordfish, weakfish or whiting. Small fish may be left whole. Large fish are cut in 1-inch slices or made into fillets.

Roll fish in seasoned flour, cornmeal or fine bread crumbs. Fry in small amount of fat in heavy frying pan, turning fish with spatula to brown both sides. Allow 10 to 15 minutes for total cooking, according to thickness of slice. Place on hot platter, garnish with slices of tomato, cucumber or lemon wedges, and serve with a tart sauce. *Allow ⅓ to ½ pound per portion.*

OVEN-FRY FISH

Follow recipe for Fried Fish, only omit the fat, flour, egg and water. Dip fish fillets in well-salted milk, using 1 tablespoon salt to 1 cup milk. Then roll pieces in very fine dry bread crumbs. Place in greased pan. Sprinkle lightly with olive oil. Bake in 450° F. (very hot) oven for about 10 minutes or until browned and flaky tender. Garnish and serve with lemon wedges.

BAKED MACKEREL, ESSEX STYLE

1 fresh mackerel (2 lb.)
2 tablespoons butter
1 large onion, thinly sliced
**2 tomatoes, sliced or 1 cup canned
   Italian tomatoes**
celery salt
½ cup heavy cream
¼ teaspoon salt
dash of pepper

Makes about 4 portions.

Split fish, clean and remove head and tail. Wash and dry. Place, skin side down, in greased baking pan. Dot with butter.

Arrange very thin slices of onion, with slices overlapping, on fish, then cover with tomato slices. Sprinkle with celery salt.

Bake, covered, in 350° F. (moderate) oven for 20 minutes. Pour cream over fish, sprinkle with salt and pepper. Bake, uncovered, 10 minutes longer.

BOILED HALIBUT

**2 pounds halibut or other white
   fish (thick piece)**
2 quarts water
1 small onion, sliced
1 small carrot, sliced
2 sprigs parsley
1 teaspoon salt   1 bay leaf
2 whole cloves
2 tablespoons vinegar
Mustard or Egg Sauce (*page* 110)

Makes 4 to 6 portions.

Cod, haddock, pickerel, pike, striped bass, fillets of flounder and sole may be used. Wipe fish, wrap in cheesecloth and tie.

Put water, vegetables, seasonings and vinegar in kettle, and heat to boiling. Add fish, cover and simmer 10 minutes. Do not boil. Remove fish from cloth and place on hot platter. Garnish as desired and pour sauce over fish.

FILLET OF HADDOCK, MARINARA

1 recipe Marinara Sauce (*page* 111)
1½ pounds fillet of haddock

Makes 4 to 6 portions.

Make savory sauce in heavy frying pan. Wipe fish, lay in sauce and cover. Simmer for 10 to 15 minutes, basting frequently. Arrange on hot platter. Pour on sauce.

SALMON OR TUNA LOAF

Follow recipe for Planked Salmon Loaf (*page* 132), only turn into greased loaf pan. Set in pan of hot water and bake in 350° F. (moderate) oven about 30 minutes, or until firm. Sprinkle crumbs over top 10 minutes before loaf is done. Serve with Egg Sauce (*page* 110).

BOILED SHRIMPS

Wash shrimps in cold water and drop into boiling salted water, adding 2 teaspoons salt to each quart of water. Simmer 5 minutes, or until shells turn pink. Drain, remove shell of round tail with pointed knife and fingers, then cut along outside to remove intestinal vein. Serve creamed, sautéed, in baked dishes, salads and cocktails. Remove vein from canned shrimps and wash. *One pound shrimps in shell makes about 2 cups, shelled, or 4 portions.*

BOILED LOBSTER

Grab clean live lobsters just behind the claws. Straighten tail and plunge it head first into large kettle of rapidly boiling salted water, using 1 tablespoon salt for each quart of water. Cover and simmer 15 to 20 minutes. The lobster turns red and the tail draws up under the body. Remove with tongs and drop into cold water until cold enough to handle.

To serve hot or cold in shell, leave claws intact. Turn on back, cut open lengthwise from head to end of tail and remove stomach and intestinal vein. Garnish with watercress and serve with hot melted butter or mayonnaise. *Allow ½ medium or 1 small lobster per portion.*

To remove meat, crack large claws with nut cracker and pick out meat with fork. Pull out tail meat in one piece and meat from body in large pieces. The liver or green part is edible, also the coral in the female lobster. The lungs or spongy tissue are discarded. Use silver or stainless steel knife. Use meat in cocktails, salads or hot dishes. *One medium-sized lobster (2 lb.) makes about 1½ cups diced meat.*

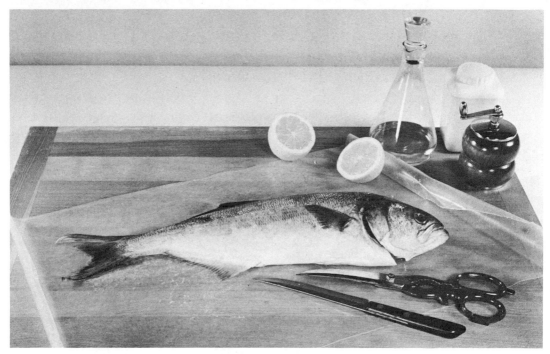

A whole bluefish to be boned (*page* 298), then broiled (*page* 104).

One way to serve crab is in a "shell" of aluminum foil. Follow recipe for Boiled Hard-shell Crabs (*page* 108), season meat as desired with any or all of the following: salt and pepper, Worcestershire sauce, tobasco, small minced onion, minced clove of garlic, chopped parsley, a pinch of rosemary and basil. Fill "shells," top with bread crumbs and dot with butter. Bake at 375° F. until lightly browned.

BOILED HARD-SHELL CRABS

Follow recipe for Boiled Lobster (*page* 106), only use washed live crabs. Simmer 15 minutes. The shell turns a strawberry pink and the meat a milky white. To remove meat, force upper and lower shells apart and remove or scrape away spongy, fibrous material (gills, sand bags and intestines). Flake meat from bony tissue and claws. Serve hot with butter, or use in salads, and hot dishes. One crab (½ lb.) yields about ½ cup flaked meat; or *allow 1 crab per portion.*

LOBSTER À LA NEWBURG

2 pounds lobster, cooked and diced,
   or 1 can (No. 1)
2 tablespoons butter
1 tablespoon flour
1 cup thin cream
2 egg yolks, beaten
½ teaspoon salt
dash of paprika   dash of nutmeg
4 to 6 slices hot toast, buttered, or
   4 to 6 patty shells

Makes 4 to 6 portions.

Cook and dice lobster as for Boiled Lobster. Cook slowly in butter 3 minutes, then stir in flour. Add cream gradually and stir until thickened. Then cook 2 minutes.

Stir in small amount of sauce into egg yolk. Then return to lobster mixture, stirring constantly for 1 minute. Remove at once from heat and add seasonings.

Serve on hot toast or in patty shells, as desired.

FRIED SOFT-SHELL CRABS

1½ pounds fat for frying
4 to 8 soft-shell crabs, washed and
   cleaned
salt and pepper
1 egg, slightly beaten
1 tablespoon water
½ cup fine bread crumbs
lemon wedges
Tartar Sauce (*page* 112)

Allow 1 to 2 crabs per portion.

Put fat in heavy kettle, adjust thermometer and heat slowly to 375° F.

Wash and prepare crabs, sprinkle with salt and pepper, and dip in mixture of egg and water. Roll in crumbs and put in frying basket.

Put basket in hot fat (375° F.) and fry for 3 or 4 minutes, or until golden brown. Drain on unglazed paper and serve at once with lemon and tartar sauce.

To prepare live, soft-shell crabs, wash and place, face down, on board. Then pull back soft shell of tapering point on either side of back, one at a time, and scrape out fibrous spongy material underneath. Then turn over and pull off tail and scrape off spongy portion beneath. Wash and drain.

CREAMED OYSTERS

2 cups Medium White Sauce
  (*page* 109)
2 cups oysters *
1 teaspoon chopped parsley
dash Worcestershire sauce

* One cup contains about: 14 small, 10 medium, 8 or 9 large oysters.

Makes about 4 portions.

Prepare sauce and keep hot.

Examine oysters for bits of shell. Heat in their own liquor about 3 minutes, or until plump and edges curl. Add to sauce. Season with additional salt, if necessary. Add parsley and Worcestershire sauce.

SAUCES

CREAM OR WHITE SAUCE

	Thin	*Medium*	*Thick*
butter	1 to 2 tablespoons	2 tablespoons	¼ cup
flour	1 tablespoon	2 tablespoons	¼ cup
milk or light cream	1 cup	1 cup	1 cup
salt	¼ teaspoon	¼ teaspoon	¼ teaspoon
pepper	dash	dash	dash

Melt butter in top part of double boiler over low heat. Stir in flour.

Add milk gradually, blending well. Cook over low heat, stirring constantly, until mixture boils and thickens. Then cook slowly about 3 minutes longer, stirring occasionally. Add seasonings. Cover and place over boiling water to keep hot.

Use Thin White Sauce for cheese sauce, cream soups and cream toast. Use Medium White Sauce for meat, fish and vegetable sauces, creamed scalloped dishes. Use Thick White Sauce for soufflés and croquettes.

Makes about 1 cup sauce.

Caper Sauce—Add 2 to 4 tablespoons chopped capers to 1 cup Medium White Sauce and add additional salt to taste. Serve with fish. *Makes about 1¼ cups sauce.*

Cheese Sauce—Make 1 cup Thin White Sauce. Add ½ cup grated American cheese. Heat in double boiler until cheese is melted. *Makes about 1¼ cups sauce.*

Cheese-Chive Sauce—Add 1 tablespoon minced chives to Cheese Sauce.

Serve with fish, eggs or on toast. *Makes about 1¼ cups sauce.*

Egg Sauce—Add 2 hard-cooked eggs (*page* 36), diced, to 1 cup Medium White Sauce and additional salt, if desired. Serve with boiled fish. *Makes about 1½ cups sauce.*

Parsley Sauce—Add ½ teaspoon grated onion and 1 tablespoon chopped parsley to 1 cup Medium White Sauce. Serve with fish. *Makes about 1 cup sauce.*

MUSHROOM SAUCE

½ pound mushrooms, sliced thin
3 tablespoons butter
3 tablespoons flour
1½ cups Brown Stock (*page* 80), or canned bouillon, or bouillon cubes and water
½ teaspoon salt   dash of pepper

Makes about 1½ cups sauce.

Slice mushrooms. Sauté in butter 5 minutes. Stir in flour gradually. Add beef stock slowly, and continue stirring until mixture boils and thickens. Cook slowly 3 minutes longer, stirring occasionally. Season.

Serve with steak, roast beef, veal, chicken.

MUSTARD SAUCE

3 tablespoons butter
2 tablespoons flour
½ teaspoon salt
1 teaspoon dry mustard
¼ teaspoon nutmeg
1½ cups hot water
1 egg yolk, slightly beaten

Makes about 1½ cups sauce.

Melt butter over low heat. Mix together flour and seasonings, then stir into butter. Add water gradually, stirring constantly until mixture boils and thickens. Then cook slowly 3 minutes longer.

Remove from heat and stir slowly into egg yolk. Serve hot.

Use with boiled fish, ham or corned beef.

MARINARA SAUCE

1 clove garlic, minced
2 tablespoons olive oil
3 cups canned tomatoes
⅛ teaspoon thyme
1 bay leaf, crushed
⅛ teaspoon ground sweet basil
6 whole cloves

Makes about 2½ cups sauce.

Sauté garlic in olive oil about 5 minutes, or until lightly browned. Add tomatoes and seasonings, and bring to a boil. Cover and simmer for 30 minutes, or until mixture is somewhat thickened. Use with fish or spaghetti.

TOMATO SAUCE

1 can (No. 2) or 2½ cups tomatoes
1 small onion, sliced
¼ teaspoon pepper
½ teaspoon celery salt
2 tablespoons butter
2 tablespoons flour
½ teaspoon Worcestershire sauce

Makes about 1½ cups sauce.

Cook tomatoes, onion and seasonings 10 minutes. Rub through sieve or colander.

Melt butter, stir in flour. Add sieved tomatoes slowly, stirring constantly until boiled and thickened. Stir in Worcestershire.

GREEN SAUCE

1 egg, cooked (*page* 36)
½ cup chopped parsley
1 small onion, minced
1 clove garlic, minced
¼ teaspoon chopped chives
2 tablespoons olive oil
1 tablespoon lemon juice
½ teaspoon salt
⅛ teaspoon pepper
1 egg, well beaten

Makes about ½ cup sauce.

Cook egg 3½ to 4 minutes. Mash well.

Prepare vegetables, then add to egg, rubbing well with spoon.

Stir in olive oil, lemon juice and seasonings. Beat egg well and fold into sauce mixture. Serve with hot or cold boiled fish.

DEVIL SAUCE

¾ cup tomato ketchup
¼ cup Worcestershire sauce
dash of tabasco

Makes 1 cup sauce.

Heat ingredients to scalding. Serve hot with corned beef hash, or smoked meats.

RAISIN SAUCE

⅓ cup firmly packed brown sugar
1 tablespoon flour
1½ teaspoons dry mustard
dash each of salt and pepper
1¾ cups boiling water
¼ cup vinegar
½ cup seedless raisins
1 teaspoon grated orange rind
2 tablespoons butter

Mix sugar, flour, mustard, salt and pepper. Add water and vinegar gradually and boil, stirring until thickened. Then simmer slowly 5 minutes. Add raisins and orange rind, and cook 2 minutes longer, or until raisins are plump. Stir in butter.

Serve hot with ham or tongue.

Makes about 2 cups sauce.

CURRANT-ORANGE SAUCE

1 cup currant jelly
½ cup orange juice
½ cup minced fresh mint

Beat jelly with fork, while adding juice and mint. Chill 1 hour. Serve with meats.

Makes about 1½ cups sauce.

NEVER-FAIL HOLLANDAISE

2 tablespoons flour
4 tablespoons butter, melted
1 cup water, or White Stock (*page* 109), or canned chicken bouillon
¼ teaspoon salt
¼ teaspoon paprika
2 egg yolks, slightly beaten
2 tablespoons lemon juice

Stir flour into 2 tablespoons melted butter in top of double boiler. Add liquid slowly, stirring constantly until mixture is smooth and thick. Add seasonings. Keep water in lower part of boiler below boiling. Stir 2 tablespoons sauce into egg yolks, then stir mixture into remaining sauce. Stir in lemon juice and remaining butter. Cook 1 minute.

Makes about 1½ cups sauce.

Serve with cooked vegetables and fish.

TARTAR SAUCE

1 cup mayonnaise
1 tablespoon chopped capers
1 tablespoon chopped olives
1 tablespoon chopped parsley
1 tablespoon chopped pickles

Combine ingredients just before serving.

Serve with hot or cold fish, or use as dressing for fish salad.

Makes about 1¼ cups sauce.

LEMON BUTTER

¼ **cup butter, melted**
1½ **tablespoons lemon juice**
1 **teaspoon chopped parsley**
dash of nutmeg

Makes about ⅓ cup sauce.

Combine ingredients. Serve warm with broccoli, asparagus, chops, and fish.

MINT SAUCE

½ **cup chopped fresh mint**
1 **cup water**
¼ **cup vinegar**
2 **tablespoons sugar**
½ **teaspoon salt**

Makes about 1 cup sauce.

Simmer ¼ cup mint and remaining ingredients together 5 minutes. Strain, cool and add remaining mint. Serve with lamb.

FLUFFY CUCUMBER SAUCE

1 **medium-sized cucumber**
½ **cup heavy cream, sweet or sour,**
   whipped
½ **teaspoon salt**
1 **tablespoon vinegar**

Makes about 1¾ cups sauce.

Chop and drain cucumber. Whip cream until stiff. Fold in cucumber, salt and vinegar. Serve with cold meats and fish.

VEGETABLES

COOKING OF VEGETABLES

Well-cooked vegetables are cooked until just tender or slightly crisp—the starch is cooked and the cellulose softened. As much as possible of the original minerals and vitamins are conserved and the natural color and flavor are retained or improved. Over-cooked vegetables are faded in color, soft, mushy, strong.

Selection and Storage—Select only fresh, crisp vegetables. When buying, try to pick out vegetables of uniform size so that cooking will be uniform. Wash quickly, dry thoroughly (if not to be used immediately), and store in refrigerator containers or plastic bags in refrigerator. Spinach and other greens are washed in several waters to remove all traces of sand and grit. Tight-headed vegetables, such as artichokes, Brussels sprouts, broccoli, cabbage and cauliflower, are soaked briefly in salted water to draw out small insects. Do not soak other vegetables. Long soaking periods result in loss of vitamins and minerals. Thick-skinned vegetables, such as potatoes, rutabaga or winter squash, are stored, unwashed, in a cool dry place.

Preparation of Vegetables for Cooking —Prepare vegetables just before cooking. Whenever possible, cook vegetables whole and in their skins. Slicing, dicing or shredding shortens cooking time but increases the loss of vitamins and minerals. When you must use this method, cut in uniform pieces so that they will cook evenly. Husk or shell corn, peas or lima beans just before cooking. (In fact, at least one authority recommends cooking these vegetables in their husks or pods.) The coloring material in red vegetables is soluble in water, therefore beets are washed, and the skins and 1 inch or more of top and roots are left on to prevent loss of color (also lessens loss of flavor and food value).

Methods of Cooking Vegetables—Vegetables are steamed, baked, broiled, panned or boiled. Whichever method you choose, do not overcook. Save any cooking liquid for use in soups, sauces and gravies. Vinegar or lemon juice added to the cooking liquid of red vegetables will help preserve their color. But don't add baking soda to brighten green vegetables as it will destroy the vitamin C content of the vegetable. Modern cooking authorities recommend adding salt just before serving rather than during cooking. Salt, they say, draws out some of the vegetable juices into the cooking water, resulting in the loss of flavor and food value.

Quick-frozen vegetables need no additional preparation. They may be cooked just thawed, or solidly frozen. Follow directions on package.

Canned vegetables are ready for use and can be substituted for fresh ones in most recipes. Open can shortly before using. Drain and use liquid for soups.

Dried vegetables require soaking for several hours or overnight in cold water to restore water. Sort and rinse thoroughly before soaking.

Methods of Serving Boiled or Steamed Vegetables—Vegetables may be served in a variety of ways such as: buttered, allowing 1 to 2 tablespoons butter, cream or other fat per cup of vegetable; glazed with butter or other fat and sugar; prepared with sauce such as white sauce, cheese sauce or Hollandaise; creamed and baked au gratin; scalloped and baked; fried in a small amount of fat, or in deep fat; diced or puréed in croquettes, soufflés, or timbales; used with stock or milk in soups.

STEAMED VEGETABLES

Steaming in live steam or in steam from vegetable juices conserves most of the food value and flavor of the vegetable. With live steam, place washed, prepared vegetable on a rack with just enough water in the bottom of your pan to generate steam. Cover and steam for the length of time required for the individual vegetable (*page* 118).

A "waterless" cooker or heavy kettle with tight-fitting cover (a frying pan is excellent) allows vegetables to "steam in their own juices." With a "waterless" cooker, the water left on the vegetable after washing is usually sufficient for cooking. (If vegetable has been washed, dried and stored in refrigerator, rinse under water before cooking.) With other type kettles, 2 to 3 tablespoons of water or vegetable oil and several lettuce leaves, drenched under the faucet and placed on top of the vegetable, will be needed. A tight-fitting cover that prevents the escape of steam is an absolute necessity. Place the kettle with prepared vegetable over medium heat until the cover is hot to touch (about 5 minutes). Reduce the heat to low and continue cooking for the time specified on the table (*page* 118). Drain, only if necessary, and reserve stock for soups, gravies and sauces. Season and serve.

BAKED VEGETABLES

Beets, carrots, parsnips, potatoes (white and sweet), onions, squash and tomatoes lend themselves well to baking. All, except onions, can be scrubbed well and baked in their skins. Winter squash is generally cut in pieces, acorn squash in half, seeds removed and then baked in the shell. Beets should be peeled just before serving. Bake in a 350° F. (moderate) oven, in covered containers (except potatoes in jackets), for the time speci-fied on the table (*page* 118). Season and serve.

Frozen vegetables can be cooked in a small amount of boiling water in a covered container in the oven. Set the temperature at 350° to 375° F. and cook for 30 to 45 minutes, or until just fork-tender. In like manner, cooked vegetables can be reheated, or canned vegetables heated—in a 350° to 375° F. oven for 15 to 20 minutes.

BROILED VEGETABLES

Fresh or canned mushrooms, cooked parsnips (halves or thick slices), cooked sweet and white potatoes (halves or thick slices), and raw tomatoes (halves or thick slices) can be broiled. Place vegetable on greased broiler rack, brush with butter and broil for the last few minutes that meat is cooking. Broil on one side only. Season and serve.

PANNED OR BRAISED VEGETABLES

Succulent vegetables such as cabbage, corn (cut), eggplant, green pepper, mushrooms, onions, summer squash or zucchini (Italian squash) can be cooked in a small amount of fat and the juice of the vegetable or a very small amount of added liquid. Wash vegetable. Shred or cut in thin slices. Cook slowly in 1 to 2 tablespoons butter or other fat in heavy frying pan about 5 minutes, stirring constantly. Then cover and cook in own juices or 1 to 2 tablespoons water or milk until just tender, stirring occasionally. Season to taste.

BOILED VEGETABLES

When you boil, put the vegetable on to cook in the least possible amount of boiling water, preferably in a wide, shallow, heavy-duty pan. Cover pan, bring quickly to boil. Turn heat low and simmer gently until just fork-tender. Vegetables cooked in this fashion are almost steamed rather than boiled. Do not overcook. Use about ½ inch water in pan—½ to 1 cup—for family-size amount of most quick-cooking vegetables. Use more water for the strong-tasting vegetables which require longer cooking. (But remember, too great heat and too long cooking causes the too strong, disagreeable odor and taste, and the discoloration of these vegetables.) With a few exceptions, no draining should be necessary. Season and rush to table.

Can you identify these vegetables? Starting from the top, left to right:

Chicory, celery cabbage, Belgian endive, escarole, collards, chives, artichoke, cauliflower, garlic, green onions, leeks, green cabbage, broccoli, shallots, zucchini, turnips, rutabaga, kohlrabi, parsnips, summer squash, mushrooms, dandelion, kale, okra, celery knob, mustard greens.

SERVING YIELD AND TIME TABLE FOR COOKING VEGETABLES

Vegetable	Amount As purchased	Time in Minutes* Boiling	Steaming	Baking	Cooked Yield Servings
Artichokes, French or globe, whole	4 medium	35 to 45	45 to 60		4
Asparagus, whole	1 lb.	10 to 20	12 to 30		4 (4–5 stalks)
Beans, green and wax	1 lb.	15 to 30	20 to 35		5 (½ cup)
lima in pod	1 lb.				2 (⅓ cup)
lima, shelled	1 lb.	20 to 30	25 to 35		6 (⅓ cup)
Beets, young, whole	1 lb.	30 to 45	40 to 60	40 to 60	4
old, whole	1 lb.	45 to 90	50 to 90	40 to 60	4
Beet greens	1 lb.	5 to 15			4
Broccoli, stalks and buds	1 lb.	10 to 20	15 to 20		3
Brussels sprouts	1 lb. (1 qt.)	10 to 20	10 to 20		5
Cabbage, shredded	1 lb.	3 to 10	8 to 12		4 (½ cup)
Carrots, young, whole	1 lb.	15 to 25	20 to 30	35 to 45	5
young, sliced	1 lb.	10 to 20	15 to 25	30 to 40	5 (½ cup)
old, whole	1 lb.	20 to 30	40 to 50	60	5
old, sliced	1 lb.	15 to 25	25 to 30		5 (½ cup)
Cauliflower, whole	1 lb.	20 to 30	25 to 30		3
flowerets	1 lb.	8 to 15	10 to 20		3 (½ cup)
Celery, diced	1 lb. (2 medium bunches)	15 to 20	25 to 30		4 (½ cup)
Corn, on cob	12 medium	5 to 15	10 to 15		6
Eggplant, sliced	1 lb.	10 to 20	15 to 20		5 (½ cup)
Onion, small, whole	1 lb.	15 to 25	25 to 35		4
Parsnips, whole	1 lb. (4 medium)	20 to 40	30 to 45	30 to 45	4
Peas, green	1 lb. (in pod)	8 to 20	10 to 20		2 (½ cup)

SERVING YIELD AND TIME TABLE FOR COOKING VEGETABLES

Vegetable	Amount	Time in Minutes*			Cooked Yield
	As purchased	Boiling	Steaming	Baking	
Potatoes, sweet, whole	1 lb.	25 to 35	30 to 35	30 to 45	3 (medium)
sweet, quartered	1 lb.	15 to 25	25 to 30		
white, whole	1 lb.	25 to 45	30 to 45	45 to 60	3 (medium)
white, quartered	1 lb.	15 to 25	20 to 30		
Rutabaga, diced	1 lb.	20 to 30	35 to 40		4
Spinach	1 lb.	3 to 10	5 to 12		4
Squash, summer, sliced	1 lb.	10 to 20	15 to 20	30	3
winter, 2 inch pieces	1 lb.	20 to 40	25 to 40	40 to 60	2
Tomatoes	1 lb.	7 to 15		15 to 30	3 (cooked)
	1 lb.				4 (raw)
Turnips, sliced	1 lb.	15 to 20	20 to 25		4 (½ cup)

* The length of time required for a given vegetable to cook by any method cannot be stated exactly because the time differs with the variety and maturity of each, the length of time and temperature at which the vegetable has been held since it was harvested, and the size of the pieces into which it has been cut.

ASPARAGUS OR BROCCOLI HOLLANDAISE

1½ pounds asparagus, cooked
(*page* 118), **or 1 medium bunch
broccoli, cooked** (*page* 118)
Never-Fail Hollandaise (*page* 112)

Makes about 4 portions.

Cook vegetable. Lift out with tongs and drain on towel or absorbent paper. Arrange in hot dish and cover with napkin.

Make sauce while vegetable is cooking. Serve hot in bowl. Brussels sprouts, cauliflower or scallions may be substituted.

VEGETABLES WITH CHEESE SAUCE

Follow recipe for Asparagus or Broccoli Hollandaise (above), only substitue Cheese or Cheese-Chive Sauce (*pages* 109 to 110) for Never-Fail Hollandaise. Use cooked asparagus, broccoli, Brussels sprouts, cauliflower or scallions. *Makes about 4 portions.*

BOSTON BAKED BEANS

I quart pea or navy beans
½ pound fat salt pork
I small onion
2 tablespoons brown sugar
2 teaspoons salt
¾ teaspoon dry mustard
¾ cup molasses
boiling water

Pick over beans. Soak overnight in cold water to cover. Cook slowly in water in which beans were soaked for 40 to 60 minutes, or until tender. To test, take several beans in spoon and blow on them. If skins pop, the beans are done. Drain and save cooking water.

Cut pork in half and place ½ on bottom of bean pot. Pour in beans and bury onion in center. Cut several gashes through rind of remaining pork but do not sever. Press into beans, leaving rind on top. Mix brown sugar, salt, mustard, molasses and I cup boiling water. Pour over beans. Cover with hot water, using reserved cooking water.

Bake, covered, in 250° to 275° F. (very slow) oven for 6 to 8 hours, adding water, when necessary, to keep beans covered. Bake, uncovered, the last ½ hour to brown pork and beans.

Makes 6 to 8 portions.

SWEET CARROTS

6 to 8 medium-sized carrots, sliced
   crosswise
½ cup boiling water
¼ teaspoon salt   ½ cup sugar
4 tablespoons butter

Cook carrots in boiling salted water 10 minutes. Add ½ cup sugar and simmer, covered, 10 minutes. Pour off liquid. Fold in butter.

Makes about 4 portions.

BROILED MUSHROOMS

Wash and drain 12 large mushroom caps, do not peel. Brush with melted butter or oil and sprinkle with salt, pepper and nutmeg. Broil, cap side up, 6 to 8 minutes. Serve, cap side up, on buttered toast or as garnish for meat.
Makes about 4 portions.

CORN FRITTERS

1¾ cups sifted flour
2 teaspoons double-action baking
   powder
¾ teaspoon salt
1 egg, beaten   ¾ cup milk
1 cup drained, canned kernel corn
1 tablespoon butter, melted
   fat for frying

Makes about 8 fritters.

Sift flour, baking powder, and salt into bowl. Combine egg, milk, corn and butter. Stir into flour mixture.

Put enough fat into frying pan to make an inch layer when melted. Heat. Drop batter from tip of large spoon into hot fat (350° to 375° F.) and fry 4 to 5 minutes, or until golden brown, turning when brown on one side. Drain.

SAUTÉED EGGPLANT

½ eggplant   salt and pepper
flour   3 tablespoons fat

Makes about 4 portions.

Pare and slice eggplant in ¼-inch slices. Sprinkle with salt and pepper. Dip in flour. Sauté in hot fat 10 minutes, or until tender and browned, turning frequently.

SAUTÉED SUMMER SQUASH AND ZUCCHINI

Follow recipe for Sautéed Eggplant, only wash and do not pare. *One medium summer squash or zucchini will make about 4 portions.*

POTATOES AU GRATIN

3 cups cubed cooked potatoes (*page 119*)
1½ cups Medium White Sauce
   (*page* 109)
1 cup grated cheese
¼ cup dry bread crumbs
1 tablespoon butter, melted

Makes about 4 portions.

Cook potatoes. Dice. Put into buttered casserole.

Make sauce. Stir in cheese and pour over potatoes. Sprinkle with buttered crumbs. Bake in 350° F. (moderate) oven 15 minutes, or until brown.

CABBAGE, ASPARAGUS OR CAULIFLOWER AU GRATIN

Follow recipe for Potatoes au Gratin, only substitute chopped, cooked cabbage, broken asparagus, or cauliflower flowerets for potatoes.

BAKED POTATOES

(White or Yellow)

Select uniform, medium-sized to large potatoes. Scrub, remove blemishes, rinse. Place in shallow baking pan or on rack. Rub with melted fat if soft skin is desired. Bake in 400° F. (hot) oven 45 to 60 minutes. To test, pick up with cloth and squeeze; if soft, they are done. Cut gashes, cross shape, on top. Insert square of butter in opening and dust with paprika. Serve in hot dish. *Allow 1 potato per portion.*

STUFFED BAKED POTATOES

4 medium-sized Baked Potatoes
3 tablespoons butter
½ teaspoon salt
¼ teaspoon white pepper
¼ cup hot milk
**2 teaspoons finely minced onion or
chives**
**1 egg white, stiffly beaten
(optional)**
grated cheese, if desired

Bake potatoes. Cut slice from top of each. Scoop out insides and mash well with fork. Add butter, salt, pepper, milk and onion, beating until fluffy. Fold in egg white. Pile lightly into shells.

Bake 5 to 8 minutes to brown lightly. Sprinkle with grated cheese before baking, if desired.

Makes 4 portions.

FRANCONIA OR BROWNED POTATOES

Pare medium-sized potatoes and cook in a small amount of boiling salted water for 15 minutes. Drain and place in pan in which meat is roasting. Bake about 30 minutes, or until tender and lightly browned, turning once. Serve on hot platter with roast. Allow 1 to 2 potatoes per portion.

FRENCH FRIED POTATOES

(Helps in Deep-Fat Frying, *page 57*)

Wash and pare small potatoes and cut lengthwise into strips about ⅜ inch thick. Soak in cold water ½ to 1 hour. Drain, wipe very dry between towels or paper towels and place just enough in bottom of frying basket or sieve to cover sparsely. Immerse in hot deep fat (385° to 395° F.) and cook 3 to 5 minutes, or until a golden brown, keeping potatoes in motion. Hold basket over kettle for fat to drip, then turn out on absorbent paper to drain. Sprinkle with salt and serve hot. *Allow 1 to 2 potatoes per portion.*

POTATO CHIPS

Follow recipe for French Fried Potatoes, only slice potatoes very thin, using a vegetable slicer. Separate chilled and dried slices. Place loosely in bottom of basket. Fry for 2 to 3 minutes, keeping potatoes in motion.

SHOESTRING OR JULIENNE POTATOES

Follow recipe for French Fried Potatoes, only cut potatoes in match-like sticks. Fry for 2 to 3 minutes, keeping potatoes in motion.

GERMAN FRIED POTATOES

5 medium-sized potatoes, pared
  and sliced thin
3 tablespoons fat, melted
¾ teaspoon salt   dash of pepper

Makes about 4 portions.

Prepare potatoes, add to melted fat in heavy frying pan. Season. Sauté slowly about 15 minutes, or until evenly browned, turning over occasionally. Cover and cook 15 minutes longer, or until done.

HASHED BROWN POTATOES

3 cups finely chopped cooked
  potatoes (*page* 119)
½ teaspoon salt
¼ teaspoon pepper
¼ teaspoon paprika
¼ cup milk
3 tablespoons fat

Makes 4 to 6 portions.

Cook potatoes and dice. Add seasonings and milk. Add to hot fat in heavy frying pan and pat evenly.

Cook slowly, without stirring, about 15 minutes, or until browned on bottom. With broad spatula fold over as with an omelet.

MASHED POTATOES

(White or Yellow)

4 to 6 cooked potatoes (*page* 119)
3 tablespoons butter
⅓ to ½ cup hot milk
salt and pepper
paprika or parsley

Makes about 4 portions.

Cook potatoes. Force through ricer, or mash well with wire or wooden masher, using strong rotary motion. Add butter and milk, beating with large spoon until fluffy and smooth. Season well. Pile into hot serving dish. Dot with additional butter, if desired. Sprinkle with paprika or parsley.

FRENCH FRIED ONION RINGS

(See French Fried Potatoes, *page* 122)

3 large mild onions
⅓ cup milk   ⅓ cup flour
⅛ teaspoon salt   dash of pepper

Makes about 4 portions.

Peel onions and cut in ¼-inch thick slices. Dip in milk, then in seasoned flour.

Fry in hot deep fat (375° to 385° F.) for 4 to 6 minutes, or until lightly browned. Drain.

MASHED RUTABAGAS, TURNIPS OR WINTER SQUASH

Follow recipe for Mashed Potatoes, only use cooked rutabagas or turnips (*page* 119) or winter squash (*page* 119), and omit milk.

PARSLEY POTATOES

Cook 1 pound new potatoes (*page* 119). Drop into 2 tablespoons melted butter to coat evenly and place in hot dish. Pour remaining butter over top and sprinkle about 2 tablespoons minced parsley over top. *Makes about 4 portions.*

SOUTHERN CANDIED SWEET POTATOES

4 cooked sweet potatoes (*page* 119),
peeled and halved
3 tablespoons butter
½ cup firmly packed brown sugar

Makes 4 portions.

Prepare potatoes. Melt butter in frying pan. Sprinkle ½ of sugar over top. Lay potatoes in pan and sprinkle with sugar.

Cook, covered, over very low heat about 20 minutes, or until golden brown and syrupy, turning several times.

GLAZED CARROTS

Follow recipe for Southern Candied Sweet Potatoes, only substitute 12 to 16 cooked small carrots for potatoes. *Serves 4.*

BUTTERED SPINACH OR SWISS CHARD

Young, tender, mild-flavored, leafy vegetables such as spinach and Swiss chard are cooked in almost no water, or only the water which clings to the leaves after washing and draining. Wash about 1 ½ pounds in 3 or more waters, or until free from sand, removing roots, tough stems and wilted leaves; drain about 15 minutes. Put in large kettle, cover, and place over medium heat until cover is hot to touch. Reduce heat to low and cook until just tender. Spinach cooks in 5 to 12 minutes; Swiss chard in 15 to 25 minutes. Drain, if necessary, and reserve stock for soup or gravy. Chop or cut, add 2 to 4 tablespoons butter, and season to taste with salt and pepper. Place in hot dish and garnish with wedges of lemon or slices of hard-cooked egg. *Makes about 2 ½ cups chopped spinach or 4 portions.*

SPINACH RING

2 cups Thick White Sauce (*page* 109)
1 small onion, sliced
2 tablespoons butter
½ cup soft bread crumbs
3 cups chopped Cooked Spinach
½ teaspoon salt
dash of pepper
⅛ teaspoon nutmeg
2 eggs, separated

Makes about 6 portions.

Prepare sauce. Sauté onion in butter in large saucepan 3 minutes. Remove from heat and stir in crumbs, spinach, white sauce and seasonings.

Beat egg whites until stiff. Beat egg yolks until mixed; then stir into spinach mixture. Fold in egg whites. Turn into well-greased, large ring mold and set in pan of hot water.

Bake in 350° F. (moderate) oven for 30 to 40 minutes, or until firm when tested with knife. Unmold on hot plate. Serve at once with creamed chicken, fish or egg.

BAKED SQUASH

Wash and split large winter squash in pieces and split acorn squash in half lengthwise. Remove seeds and stringy portion, and cut large squash in pieces for serving. Wash summer squash or zucchini, cut in half lengthwise and remove seeds. Place squash in shallow pan, spread generously with softened butter and sprinkle with salt and pepper. Bake in 350° F. (moderate) oven for 45 to 60 minutes, or until squash is soft. Strips of bacon may be used instead of butter. *Allow about ⅓ pound squash per portion.*

BAKED ZUCCHINI OR SUMMER SQUASH SLICES

Wash squash and cut in ½-inch slices crosswise. Season, then brush with butter. Bake, uncovered, in 350° F. (moderate) oven about 30 minutes, or until crusty, basting once. *Allow 3 slices per portion.*

BROILED TOMATOES

Wash 4 medium-sized tomatoes and cut in halves, crosswise. Brush cut sides with melted butter and sprinkle with salt, pepper and sugar. Broil, cut side up, about 2 minutes, or until browned. Grated cheese or buttered bread crumbs may be sprinkled over surfaces before broiling, if desired. Serve on buttered toast with Cheese Sauce (*page* 110), or use as garnish for meat, poultry or fish. *Allow* 1 *tomato per portion.*

STUFFED TOMATOES

4 firm ripe tomatoes
3 slices bacon
1 tablespoon bacon fat
2 teaspoons minced onion
¾ cup soft bread crumbs
salt and pepper
1 tablespoon butter, melted
⅓ cup dry bread crumbs

Makes 4 portions.

Wash tomatoes. Slice off stem ends. Scoop out pulp and chop. Fry bacon until crisp. Remove and dice. Pour off all but 1 tablespoon fat from pan. Add onion and sauté 2 minutes. Add crumbs, bacon and chopped pulp. Season to taste.

Fill tomatoes with mixture. Top with buttered crumbs, place in baking pan and bake in 350° F. (moderate) oven for 20 minutes, or until tender and crumbs browned.

STUFFED ONIONS

Follow recipe for Stuffed Tomatoes, only use onions, steamed until almost tender. For variety, ½ cup chopped left-over ham, beef, veal or lamb may be substituted for bacon; use less crumbs.

STUFFED PEPPERS

Follow recipe for Stuffed Tomatoes. First cut thin slice from stem end of peppers and remove seeds. Stuff and bake until tender.

STUFFED BEETS

Follow recipe for Stuffed Tomatoes, only cook beets until tender (*page* 118). Peel and scoop out centers. Cut slice from bottom of each so beets will stand level.

GLAZED TURNIPS OR PARSNIPS

6 small turnips or parsnips
water
2 tablespoons butter, melted
¾ cup brown stock
¼ teaspoon salt
1 teaspoon sugar
½ teaspoon mace

Makes about 4 portions.

Wash, peel or scrape vegetable. Cut in large cubes. Boil 5 minutes in a small amount of water. Drain.

Add turnip to remaining ingredients in heavy saucepan. Bring to a boil and simmer, covered, about 20 minutes, or until tender. Uncover and cook until sauce is reduced to a glaze.

OVEN MEALS

Whenever you light or turn on your oven, try to use the oven to its full capacity. Baking days combined with oven meals are really fuel economy days.

After food is prepared for oven cooking, you can set your minute timer and go off to do something else. The bell will remind you when the food is cooked. If you have an automatic timer, your carefully prepared meal is on its own—the oven will automatically turn on at the time you have indicated and cook the food for the time allowed—a great convenience if you are to be away for an outing and want your cooked meal to be ready upon your return. Of course, you will have to choose foods that will not spoil if not refrigerated, such as frozen or cured meats. And beware of leaving casseroles made with white sauce or eggs in the oven very long before turning on heat.

Plan foods that can be cooked at the same temperature. It is possible to alter the cooking temperatures of certain foods to fit your oven meals. Naturally, you won't try to bake biscuits at 325° F. or roast meats at 450° F., but vegetables, meats and certain desserts can be baked at temperatures lower than those designated in the recipes—allowing extra time for cooking.

Plan the length of cooking time carefully. Foods left to cook while you are away must take the same cooking time. If you are home, meats or other foods taking longer cooking periods are put in the oven first, and the remainder of the dinner added later.

Foods with syrups, and desserts are usually cooked on the upper oven rack. Vegetables, that are generally not baked, can be cooked or heated in a small amount of water in a covered casserole, at any oven temperature from 250° to 500° F.—the higher the temperature the shorter the cooking period. However, when possible, it is recommended that vegetables be cooked at 350° F. about 60 minutes. Frozen vegetables cook in less time—350° to 375° F. oven for 30 to 45 minutes.

OVEN MEAL 1

Food	Approximate Oven Time	Oven Temperature	Recipe on Page
Baked Stuffed Pork Chop	60 minutes	350° F.	93
Frozen carrots and peas	40 minutes	350° F.	114
Raisin-Nut Bread	60 minutes	350° F.	69
Baked Apples	40 minutes	350° F.	26

OVEN MEAL 2

Food	Approximate Oven Time	Oven Temperature	Recipe on Page
4 pound Rib Roast	1 ½ to 2 hours	325° F.	85
Franconia Potatoes	30 minutes	325° F.	122
Frozen chopped broccoli	40 minutes	325° F.	114
Danish Apple Cake	1 ¼ hours	325° F.	154

BROILER MEALS

Broiler meals add variety to your menus as well as saving cooking fuel. Tender cuts of meat (except veal and fresh pork), variety meats, poultry and fish can be broiled satisfactorily.

The excess fat is trimmed from meats,

and the remaining fat is cut at 1-inch intervals to make meat lie flat during broiling. Chicken, variety meats and non-oily fish are brushed with butter or oil before broiling.

Vegetables, except mushrooms and tomatoes, are pre-cooked before broiling. Fruits and vegetables are brushed with butter or oil and added during the last 5 to 8 minutes of broiling, and are broiled on one side only. Cooked or canned vegetables can be heated in a small amount of boiling water or liquid from can on the bottom of the broiler shelf while other foods are broiling. Use a covered pot or casserole. Broiling time is insufficient to cook vegetables in this manner.

BROILER MEAL 1

Food	Approximate Broiling Time	Recipe on Page
Ham Steak	20 minutes	93
Sweet potatoes	5 to 8 minutes	119 (cooking)
Pineapple slices	5 minutes	above (broiling)
Canned green beans	20 minutes	

The pineapple slices are placed on top of meat during last 5 minutes of broiling. The green beans are heated in a small amount of liquid from can in a covered casserole on bottom shelf of broiler.

BROILER MEAL 2

Food	Approximate Broiling Time	Recipe on Page
Sirloin Steak—1 ½ inches	16 minutes	82
Browned potatoes	6 to 8 minutes	119 (cooking)
		above (broiling)
Broiled Tomatoes	2 minutes	126
Broiled Mushrooms	6 to 8 minutes	120

PLANKED DINNERS

Almost any meat, fish, poultry or game which is ordinarily broiled, roasted or baked can be cooked and served on a plank, usually of oak or hickory.

Use clean, well-seasoned plank, brush with oil and heat in 350° F. (moderate) oven about 10 minutes before using. If used for broiling, have broiler oven moderately hot. Do not put plank too near flame.

To season a new plank, wipe clean with dry cloth and brush top and edges with oil. Heat in 350° F. (moderate) oven about 5 minutes for oil to pene-

trate wood. Repeat process twice, or until wood has absorbed all oil.

To clean plank, scour with steel wool to loosen all food particles and wash quickly with clean, hot soapy water. Do not allow board to soak. Rinse with hot, clear water, wipe with cloth and dry at room temperature—never in heat.

Sizzling platters of aluminum with grooved compartments and detachable wooden handles for service at table may be used instead of planks.

SERVICE SUGGESTIONS FOR PLANKED DINNERS

Choose, from one or all of the groups listed below, 3 or more vegetables and fruits of contrasting color, shape and texture, with a pleasing blend of flavors.

Vegetables or fruits, one or several, to be arranged on plank and browned in oven or under broiler about 10 minutes before dish is done:

Mashed vegetables, brushed with melted butter, egg or milk

Cooked fruit or vegetable halves or slices; tomato slices, brushed with butter, sprinkled with sugar

Mushroom caps, brushed with butter

Cooked vegetables, one or several, to be arranged on plank for serving:

Buttered peas, lima or kidney beans, string beans

Baked stuffed onions, green peppers, tomatoes, beets or turnips

Cauliflower flowerets or Brussels sprouts with buttered crumbs

French fried or fried onion rings, asparagus tips, julienne potatoes

Baked or sautéed summer squash slices, eggplant

Buttered, diced carrots, beets, turnips, rutabagas, asparagus tips

Buttered potato balls

Uncooked vegetables or fruits for garnish, one or several:

Parsley or watercress, cucumber, onion, or tomato slices, radishes, scallions, lemon or lime wedges

Who could resist it? A juicy tender planked steak surrounded by vegetables. Planking adds both style and flavor to foods.

PLANKED STEAK FOR FOUR

(See Planked Dinners, *page* 130)

**club steak, or porterhouse, 1½
    inches thick (2½ or 3 lb.)**
3 cups Mashed Potatoes (*page* 123)
12 mushroom caps
butter   salt and pepper
2 cups buttered peas

Broil steak (*page* 82) browning on both sides, until about ½ done, according to desired degree of doneness.

Then place browned steak on heated, oiled plank. Flank potatoes on ends and mushrooms on sides of plank. Brush with butter and season steak and mushrooms with salt and pepper.

Place in 350° F. (moderate) oven and bake until potatoes are browned and meat is done.

Just before serving, place peas on plank and garnish with parsley. Place plank on large tray or in holder and serve at once.

Makes about 4 portions.

PLANKED SALMON LOAF

(See Planked Dinners, *page* 130)

2 cups or 1 can (No. 1) salmon
½ cup dry bread crumbs
2 eggs, slightly beaten
¼ cup light cream
4 tablespoons butter, melted
1 tablespoon lemon juice
1 tablespoon minced parsley
1 teaspoon scraped onion
½ teaspoon salt   dash of pepper
⅓ cup soft bread crumbs, buttered
Baked Zucchini Slices (*page* 125)
Parsley Potatoes (*page* 125)
Buttered String Beans (*page* 118)
parsley sprigs
Cucumber Sauce (*page* 113)

Makes about 4 portions.

Heat oiled plank 10 minutes. Drain salmon and break fish in pieces. Add crumbs, egg, cream, butter, lemon juice and seasonings, and mix well.

Shape into round-topped small loaf on center of hot plank.

Bake in 350° F. (moderate) oven for 40 minutes. Then sprinkle buttered crumbs over loaf and brown in oven or under broiler about 5 minutes.

Arrange zucchini slices, potatoes and string beans on plank and garnish with parsley. Serve with bowl of cucumber sauce.

SALISBURY SIZZLING PLATTER

1¼ pounds lean beef, ground
2½ tablespoons lemon juice
1 teaspoon salt
¼ teaspoon celery salt
¼ teaspoon pepper
2 apples, cored and halved, crosswise
2 medium-sized onions, peeled and cut in thirds, crosswise
6 tablespoons butter, melted
4 tablespoons brown sugar
4 sweet potatoes, boiled (*page* 119) and halved, lengthwise

Makes about 4 portions.

Mix meat with lemon juice and seasonings. Shape lightly on greased aluminum platter into 2-inch thick steak.

Arrange apples and onion pieces on platter around meat. Brush with butter. Sprinkle apples with brown sugar.

Place platter in 350° F. (moderate) oven and bake about 30 minutes, basting all several times with butter.

About 10 minutes before platter is done, arrange sweet potato halves on platter. Brush with butter and sprinkle generously with brown sugar. Serve platter, sizzling hot.

Salads Every Day in the Year

Salad is the most adaptable of all dishes. An appetizer-salad starts a meal with just enough zest. A dinner salad, cold greens or a mixture of crisp vegetables with a thin, sharp dressing, gives "lift" to the middle of a meal, and a salad-dessert, just a trifle sweet, gives a fillip to a meal that has, perhaps, been on the heavy side. More than all that, a luncheon or supper salad of meat, poultry, egg, potato or mixed vegetables is a delicious main dish. If your dinner begins with a salad, serve crisped, raw vegetable relishes in place of the dinner salad.

What Makes a Good Salad? A well-made salad is cold, crisp, colorful, refreshingly tart in flavor, and simple in arrangement and service. The ingredients are cut or sliced into pieces large enough to be distinct and recognizable. The ingredients for any salad, except a molded one, are tossed and tumbled together lightly. A salad should never be stirred for stirring bruises delicate fruits and vegetables.

Preparing Fruits and Vegetables. Fruits and vegetables for salads must be thoroughly chilled. All fruits and vegetables, except greens, may be marinated in a French dressing, lemon juice, or the vinegar from sweet pickles or capers, before being mixed with mayonnaise or other dressing. Greens, for tossed salads, are first coated with oil, to seal in moisture and allow other seasonings to permeate as they are added.

SALAD DRESSINGS

FRENCH DRESSING

1 small onion or 1 clove garlic
¼ cup vinegar or lemon juice
¾ teaspoon salt
⅛ teaspoon pepper
½ teaspoon paprika
1 tablespoon sugar
¾ cup olive or salad oil

Makes about 1 cup dressing.

Chop or mince onion or garlic in bowl. Add vinegar, crush thoroughly with fork, and let stand 20 minutes. Strain.

Measure seasonings into large bottle or small deep bowl. Add vinegar and oil, and shake or beat thoroughly with rotary beater. Store, covered, in refrigerator or cold place. Always shake well before using.

ROQUEFORT DRESSING

To ½ cup French Dressing add: 1 ounce soft or 5 tablespoons grated dry Roquefort cheese. Soften cheese with 1 tablespoon dressing, then stir in remaining dressing. *Makes about ¾ cup dressing.*

CHIFFONADE DRESSING

To ½ cup French Dressing add: 1 tablespoon each chopped green pepper, pimiento and sour pickle, 1 teaspoon minced chives or onion, and 1 hard-cooked egg, finely chopped. *Makes about ¾ cup.*

MAYONNAISE

1 egg or 2 egg yolks
½ teaspoon salt
½ teaspoon dry mustard
¼ teaspoon paprika
dash of cayenne
2 tablespoons vinegar or lemon
  juice
1 cup olive or salad oil
cream, plain or whipped; or fruit
  juice to dilute dressing, if necessary

Makes about 1½ cups dressing.

Break egg into small deep bowl and stir in seasonings with rotary beater. Add 1 tablespoon vinegar and beat very thoroughly. Beat in ¼ cup oil gradually, about 1 tablespoon at a time, until mixture becomes thick, beating thoroughly after each addition.

Beat in remaining 1 tablespoon vinegar, then the oil gradually, about 2 tablespoons at a time, beating thoroughly after each addition, adding oil faster as mixture thickens. Dilute as desired.

NOTE: If oil is added too rapidly, mayonnaise sometimes curdles and remains thin. If so, start with a second egg, beat in curdled mixture gradually, and proceed as directed.

FLUFFY CREAM MAYONNAISE

To ½ cup mayonnaise add: ¼ cup heavy cream, sweet or slightly sour. Whip cream until thick and fold into mayonnaise. Serve with fruit or vegetable salads. *Makes about 1 cup dressing.*

RUSSIAN DRESSING

To ½ cup mayonnaise add: 2 teaspoons each chopped green pepper and celery, 1 tablespoon chopped pimiento, ½ teaspoon minced onion or chives, 2 tablespoons chili sauce, ½ teaspoon paprika. Hard-cooked egg yolk, forced through sieve, may be added. Serve with lettuce, tomato and other vegetable salads. *Makes ¾ to 1 cup dressing.*

THOUSAND ISLAND DRESSING

To Russian Dressing add: 1 tablespoon ketchup, 2 tablespoons chopped sour pickles or ripe olives and 1 teaspoon capers. Serve with vegetable or fish salads. *Makes 1 to 1¼ cups dressing.*

SOUR CREAM DRESSING

½ cup sour heavy cream
2 tablespoons sugar
¼ teaspoon salt
⅛ teaspoon celery salt
dash of cayenne
2 tablespoons vinegar or lemon
   juice

Makes about ⅔ cup dressing.

Cream may or may not be whipped. Add seasonings and mix well. Stir in vinegar or lemon juice gradually.

Serve with vegetable salads and coleslaw.

HORSERADISH SOUR CREAM DRESSING

Follow recipe for Sour Cream Dressing (*see above*), only substitute 1 to 2 tablespoons prepared horseradish for vinegar.

COOKED SALAD DRESSING

2 tablespoons flour
1 tablespoon sugar
1 teaspoon salt
⅛ teaspoon pepper
dash of cayenne
1 teaspoon dry mustard
1 egg, slightly beaten
¾ cup milk or water
2 tablespoons butter
¼ cup vinegar

Mix flour, sugar, and seasonings in top of double boiler. Stir in egg, then milk.

Place over boiling water and cook 10 minutes, or until thickened, stirring constantly. Stir in butter and vinegar. Chill. Thin with plain or whipped cream, or fruit juices before using, as desired.

Makes about 1 cup dressing.

COOKED FRUIT DRESSING

Follow recipe for Cooked Salad Dressing with the following changes: increase sugar to ½ cup; substitute orange, pineapple, cherry or plum juice for milk, and lemon juice for vinegar. Fold in whipped cream before using.

SALADS

CARROT STRAWS

Use tender young carrots. Wash and scrape or peel. Cut in quarters, then in smaller wedges or sticks, according to size. Wrap in clean cloth and chill.

CELERY—FRENCH ENDIVE

Use tender bunches of celery or celery hearts (celery with outer stalks removed). Remove coarser stalks for soup, cooked vegetable or salad. Scrub, remove coarser leaves, cut all brown spots from roots and wash. Wrap in a clean towel and chill in refrigerator for several hours to crisp.

CELERY, CLUB STYLE

Trim root ends of crisp, tender, white celery hearts, and cut hearts lengthwise in quarters or thirds.

Salads every day of the year. Fresh strawberries, bananas, oranges and apples combined with canned fruits and served on crisp salad greens as a fruit salad or a salad-dessert (*page* 146).

Crisped, raw vegetable relishes as appetizers or in place of a dinner salad—radish roses, celery, curled carrots and olives (*page* 136).

Green Salad Bowl with your own interesting additions and a dressing made with oil and lemon or vinegar (*page* 139), served as a main course at lunch or the salad course with dinner.

STUFFED CELERY

Use crisp, tender, white celery stalks. Dry on absorbent paper or clean towel, and fill grooves with one of the following smooth mixtures: cream cheese, moistened with cream or mayonnaise, and scraped onion or minced chives, pimiento or parsley; cream cheese and Roquefort cheese, moistened with cream; chopped hard-cooked egg, mayonnaise and chopped stuffed olives or nut meats.

STUFFED FRENCH ENDIVE

Use crisp, tender blades of French endive or chicory. Wash and dry. Fill blades with one of mixtures used for Stuffed Celery.

CUCUMBER SLICES

Wash and pare chilled cucumber. With four-tined fork score around cucumber lengthwise; then cut in very thin slices. Serve with salt and pepper. Or slice tender cucumber without paring.

RADISH ROSES

Select firm, red radishes, uniform in size and with unwilted leaves. Wash and leave about 1 inch of tops on each. Cut a thin slice from root end. With a sharp thin knife cut 5 or 6 strips of red peel from root end, almost down to the stem. Chill in ice water; peel will open. Serve crisp.

SCALLIONS

Wash well, peel if skin is loose or shrivelled. Cut off root ends and trim stem, leaving 2 to 3 inches. Wrap tightly if placed in refrigerator.

APPETIZER-SALADS

Serve any small tart salad, either seafood, vegetable or fruit, at the beginning of a meal—just enough to whet the appetite. Serve it with small crisp crackers, pretzels, cheese sticks, Cheesies (*page* 268), tiny sandwiches or canapés, etc. A few interesting combinations follow:

Cream cheese, anchovy paste, scraped onion, mayonnaise. Make into small balls and serve on crisp lettuce with pretzels.

Cream cheese, scraped onion, mayonnaise. Make into smooth paste, spread thick over slices of tomato. Serve on watercress with tiny cucumber sandwiches.

Crabmeat flakes, minced cucumber, radishes and chives, hard-cooked egg yolks, chopped, lemon juice to moisten. Make into mixture. Fill tender chicory or French endive blades or small, hollowed-out tomatoes. Serve 2 or 3 blades, or 1 tomato on a plate with crisp crackers.

Shrimps, cleaned, sliced ripe or stuffed olives, small pineapple slices. Place pineapple on crisp lettuce, top with 3 shrimps and fill center with olives. Serve with French dressing and Cheesies (*page* 268).

GREEN SALAD BOWL, ITALIAN STYLE

Use one, two or more greens:
  lettuce, leaf or head
  romaine
  chicory or French endive
  curly endive
  escarole   watercress
  tender spinach leaves
  Chinese or celery cabbage
1 garlic bud
piece of dry bread
2 to 4 tablespoons olive oil
⅛ to ¼ teaspoon salt
1 to 2 tablespoons lemon juice

Select greens. Remove all wilted leaves and wash thoroughly. Drain, roll in cloth and crisp in refrigerator. When ready to serve, break greens with fingers into large salad bowl; cut or shred celery cabbage.

Split garlic clove and rub on a piece of dry bread. Add garlic bread to salad greens. Dribble oil over greens, toss lightly with spoon and fork (use wooden ones, if available), or two forks to coat with oil. Then sprinkle with salt and lemon juice or vinegar, tossing gently to mix well. Remove garlic bread before serving.

ADDITIONS TO SALAD BOWL

One or several of the following may be added to greens: sliced Bermuda onions, cucumbers, green peppers, radishes, stuffed olives or tomatoes; or chopped onions, scallions, pimiento, green or ripe olives or chopped chives or leeks with tops; or your favorite seasoning and herbs, such as sweet basil and paprika or a few tender leaves of fresh thyme.

COLESLAW

2 to 3 cups shredded cabbage, washed, dried and chilled
1 teaspoon minced onion, if desired
Sour Cream Dressing (*page* 135), **or Cooked Salad Dressing** (*page* 136), **diluted with milk or cream**
salt and pepper

Place chilled cabbage in salad bowl. Add onion, if desired, or rub bowl with garlic for flavor before mixing salad in it.

Pour dressing over cabbage and toss together lightly. Season to taste.

ADDITIONS TO COLESLAW

Add one or several of the following: chopped celery, sliced radishes or raw cauliflower, diced cucumbers, grated carrot, drained diced pineapple, diced apples, sliced eggs.

FRESH VEGETABLE SALADS

2 to 3 cups prepared fresh vegetables, 3 or more combined
French Dressing (*page* 134), **or Roquefort Dressing** (*page* 134), **Sour Cream Dressing** (*page* 135), **or Mayonnaise** (*page* 134)

lettuce, romaine, curly endive, chicory or watercress

Allow ½ to ⅔ cup per portion.

Use fresh vegetables in desirable combinations. Prepare for salad and chill. Before serving, put vegetables in bowl, rubbing it first with cut garlic if you wish. Lemon juice sprinkled over shredded carrot adds flavor. Add small amount of dressing, tossing together lightly.

Serve on crisp lettuce with additional dressing. Or serve in salad bowl.

For each fresh vegetable salad below, use vegetables in amounts, as desired; prepare and mix lightly with dressing:

VEGETABLE SALAD, ITALIA

Broken or sliced cauliflower, tomato wedges, diced celery and green pepper slices.

JULIENNE BERMUDA SALAD

Julienne carrots and celery, sliced Bermuda onions and stuffed olives.

SUMMER GARDEN SALAD

Sliced cucumber, sliced radishes, shredded cabbage and carrots.

CRISP SPRING SALAD

Thinly sliced, crisp cucumbers, red radishes, and scallions or young onions on watercress; serve with Chiffonade Dressing (*page* 134).

COOKED VEGETABLE SALADS

2 to 3 cups cooked vegetables, 3 or more combined

Prepare vegetables for one of salads listed below, or choose any other combination of vegetables, in amounts as desired. Chill.

French Dressing (*page* 134)
lettuce, romaine, curly endive, or chicory
Chiffonade Dressing (*page* 134), **or Mayonnaise** (*page* 134)

Allow ½ to ⅔ cup per portion.

Marinate in French dressing, separately or combined, ½ hour or longer. Bowl may be rubbed with garlic before adding vegetables.

Serve in salad bowl, or on crisp lettuce leaves with any desired dressing.

QUICK VEGETABLE SALAD

Peas, diced carrots, julienne string beans and raw celery strips.

VEGETABLE MEDLEY SALAD

Cauliflower flowerets, diced beets, diced raw cucumber and sliced raw green pepper.

LUNCHEON VEGETABLE SALAD

Kidney beans, diced cauliflower, broken asparagus tips, chopped green pepper and pimiento strips.

INTERESTING SALAD ADDITION

One or several of the following may be added to the salad: sliced or diced hard-cooked eggs, stuffed olives, pickles, or pimiento; fresh celery, cucumbers, green peppers, radishes, scallions, and tomatoes.

POTATO SALAD

2 cups cubed cooked potatoes (*page 119*)
½ cup diced celery
½ cup diced cucumber
¼ cup sliced radishes
1 tablespoon minced onion or chives
½ cup French Dressing (*page 134*)
2 Hard-Cooked Eggs (*page 36*)
½ teaspoon salt
dash of pepper
Mayonnaise or Cooked Salad Dressing (*pages 134 and 136*)
crisp lettuce

Makes about 4 portions.

Mix potatoes and vegetables in large bowl, rubbing bowl with cut garlic, if desired.

Add French dressing, cubed or sliced eggs, and seasonings, tossing together lightly. Cover and chill in refrigerator for at least 1 hour.

Add just enough mayonnaise to moisten, mixing gently to avoid mashing potato. Arrange in salad bowl lined with crisp lettuce leaves.

Chopped green pepper, pimiento, or stuffed olives or sweet pickles may be added, as desired.

STUFFED TOMATO OR BEET SALAD

medium-sized ripe tomatoes, peeled, if desired; or cooked beets (*page 118*)

diced cucumber, celery, chopped olives; or
shredded cabbage, fresh pineapple or diced apple; or
diced apple, banana and minced onion; or
diced celery, broken walnut meats, chopped ripe olives; or
cubed shrimps, diced avocado or cucumber
Mayonnaise (*page 134*)
salt and pepper
crisp lettuce or watercress

Allow 1 tomato or beet per portion.

Scoop out centers from stem ends of tomatoes. Chill. Cut slices from root ends of beets. Scoop out centers from stem ends, leaving thin walls. Chill.

For filling, chop centers of tomatoes or beets, according to salad, and mix with one of the vegetable or fruit combinations suggested, or any other combination. Moisten with mayonnaise and season to taste.

Serve cold on crisp lettuce with a spoonful of dressing on top.

DEVILED EGG SALAD

8 Hard-Cooked Eggs (*page* 36)
1 tablespoon minced onion or chives
1 tablespoon minced celery
¼ teaspoon salt
dash of paprika
1 teaspoon horseradish
Mayonnaise (*page* 134)
crisp lettuce
celery or radishes

Makes 4 to 6 salads.

Cut eggs in halves, lengthwise. Remove yolks and mash with silver fork.

To egg yolks add onions, celery, seasonings, and mayonnaise to moisten.

Fill egg whites. Arrange halves or quarters on crisp lettuce and garnish with celery or radishes.

EGG AND ANCHOVY SALAD

Follow method for Deviled Egg Salad, only add the following to mashed egg yolks: 4 tablespoons cream cheese, 3 tablespoons anchovy paste, 1 tablespoon chopped ripe olives, dash of cayenne and 4 tablespoons mayonnaise.

EGG AND NUT SALAD

Follow method for Deviled Egg Salad, only add the following to mashed egg yolks: ½ cup each chopped nuts and celery, salt, 6 tablespoons mayonnaise or Russian Dressing (*page* 135).

MOLDED VEGETABLE SALADS

(Basic Vegetable Salad Mold)

1 package lemon-flavored gelatin
1 cup hot water
½ cup cold water or orange juice
¼ cup vinegar
1½ teaspoons grated lemon rind
1½ to 2 cups prepared vegetables
1 teaspoon salt
3 tablespoons lemon juice
crisp lettuce leaves or romaine
Mayonnaise (*page* 134) **or French Dressing** (*page* 134)

Makes 4 to 6 portions.

For gelatin base, dissolve gelatin in 1 cup hot water as directed on package. Add water or orange juice, vinegar and lemon rind. Chill until slightly thickened.

Prepare vegetables for one of salads suggested below. Add salt and lemon juice, and chill. Fold into slightly thickened gelatin and pour into large plain or ring mold, individual molds, or shallow pan. Chill until firm.

Unmold or cut in squares, and serve on crisp lettuce with mayonnaise or any dressing, as desired.

For each molded vegetable salad below, add the prepared vegetables listed to gelatin base (*page* 143).

BATIK VEGETABLE SALAD MOLD

Thinly sliced celery, shredded raw carrots and beets, and minced onion. (Use ½ cup orange juice in gelatin base.)

PINCH-PENNY VEGETABLE MOLD

Shredded cabbage, finely chopped green pepper, sliced radishes and minced onion.

PINEAPPLE-VEGETABLE MOLD

Shredded cabbage, diced cucumber, grated cooked pineapple, drained. (Use ½ cup pineapple juice instead of water in gelatin base.)

FLORIDA SALAD MOLD

Grated raw carrots and diced grapefruit sections. (Use grapefruit juice instead of orange juice in gelatin base.)

CABBAGE-OLIVE MOLD

Shredded cabbage, diced celery, chopped green pepper, sliced stuffed olives and minced onion.

Golden Glow Fruit Molds make attractive individual salads (*page* 145).

VEGETABLE BOUQUET MOLD

Diced pickled beets, diced celery, shredded cabbage, minced onion. (Use pickled beet juice instead of orange juice in gelatin base; if too sour, add half water.)

MOLDED FRUIT SALADS OR DESSERTS (SELF-LAYERED)

1 tablespoon gelatin
2 tablespoons cold water
1 cup boiling water
¼ cup lemon juice
½ cup orange juice, or juice of fruit used
dash of salt
1 to 1½ cups prepared fruits
crisp lettuce
Mayonnaise (*page* 134), **Cooked Dressing** (*page* 136) **cream or Custard Sauce** (*page* 162)

Makes 4 to 6 portions.

For gelatin base, soak gelatin in cold water 5 minutes. Add boiling water, stirring until dissolved. Add lemon and other fruit juice, and salt. Cool.

Prepare fruits for one of salads suggested below. Add to gelatin bases. Pour into large plain or ring mold, individual molds, or shallow pan. Chill until firm.

For salad, unmold or cut in squares, and serve on crisp lettuce with dressing, as desired. For dessert, unmold or cut in squares, and serve with cream or sauce.

For each molded fruit salad or dessert, add prepared fruits to gelatin base (*above*); the canned fruit sinks and the fresh fruit floats:

WINTER FRUIT SALAD MOLD

Canned pineapple wedges, cubed red apple, chopped nuts.

MOLDED CHERRY SURPRISE

Canned white cherries stuffed with pecan meats, cubed orange sections.

GOLDEN GLOW FRUIT MOLD

Sliced canned peaches or pears, cubed grapefruit, sliced bananas.

ORANGE-BERRY OR CHERRY MOLD

Orange or kumquat marmalade, fresh strawberries or cherries, or white grapes halved and seeded.

FROZEN FRUIT SALAD

1 cup crushed, canned pineapple
¼ cup orange marmalade
1 cup diced, canned peaches
1 cup seeded, white cherries or grapes
10 marshmallows, diced
½ cup salted almonds
½ cup Mayonnaise (*page* 134)
1 cup heavy cream, whipped

Makes 6 to 8 portions.

Mix pineapple and marmalade. Add other fruits, marshmallows and nuts. Toss together. Chill.

Fold mayonnaise into cream. Then fold into fruit mixture. Turn into freezing tray of automatic refrigerator for 4 hours, or until frozen. Unmold, cut in 1-inch slices. Serve with additional mayonnaise.

FRUIT SALADS OR SALAD-DESSERTS

Almost any firm and ripe fruit, fresh or canned, can be used alone or in combination in salads or salad-desserts. Dip fresh fruits such as apples, avocados, bananas, peaches and pears, in lemon or other tart juices to prevent discoloration. Marinate prepared fruit in French dressing or lemon juice, if desired, then chill. Mix together fruit and dressing by tossing lightly with spoon and fork. Serve on crisp lettuce or other green. *Allow ½ to ¾ cup per salad.*

WALDORF SALAD

2 cups cubed tart apples mixed with 2 tablespoons lemon juice, 1 cup diced celery, ½ cup walnut meats, dash of salt, ⅓ cup mayonnaise (about). Mix together just before serving. Serve on crisp lettuce and sprinkle with paprika.

FRUIT SALAD BOWL

½ cup pineapple wedges, ½ cup halved and seeded white grapes, ½ cup melon balls, ½ cup sliced bananas, dipped in 2 tablespoons pineapple juice, ¼ cup red cherries. Arrange fruit in separate piles in bowl, sprinkling cherries over top. If desired, mix each fruit with dressing before arranging in bowl. Serve with Fluffy Cream Mayonnaise (*page* 135).

AVOCADO SALAD

1 avocado, peeled or pared, cut in slices lengthwise, and marinated in 2 tablespoons lemon or lime juice; sections from 2 oranges or 1 grapefruit

(*page* 27). Arrange in alternate layers on crisp curly endive or lettuce and serve with French dressing or mayonnaise.

ORANGE AND ONION SALAD

2 seedless oranges, peeled and sliced crosswise, ½ Bermuda onion, thinly sliced. Arrange on crisp lettuce and serve with French dressing.

FRUIT AND CHEESE SALAD

4 canned peach or pear halves, 8 apricot halves or 4 pineapple slices; ½ cup cottage cheese mixed with 2 tablespoons cream and dash of salt; 4 tablespoons minced celery, 4 tablespoons chopped nut meats, 2 tablespoons minced ripe olives. Spread rounded side of halved fruit or pineapple slices with cheese and dip in mixture of celery, nuts and olives. Serve on crisp lettuce with French dressing.

GRAPEFRUIT AND SHRIMP SALAD

Sections from 1 large grapefruit (*page* 27); 1 avocado, peeled or pared, and sliced lengthwise, then marinated in grapefruit juice; 1 cup shrimps, intestinal vein removed, washed and dried. Arrange simply on crisp lettuce or watercress. Serve with French dressing. Or dice fruit and shrimps, add dressing and toss together lightly. Serve on crisp lettuce.

MEAT SALADS

1½ cups cubed, cooked meat
1 cup diced celery
½ cup diced cucumber
2 tomatoes, sliced
1 tablespoon minced onion or chives
1 tablespoon chopped pimiento
salt and pepper
French Dressing (*page* 134)
Mayonnaise (*page* 134)
crisp lettuce or romaine

Makes about 4 portions.

For meat use beef, veal, pork, ham, tongue, sweetbreads, poultry, or game. Prepare one meat, then vegetables. Mix lightly, sprinkle with salt and pepper, and marinate with French dressing ½ hour or longer. Then mix with mayonnaise, tossing lightly.

Serve in large bowl lined with crisp lettuce, or on crisp lettuce on plates, with additional mayonnaise. Garnish with radish roses, pickles, or parsley, as desired.

CHICKEN AND VEAL SALAD

1½ cups cubed, cooked chicken
½ cup cubed, cooked veal
1 cup diced celery
½ cup diced pineapple
12 ripe olives, chopped
Mayonnaise (*page* 134)
salt and pepper   crisp lettuce

Makes about 4 *portions.*

Mix chicken, veal, celery, pineapple and olives with mayonnaise, tossing lightly. Season to taste.

Serve in bowl lined with crisp lettuce, or serve on crisp lettuce on individual plates with additional dressing. Garnish.

FISH OR SEAFOOD SALAD

2 Hard-Cooked Eggs (*page* 36)
1 cup cubed or flaked crabmeat,
    lobster, shrimp, tuna or salmon
1 cup diced celery
½ cup diced cucumber
2 tablespoons chopped green pepper
French Dressing (*page* 134)
Mayonnaise (*page* 134)
crisp lettuce
2 tomatoes, quartered

Makes about 4 *portions.*

Cook eggs, chill quickly. Remove shells and cut in quarters.

Prepare one fish, then vegetables. Add French dressing, toss together lightly and let stand ½ hour in refrigerator.

Just before serving mix with a small amount of mayonnaise, and season to taste. Serve on crisp lettuce with additional dressing. Garnish with tomatoes and eggs.

Desserts
for Every Occasion

Before deciding upon the dessert, it is important that you consider the meal as a whole. The dessert may contribute its own share of the nourishment, as well as flavor and beauty.

A slim meal will not leave that slim feeling behind if a dessert on the substantial side such as fruit roly-poly, shortcake, or pie, is served. On the other hand, with a more hearty meal, serve something on the light and dainty order for dessert: fruit with cheese, a cool, tart lemon snow pudding, ambrosia or a fruit whip. Many times we like to start a meal with fruit. If we end it, then, with a Bavarian cream, another sweet made of gelatin, or an ice, we have exactly the right cooling finish. Frozen desserts are very adaptable. They can be just a cold refreshing fluff and nothing more, or a nourishing frozen cream, contributing good food value and much needed milk to the meal.

Additional recipes may be found in other sections—Salads, The Cooky Jar and the Cake Box, It's Fun to Entertain, Your First Party—to name only a few.

BLANC-MANGE

¼ cup sugar
3 tablespoons cornstarch or
  6 tablespoons cake flour
¼ teaspoon salt
2 cups milk
1½ teaspoons vanilla
cream or fruit juice

Combine sugar, cornstarch and salt in saucepan. Add milk gradually, blending well. Cook over low heat until mixture boils, stirring constantly to avoid scorching. Cook 1 more minute. Remove from heat.

Add the vanilla and turn into individual molds, rinsed in cold water. Chill. Unmold and serve with cream or fruit juice.

Makes 4 portions.

CHOCOLATE BLANC-MANGE

Follow recipe for Blanc-Mange, only use ¼ cup more sugar and add 2 squares chocolate (2 ounces), shaved, to sugar-cornstarch mixture. Use only ½ teaspoon vanilla. *Makes 4 portions.*

COCONUT, FRUIT OR NUT BLANC-MANGE

Add ½ cup coconut to milk, or ¾ cup chopped dates, nuts or raisins. *Makes 4 to 6 portions.*

TAPIOCA CREAM

2 egg yolks, slightly beaten
2 cups milk
2 tablespoons sugar
3 tablespoons quick-cooking
   tapioca
1/4 teaspoon salt
1 teaspoon vanilla
2 egg whites, beaten stiffly but not
   dry
2 tablespoons sugar
cream or fruit

Mix egg yolks, milk, sugar, tapioca and salt in saucepan. Cook over low heat until mixture boils, stirring constantly to avoid lumping and scorching. Remove from heat. Cool slightly. Stir in vanilla. Fold in meringue made of beaten egg whites and sugar. Spoon into sherbet glasses or dessert mold. Serve with cream, crushed fruit, canned fruit or Fruit Sauce (*page* 163).

Makes 4 portions.
To vary—Fold in 1/4 cup peanut brittle, or 3/4 cup chopped nut meats, dates or prunes.

CREAMY RICE PUDDING

4 cups milk, scalded
1/2 cup rice
1/2 cup seedless raisins
1/2 cup sugar
1/2 teaspoon salt
cream, or fresh or stewed fruit

Makes 4 to 6 portions.

Scald milk in double boiler. Follow package directions for washing rice. Stir rice into milk. Cover and cook 1 hour, stirring occasionally. Add raisins, sugar and salt. Continue cooking 1 hour, or until rice is tender. Serve with cream.

BAKED CUSTARD

3 cups milk, scalded
3 eggs, slightly beaten, or 6 egg
   yolks
1/3 cup sugar
1/4 teaspoon salt
1/2 teaspoon vanilla, or 1/4 teaspoon
   nutmeg

Scald milk in double boiler.

Beat together eggs, sugar and salt; stir in milk gradually. Add vanilla or sprinkle top with nutmeg. Turn into custard cups or 1 1/2 quart casserole. Set in pan of hot water (1 inch up on side). Bake in 350° F. (moderate) oven, 30 to 60 minutes, until knife thrust into center comes out clean. Remove immediately from heat. Serve chilled in same cups or spoon into sherbets at time of serving.

Makes 6 small custards.

To vary—Add one to each cup: 1 tablespoon chopped nut meats, dates, coconut or jelly.

MAPLE OR CARAMEL CUSTARD

Follow recipe for Baked Custard with following change: add 1 tablespoon maple or caramel syrup to each cup, then fill with custard mixture, pouring it against a spoon. Syrup spreads over baked custard when mold is inverted.

LEMON SNOW PUDDING

1 tablespoon gelatin
¼ cup cold water
1 cup boiling water
⅔ cup sugar   dash of salt
½ teaspoon grated lemon rind
¼ cup lemon juice
2 egg whites, stiffly beaten
Custard Sauce (*page* 162)

Makes 6 portions.

Soak gelatin in cold water 5 minutes. Add hot water, stirring until dissolved. Stir in sugar, salt, lemon rind and juice. Chill.

When slightly thickened, beat with rotary beater until light and frothy. Beat egg whites until stiff; then whip into gelatin mixture. Continue beating until mixture holds shape. Turn into mold or individual sherbets and chill until firm. Unmold. Serve with custard sauce.

FRUIT BAVARIAN

1 tablespoon gelatin
¼ cup cold water
1 cup hot fruit juice
½ cup sugar
1 tablespoon lemon juice
1 cup crushed strawberries, raspberries, peaches, apricots, or canned crushed pineapple
1 cup heavy cream, or ½ cup evaporated milk, whipped stiff

Makes 8 portions.

Soak gelatin in water 5 minutes. Dissolve in hot fruit juice. Add sugar, lemon juice and fruit. Chill until mixture is partially set. Beat with rotary beater. Fold whipped cream into slightly thickened gelatin mixture. Turn into mold or individual molds. Chill until firm. Unmold, garnish with fruit and serve with additional cream, plain or whipped.

WHIPPED EVAPORATED MILK

Drop can of milk into boiling water and boil 1 minute. Chill quickly and keep in refrigerator until ready to whip. Whip as for cream. It is less rich than cream and about trebles in bulk in whipping.

JELLIED RASPBERRY GRAPEFRUIT

2 small grapefruit
I cup sugar

Cut off all rind and white skin, remove sections, cut in thirds and place in shallow pan. With hand squeeze out all juice left in membrane and pour over fruit. Sprinkle sugar over fruit, mix well and let stand 10 minutes.

I package raspberry-flavored
  gelatin
I ½ cups hot or boiling water

Follow directions on package for dissolving gelatin in water. Pour over fruit, mix well and chill until thickened, stirring occasionally.

¾ cup Custard Sauce (*page* 162)

Makes 6 to 8 portions.

To serve pile lightly in sherbet glasses and serve plain or with custard sauce.

SUNNY-SIDE-UP MOLDS (SELF-LAYERED)

I package orange-flavored gelatin
2 cups hot or boiling water
6 canned peach halves
I ½ cups sliced bananas
I tablespoon lemon juice
½ cup heavy cream, whipped

Follow directions on package for dissolving gelatin in water. Cool.

Place peach half, rounded side down, in each of 6 individual molds. Nearly fill molds with cooled gelatin. Slice bananas and sprinkle with lemon juice. Add to molds. Chill until firm. Unmold. Top with whipped cream.

Makes 6 molds.

CHEESE TORTE

½ recipe Zwieback Pastry (*page*
  166)
⅓ cup sugar   I tablespoon flour
⅛ teaspoon salt
2 ½ packages (3 oz. each) cream
  cheese
I ½ teaspoons vanilla
2 eggs, separated
⅓ cup light cream

Makes I (9-inch) pie.

Make pastry and press into 9-inch pie pan. Do not bake.

Combine sugar, flour and salt. Beat cheese, vanilla, egg yolks and cream until smooth and light. Stir in sugar and flour mixture. Beat egg whites until stiff. Fold into cheese mixture. Turn into the unbaked crumb crust.

Bake in 350° F. (moderate) oven 30 minutes, or until firm. Serve cold.

TUMBLE TORTE

2 cups sifted flour
2 teaspoons double-action baking powder
2 eggs, well beaten
1 cup sugar
½ cup butter, melted
1 teaspoon vanilla
1½ cups broken nut meats
1 cup quartered dates
1½ cups heavy cream

Makes about 8 portions.

Sift flour, measure 2 cups into sifter. Add baking powder, mix and sift.

Beat eggs in large bowl. Beat in sugar gradually, then butter and vanilla. Stir in flour, nuts, and dates. Spread on buttered, paper-lined, small baking sheets.
Bake in 325° F. (slow) oven 30 to 40 minutes, or until done.

Crumble torte. Whip 1 cup cream until thick. Stir into torte crumbs. Chill thoroughly. Serve with remaining ½ cup cream, whipped.

DANISH APPLE CAKE

1 package (6 oz.) zwieback, crushed or finely ground
1 cup sugar
½ cup butter, browned but not burned
8 tart apples, pared, cored and sliced
½ to ¾ cup heavy cream, whipped

Makes about 8 portions.

Grind zwieback and mix with sugar. Brown butter slowly in heavy frying pan. Do not burn. Stir into the crumb mixture. Cover bottom of greased casserole with layer of crumbs. Place apples on top. Repeat layers of crumbs and apples until all are used, with layer of crumbs on the top. Bake in 325° F. (slow) oven for 1¼ hours, or until crusty. Serve with cream.

GINGERSNAP CHEESE CAKE

1 package (3 oz.) cream cheese
12 maraschino cherries
½ cup chopped walnuts

16 gingersnaps

Break up and beat cheese until soft. Cut cherries with wet scissors and chop nuts. Stir into softened cheese.

For each portion put 4 gingersnaps together, like a layer cake, with a generous amount of cheese mixture between layers. Chill in refrigerator for 3 hours.

⅔ cup heavy cream, whipped
1 tablespoon confectioners' sugar
2 teaspoons lemon juice

Makes 4 portions.

Just before serving, whip cream until thickened. Fold in sugar and lemon juice. Then spread cream over each serving, covering sides and top.

DATE MARSHMALLOW LOAF

16 large graham crackers, rolled
    fine or ground
16 marshmallows, cut in pieces
½ pound dates, pitted and sliced
½ cup chopped walnuts
¼ cup light cream
¼ cup heavy cream, whipped

Makes about 6 portions.

Prepare crackers, marshmallows, dates and nuts. Mix all together and stir in light cream. Then stir and fold in whipped cream.

Turn mixture out on waxed paper and use paper to shape into 3-inch thick roll. Cover with paper and chill in refrigerator overnight.

To serve, cut in slices and top each with additional whipped cream, if desired.

Frosting adds the glamor to Chocolate Icicle Cake (*page* 175).

Quick to make—and delicious—
Strawberry Shortcake (*page* 255).

BLACKBERRY OR BLUEBERRY ROLY-POLY

**1 recipe rich Baking Powder Bis-
cuits** (*page* 67)
2 tablespoons butter, melted
2 cups blackberries or blueberries
½ cup sugar
1½ tablespoons lemon juice
2 tablespoons butter, softened

Makes about 6 portions.

Make dough. Roll ½ inch thick. Brush with butter. Cover with fruit. Sprinkle with sugar and lemon juice. Roll and place, seam down, in greased pan. Butter. Bake in 400° F. (hot) oven 25 to 30 minutes, or until browned. Serve hot.

PEACH OR APPLE DUMPLINGS

**1 recipe rich Baking Powder Bis-
cuits** (*page* 67), **or Plain Pastry**
(*page* 164)
**6 large peaches or apples, peeled
or pared and sliced**
2 tablespoons lemon juice
½ cup sugar
3 tablespoons butter   milk
egg white, slightly beaten
cream or Lemon Sauce (*page* 162)

Makes 6 portions.

Roll biscuit dough ¼ inch thick. Cut in 6 squares. Or divide pastry into 6 pieces, roll each ⅛ inch thick.

Put fruit in center of each. Sprinkle with lemon juice and sugar, dot with butter. Fold dough over fruit, moisten edges with milk and press together to seal. Prick crust. Brush with egg white, sprinkle with sugar, put in a greased shallow pan. Bake in 425° F. (hot) oven 45 to 55 minutes, or until fruit is soft. Serve with cream or sauce.

FRUIT COBBLER

**2 cups prepared fruit: sliced
apples, peaches or apricots; berries; or pitted cherries**
½ teaspoon cinnamon
½ to ¾ cup sugar
1 tablespoon flour
**2 drops almond extract (for
apricot or peach)**
3 tablespoons butter
**½ recipe rich Baking Powder
Biscuits** (*page* 67)
cream or Hard Sauce (*page* 161)

Makes about 4 portions.

Prepare one fruit, as suggested. Combine fruit, cinnamon, sugar and flour in saucepan. Bring mixture to a boil. Stir occasionally to prevent scorching. Remove from heat. Add flavoring for apricot or peach cobbler. Put into buttered baking dish. Dot with butter.

Prepare biscuit dough, using butter or margarine for shortening. Roll ½ inch thick. Place over fruit and cut slits in dough. Bake in 425° F. (hot) oven about 30 minutes. Serve with cream or sauce.

FROZEN DESSERTS, ICE CREAMS AND ICES

Homemade ice cream is so delectable that you will want to have it on your list of "know-hows." Made in a freezer and cranked by hand or electricity, it has a texture that is incomparable.

RULES FOR MAKING ICE CREAMS AND ICES

IN A CRANK FREEZER

Prepare the ice cream mixture the day before it is to be frozen for smoothest cream and largest yield. When this is not possible, chill for at least 1 hour before freezing. When using a syrup, be sure it is cool before adding to cream.

Scald freezer and rinse in cold water. Crush ice and measure out 3 to 6 parts ice to 1 part of *coarse* rock salt. The less salt, the finer the grain of the frozen dessert or cream, but the longer it takes to freeze. Fill the ice cream container no more than ¾ full (⅔ is even safer) to allow for expansion of the frozen dessert.

To freeze—Put can and dasher in place. Cover filled container, and adjust top and crank so dasher turns readily. Fill tub with a 2-inch layer of ice. Put in remaining ice and salt in alternating layers until tub is about ¾ full. This will be slightly above the level of the mixture in the can. Pack solidly, and let stand for 5 minutes before cranking. Turn slowly at first to insure an even-grained texture. When a pull is felt, turn crank rapidly until heavy to turn and mixture is thick. (About 10 minutes.)

To pack—Drain off excess brine, wipe lid of can and remove. Take out dasher. Scrape the dasher clean. Pack mixture down solidly with spoon. Replace cover, and place cork in opening in lid. Repack in ice and salt, using 4 parts ice to 1 part salt. Top with ice. Cover with heavy paper or burlap. Let stand to ripen: 2 to 4 hours for ice cream; 1 ½ to 2 hours for ices.

RULES FOR FREEZING MOLDS

Turn mousse, parfait or pudding mixture into special mold, tin can or pail; very little space need be left for "swell." Cover tightly and seal by winding a strip of cloth, dipped in melted fat or paraffin, around edge of cover—also along bottom and seam of tin can unless it is watertight. Use a wooden pail or tub, if possible, for ice and salt mixture. Bury mold completely in coarsely cracked ice and rock salt, using 3 parts ice to 1 part of salt. If metal pail or kettle is used, wrap well in papers or rug. Allow 3 to

4 hours for mousse and parfaits to freeze and ripen; 2 to 3 hours for bombes or fancy molds of frozen creams.

RULES FOR MAKING FROZEN DESSERTS, ICE CREAMS AND ICES IN REFRIGERATOR

In order to get best results, some thickening substance must be added to the mixture to be frozen. This may be dissolved gelatin, egg yolks, flour, cornstarch or strained tapioca.

Set temperature of refrigerator according to the manufacturer's directions. Prepare mixture and pour into ice cube tray with rack removed. Put tray into place and freeze until mixture is mushy. (About 30 minutes.)

Spoon into a chilled bowl and beat with rotary or electric beater until mixture is well blended. But don't overbeat, particularly if mixture is heavy with cream. Return mixture to freezing tray and freeze until firm. (About 3 hours.) Or use individual paper cups or molds. Decorate with fruits, nuts or whipped cream put on with a pastry bag or tube.

Set temperature at normal and allow mixture to ripen for at least 1 hour before serving to improve flavor.

All set for making ice cream.

VANILLA ICE CREAM (CRANK FREEZER)

2 cups milk   1 cup sugar
2 tablespoons flour
⅛ teaspoon salt
3 egg yolks, slightly beaten
1 teaspoon vanilla
2 cups all purpose cream, lightly
   whipped

Makes about 1½ quarts ice cream.

Scald milk in double boiler. Mix sugar, flour and salt. Stir into hot milk and cook 5 minutes, stirring constantly until thick. Stir small amount slowly into egg yolks. Then stir this into remaining mixture and cook 2 minutes, stirring constantly. Chill. Add vanilla and cream.

Pour into chilled container, filling it only ⅔ full. Freeze. Repack. Ripen 3 hours.

VANILLA ICE CREAM (REFRIGERATOR)

2 teaspoons gelatin
½ cup cold water
1¾ cups evaporated milk,
   scalded
1 cup sugar
2 teaspoons vanilla
1½ cups heavy cream, whipped

Makes about 1½ quarts ice cream.

Soak gelatin in cold water 5 minutes. Add hot milk and stir until dissolved. Add sugar and vanilla, and chill.

When slightly thickened, whip until frothy. Fold in whipped cream.

Turn into freezing tray of automatic refrigerator with control set at coldest point. Freeze until mushy (about 30 minutes). Spoon into chilled bowl. Beat with rotary beater or mixer until well blended. Return to freezing tray and freeze until firm (about 3 hours). Set temperature at normal. Ripen for 1 hour before serving.

VANILLA ICE CREAM VARIATIONS
(CRANK FREEZER OR REFRIGERATOR)

Bisque—Follow recipe for Vanilla Ice Cream only add 1 cup finely chopped, toasted (unsalted) almonds to mixture.

Butterscotch—Follow recipe for Vanilla Ice Cream, but mix sugar with 2 tablespoons butter in skillet until melted and well browned. For Crank Freezer Ice Cream, blend browned mixture with flour and salt. Stir into hot milk. For Refrigerator Ice Cream, dissolve browned mixture in hot milk.

Chocolate—Follow recipe for Vanilla Ice Cream, but melt 2 squares (2 ounces) chocolate with milk as it is scalded. Increase sugar to 1 ¼ cups.

Peanut Brittle—Follow recipe for Vanilla Ice Cream, but omit sugar. Crush ½ pound peanut brittle and add to mixture. Add sugar to taste.

Peppermint Candy—Follow recipe for Vanilla Ice Cream, but omit sugar. Crush ½ pound peppermint candy and add to scalded milk. Taste for sweetness.

LEMON ICE CREAM

2 eggs
½ cup sugar
⅓ cup light corn syrup
2 cups top milk or rich milk, chilled
1 teaspoon grated lemon rind
¼ cup lemon juice

Makes about 1 quart ice cream.

Beat eggs until thick. Add sugar gradually, beating until light and fluffy. Stir in syrup, milk and lemon rind, then juice.

Turn into freezing tray of automatic refrigerator with control set at coldest point. Freeze ½ hour, or until mushy. Turn into chilled bowl and beat with rotary beater until fluffy. Then freeze 2 to 3 hours longer.

NOTE: Freeze in crank freezer, if desired.

FRUIT SUNDAE

Cut 3 ripe, chilled cantaloupes in halves and remove seeds. Fill cavities with Lemon Ice Cream (above). Top with fresh or canned raspberries. *Makes 6 portions.*

FRUIT MOUSSE

1 cup crushed strawberries, raspberries, peaches or crushed
   pineapple
¾ cup sugar
dash of salt
1 cup heavy cream, whipped
2 egg whites, stiffly beaten

Mix fruit, ½ cup sugar and salt, and chill thoroughly. Fold in cream. Beat egg whites until stiff, then beat in gradually remaining ¼ cup sugar. Fold into fruit-cream mixture.

Turn into freezing tray of automatic refrigerator, or into paper cups, and set in tray. Set control at coldest point. Freeze 2 to 4 hours, or until firm.

NOTE: If canned or frozen fruits are used, decrease sugar to at least ½ cup.

Makes about 1 quart mousse.

PINEAPPLE SHERBET

4 cups boiling water
2½ cups sugar
1½ teaspoons grated lemon rind
3 tablespoons lemon juice
2 cups canned crushed pineapple
2 egg whites, stiffly beaten

Boil water and sugar 5 minutes, cool. Add lemon rind and juice, and pineapple.

Freeze to a mush-like consistency. Then fold in egg whites and continue freezing until firm (*page* 158). Ripen 1½ hours.

Makes about 2 quarts sherbet.

To vary—Substitute one of the following in place of 3 cups of boiling water: 3 cups orange juice and 1 tablespoon grated orange rind; 3 cups raspberry juice; or 2¾ cups cranberry juice and ¼ cup orange juice.

DESSERT SAUCES

HARD SAUCE

⅓ cup butter
1 cup confectioners' sugar, sifted
½ teaspoon vanilla, or ¼ teaspoon
   almond extract
2 tablespoons cream (about), or
   maraschino juice and 2 tablespoons chopped cherries

Cream butter. Stir in sugar gradually, then flavoring and cream. Beat until fluffy. Chill until cold but not hard. Beat in ¼ cup chopped nuts, if desired.

Makes about ¾ cup sauce, or enough for 4 to 6 portions.

BUTTERSCOTCH HARD SAUCE

Follow recipe for Hard Sauce with following changes: substitute ½ cup firmly packed brown sugar for confectioners' sugar; use 3 tablespoons cream and 1 egg yolk.

CUSTARD SAUCE

1 egg or 2 egg yolks, slightly beaten
¼ cup sugar
dash of salt
1 cup milk
¼ teaspoon vanilla

Makes about 1 cup sauce.

Beat egg with sugar and salt in top part of double boiler. Stir in milk, place over boiling water and cook, stirring constantly. until mixture coats spoon. Then pour into bowl, add vanilla, chill.

CHOCOLATE SAUCE

1 cup milk
1½ squares chocolate
⅓ cup sugar
½ tablespoon flour
dash of salt   1 egg yolk
1 tablespoon butter
¼ teaspoon vanilla

Makes about 1¼ cups sauce.

Heat milk and chocolate in double boiler until chocolate is melted. Beat with rotary beater until smooth.

Mix together sugar, flour, salt, and egg yolk. Stir in milk and chocolate. Cook 5 minutes, stirring constantly. Add butter and vanilla. Serve hot or cold.

LEMON SAUCE

½ cup sugar
1 tablespoon cornstarch
⅛ teaspoon salt
1 cup boiling water
1 teaspoon grated lemon rind
3 tablespoons lemon juice
2 tablespoons butter

Makes about 1¼ cups sauce.

Combine sugar, cornstarch and salt. Stir in hot water gradually, bring to a boil and cook 15 minutes, stirring constantly until thickened, then occasionally. Remove from heat. Stir in lemon rind and juice, and butter. Serve cold or hot.

FUDGE SAUCE

1 cup sugar
2 tablespoons light corn syrup
1 ½ squares chocolate
1 cup water or milk
1 tablespoon butter   dash of salt
½ teaspoon vanilla

Makes about 1 cup sauce.

Measure sugar, syrup, chocolate and water into deep saucepan. Heat slowly, stirring until chocolate is melted.

Boil, covered, 2 minutes. Uncover and boil until a small amount forms jelly-like mass in cold water (224° F.). Remove from heat, stir in butter, salt and vanilla. Serve hot or cold.

BUTTERSCOTCH SAUCE

½ cup firmly packed brown sugar
½ cup light corn syrup
¼ cup water
4 tablespoons butter
½ cup light cream
½ teaspoon vanilla

Makes about 1 cup sauce.

Measure sugar, syrup, water and butter into saucepan. Heat slowly, stirring to dissolve sugar.

Boil until a small amount forms very soft ball in cold water (228° F.). Add cream and bring to a brisk boil. Remove from heat and stir in vanilla. Serve hot or cold.

FLUFFY CHOCOLATE SAUCE

½ cup heavy cream, whipped
4 tablespoons Fudge Sauce, or
  Chocolate Syrup (*page* 204)

Makes about 1 cup sauce.

Whip cream until thick. Fold in cold chocolate fudge sauce or syrup.

FOAMY ORANGE SAUCE

½ cup confectioners' sugar, or ¼
  cup firmly packed brown sugar
2 tablespoons butter, softened
1 egg, separated   dash of salt
1 teaspoon grated orange rind
¼ cup orange juice

*Makes about ½ cup sauce, or
enough for 4 portions.*

Stir sugar gradually into butter. Add egg yolk, salt, orange rind and juice.

Beat egg white until stiff. Fold into sugar-orange mixture. Serve at once.

FLUFFY BERRY SAUCE

Follow recipe for Fluffy Chocolate Sauce, only substitute ½ cup crushed and sweetened berries for chocolate sauce.

PASTRY

PLAIN PASTRY

Good pie crust is flaky and light, bubbly rather than smooth. The top crust and sides are delicately browned, tender but not crumbly; the bottom crust is light brown and crisp, not soggy nor moist.

Utensils Needed	*Order of Work*
Mixing bowl; flour sifter, measuring cup and set of spoons, pastry blender or 2 knives, fork; waxed paper; rolling pin and board, or canvas, and stockinette for rolling pin.	1. Assemble utensils and ingredients. 2. Mix dough, shape in ball, wrap in waxed paper and chill. 3. Preheat oven. 4. Use for pies, tarts, pastry snacks. Roll dough on lightly floured board, about ⅛ inch thick. Shape and bake.

RECIPE

2 cups sifted flour ★
½ teaspoon salt
½ to ⅔ cup shortening ★

Mix flour and salt, then sift into bowl. With pastry blender or knives cut in shortening until mixture is uniform, like tiny coated pebbles.

¼ cup cold water (about)

Makes pastry for 2-crust (8-inch) pie, 2 pastry shells, or 12 (4-inch) tarts.

★ For more tender pastry use:
  2 cups sifted cake flour
  6 to 8 tablespoons shortening

Sprinkle 1 tablespoon water over a small portion, stir lightly with fork and toss aside pieces of dough as soon as formed. Repeat, adding water each time to a new portion of mixture and using just enough to make particles hold together. Press into ball. Wrap in waxed paper. Chill. Roll out and shape.

CHEESE PASTRY

Follow recipe for Plain Pastry, only add ¼ cup grated cheese, cutting it in with shortening.

FRUIT JUICE PASTRY

Follow recipe for Plain Pastry, only substitute available fruit juice for some of water.

TWO-CRUST PIES

Divide pastry into 2 parts, 1 slightly larger. Chill smaller one in refrigerator while you roll out lower crust. Lightly flour rolling pin. Set dough on lightly floured board, and with light strokes, roll in circle, ⅛-inch thick and 1-inch larger than pie plate. Work outward from the center. Lift up occasionally with broad spatula and dust additional flour under it as needed to keep from sticking. Roll evenly so that pastry will be same thickness throughout. Fold double and lift gently into plate. Unfold and fit, being careful not to stretch. Trim edge with scissors or sharp knife flush with pan rim.

Allow plenty of filling. Heap fruit high in center to allow for settling during baking.

Roll out second piece of dough a little thinner for top crust—large enough to extend 1 inch beyond edge of plate. Make slits or prick design in center to allow for steam to escape during baking. Moisten edges of undercrust with a little water. Fold top crust double and gently fit over the filling. Unfold. There should be a ½-inch rim beyond pie plate. Trim off any extra edges. Fold top edge under lower edge of pastry and seal thoroughly by pressing around rim of pie plate. Press sealed edge with floured fork or form fluted edge by pressing dough with index finger of one hand while you pinch it on other side with thumb and index finger. Bake as directed.

For best results, measure accurately and work quickly. Be careful not to blend ingredients too thoroughly. If possible, use a "flavor saver" deep-dish pie plate for fruit pies. Make 4 slits around outer rim after you have sealed the two crusts (just below the seal). As the pie bakes, some of its juices will bubble out and give the edge of the crust a pungent flavor. And the deep plate will protect the oven from juice markings. With regular pie plates, to prevent edge of fruit pies from becoming too brown, cover with a wet strip of cloth while baking. Remove cloth when pie is baked.

ONE-CRUST PIES

Use ½ recipe and follow directions for rolling bottom crust for Two-Crust Pies (*page* 165). Fit loosely into pie plate. Trim off any uneven edges with scissors, leaving ½ inch all around edge. Fold extra pastry back and under evenly. Build up fluted edge to hold a lot of filling as directed for Two-Crust Pies. Fill and bake as directed.

PASTRY SHELLS

Follow the directions for One-Crust Pies (above). Fit into pie plate which has been slightly warmed to prevent shrinking. Dot lightly with 1 scant tablespoon butter. Prick pastry with fork tines to prevent puffing. Bake in 450° F. (very hot) oven for 10 to 12 minutes.

SALAD OIL PASTRY

(The quick, no guessing method)

2 cups sifted flour
½ teaspoon salt
½ cup salad oil
¼ cup milk

Mix flour and salt. Add oil and milk all at once. Stir quickly, until ingredients are blended.

Form into a ball. Divide into 2 parts. Flatten slightly. Roll dough between sheets of waxed paper. Remove top paper and invert rolled dough, paper and all, onto pie plate. Remove paper and proceed as for any pie.

Makes pastry for 2-crust (8-inch) pie.

ZWIEBACK PASTRY

½ package (12 oz. pkge.) zwieback,
  rolled very fine
2 tablespoons sugar
¼ cup butter, browned but not
  burned, or use softened butter

Mix zwieback and sugar. Add browned butter and mix well. Press over bottom and sides of 8- or 9-inch pie pan.

Bake in 325° F. (slow) oven about 10 minutes. Use for cooked fillings. For uncooked fillings, do not bake.

Makes 1 pastry shell.

COOKY PASTRY

Follow recipe for Zwieback Pastry, only substitute about 20 vanilla wafers for the zwieback. Makes 1 pastry shell.

ORANGE CHIFFON PIE

1 recipe Zwieback Pastry (*page* 166)

Prepare pastry and press over bottom and sides of 9-inch pie plate. Chill.

1 tablespoon gelatin
2 tablespoons cold water
½ cup boiling water

Soak gelatin in cold water about 5 minutes. Add boiling water, stirring until gelatin is dissolved.

4 egg yolks
½ cup sugar
¼ teaspoon salt

Beat egg yolks until light, then gradually beat in sugar and salt. Stir in hot gelatin mixture.

1½ teaspoons grated orange rind
1 cup orange juice
3 tablespoons lemon juice
4 egg whites
¼ cup sugar

Add grated rind and fruit juices, and cool until mixture begins to thicken.

Beat egg whites until stiff but not dry. Gradually beat in sugar and fold into gelatin mixture.

Turn into prepared pie plate and let stand in refrigerator until firm.

Makes 1 (*9-inch*) *pie or* 6 *portions.*

CRISSCROSS CHERRY PIE

1 recipe Plain Pastry (*page* 164)
2¾ cups pitted sour cherries, drained (1 quart)
1½ cups sugar *
1 to 1½ tablespoons flour, quick-cooking tapioca, ½ tablespoon cornstarch, or ⅓ cup cornflakes
1 tablespoon butter
milk, cream, or egg white

Follow directions for pastry for Two-Crust Pies (*page* 165). Drain cherries. Mix with sugar and flour. Turn into plate. Dot with butter.

Roll remaining dough ⅛-inch thick. Cut in ¾-inch strips and arrange 7 across pie. Lay 7 strips, diagonally across first strips to make diamond openings. Trim ends and press down. Moisten edge and fold border over. Press crusts together with floured fork. Then brush strips with milk. Bake in 425° F. (hot) oven 30 to 45 minutes.

* For less sour fruits, use:
  1 to 1¼ cups sugar

Makes two-crust (*8-inch*) *pie.*

Pumpkin Pie

Crisscross
Cherry Pie

DEEP-DISH APPLE PIE

½ **recipe Plain Pastry** (*page* 164)
6 to 8 apples
1 cup firmly packed brown sugar ★
½ **teaspoon salt**
3 tablespoons strong coffee ★
2 tablespoons butter
milk or cream

With 1 cup granulated sugar, use:
½ teaspoon cinnamon
2 tablespoons water (instead of
coffee)
1 tablespoon lemon juice

Makes 1 *deep-dish* (*9-inch*) *pie, or*
6 *individual pies.*

Prepare pastry. Chill until needed.

Pare, core and slice apples into baking
dish or small casseroles. Sprinkle sugar
and salt over apples; scatter coffee over
all and dot with butter.

Roll pastry into ⅛-inch thick round, 1-
inch larger than dish. Fold in half and cut
several slits near fold to permit escape of
steam. Place over filled dish. Unfold and
fold overhanging border under. Moisten
rim of dish with water. Press double edge
down against rim with floured fork. Brush
crust with milk.

Bake in 425° F. (hot) oven 45 to 55 minutes, or until apples are done.

PUMPKIN OR SQUASH PIE

½ **recipe Plain Pastry** (*page* 164)
¾ **cup firmly packed brown sugar**
¾ **teaspoon salt**
½ **teaspoon cinnamon**
⅓ **teaspoon nutmeg**
⅓ **teaspoon ginger**
⅛ **teaspoon cloves**
1 ½ **cups canned or strained cooked**
 pumpkin or squash
2 eggs slightly beaten
1 ½ **cups evaporated milk**

Makes one-crust (*8-inch*) *pie.*

Follow directions for pastry for One-Crust
Pie (*page* 166).

Combine sugar, salt and spices, and stir
into pumpkin. Beat eggs slightly. Add
milk, then stir into pumpkin mixture.
Turn into pastry-lined plate.

Bake in 400° F. (hot) oven 30 to 40 minutes. To test shake pan slightly; if firm in
center, filling is done.

CUSTARD PIE

½ **recipe Plain Pastry** (*page* 164)
3 eggs, slightly beaten
⅓ **cup sugar**
¼ **teaspoon salt**
¼ **teaspoon nutmeg, or** ½ **teaspoon vanilla**
2 cups rich milk, scalded

Makes one-crust (8-inch) pie.

Follow directions for One-Crust Pie (*page* 166).

With rotary beater, lightly beat eggs. Beat in sugar, salt, flavoring and milk. Pour into pastry-lined plate.

Bake in 400° F. (hot) oven 30 to 40 minutes, or until knife inserted comes out clean.

DATE CUSTARD PIE

Follow recipe for Custard Pie only add ½ cup chopped dates to custard.

MERINGUE COCONUT PIE OR TARTS

½ **recipe Plain Pastry** (*page* 164)
½ **cup sugar**
5 tablespoons flour
⅓ **teaspoon salt**
2 egg yolks, beaten
1½ **cups milk, scalded**
2 tablespoons butter
½ **teaspoon vanilla**
½ **cup coconut**
2 egg whites
4 tablespoons sugar
¼ **cup coconut**

Makes one-crust (8-inch) pie, or 6 (4-inch) tarts.

Follow directions for Pastry Shells (*page* 166). Bake shell.

Combine sugar, flour and salt. Stir in egg yolks. Then stir in milk gradually. Cook over boiling water 10 minutes, stirring constantly. Add butter, vanilla, and ½ cup coconut, and cool slightly. Then turn into baked shell or shells.

Beat egg whites until frothy. Beat in sugar gradually, beating until mixture falls in peaks. Pile lightly on filling. Sprinkle with coconut.

Bake in 350° F. (moderate) oven 12 to 15 minutes, or until delicately browned.

CHOCOLATE CREAM PIE

Follow recipe for Meringue Coconut Pie with following changes: use 1 whole egg instead of 2 egg yolks in filling. Omit coconut. Add 2 squares chocolate to milk, then scald. Substitute for meringue, ½ cup heavy cream, whipped and sweetened with 1 tablespoon sugar. Grate chocolate over top.

The Cooky Jar
and the Cake Box

Cooky and cake recipes are cherished by families and handed down—as heirlooms are—from generation to generation. Every recipe in this section is worthy of being cherished. Each one is a recipe of standing, tested thoroughly in a kitchen-laboratory, and through years of use in family kitchens. You may follow them all with confidence.

Cookies. Here are drop and rolled cookies, cookies baked in a sheet, and the popular refrigerator cooky. Any favorite rolled cooky dough may be chilled, sliced and baked, exactly as the refrigerator type.

Cakes. Most cakes are classified in two main groups: butter cakes, made with butter or other shortening; sponge cakes, made without shortening. The true sponge cake—Angel Food (*page* 179), for example—is made without a leavening agent, other than the air beaten into the eggs and folded into the batter. A "mock" sponge cake is leavened partly by baking powder. You will find recipes for butter and sponge cakes in this section.

Tips for Baking Days. For best results, particularly in cake making, use the ingredients called for in the recipe. Don't use oil or melt the shortening unless directed by the recipe. Cake recipes in this section call for *cake* flour. If you substitute all-purpose flour, you will not have the same, delicate cake. When the recipe says "1 cup sifted cake flour," that means that you must sift the flour once before you measure it.

170

Granulated sugar does not need sifting unless it is lumpy; brown sugar that has hardened can be rolled. Dried whole eggs may replace fresh eggs. Allow 2½ tablespoons egg powder, sifted, and 2½ tablespoons water for each fresh egg. For quick breads and cookies, egg powder can be sifted with dry ingredients and water added to other liquid in the recipe. With cakes and other foods, combine egg powder and water before using.

Careless measurements can greatly alter product. Timely tips on measuring for beginner cooks may be found on *pages* 9 and 16.

Have eggs, milk and shortening at room temperature. If shortening and sugar are to be creamed together, add sugar gradually, and cream mixture until light and fluffy. When alternating the addition of dry and liquid ingredients, always begin and end with dry ingredients to avoid a curdled batter.

Step-savers and suggestions for efficient working centers may be seen in the pictures on *pages* 12 and 13. The advice on lining the bottom of the cake pans with wax paper is timely. First butter the pan, then fit the paper into it and then butter the paper. Do not butter the sides of pan for even rising of cake. Butter gives a delicious flavor to the crust of cake and therefore is recommended, but any good cooking fat will keep the pans from sticking.

Prepare pans, check proper placing of racks and preheat oven (for 15 minutes) to correct temperature before combining ingredients. Oven-glass plates bake faster than metal pans, so reduce oven heat by 25° F. when you use glass.

Altitude. Cake recipes in this section were developed at sea level. Results will be satisfactory at altitudes under 3000 feet. As the altitude increases to 5000 feet and more, the cakes become increasingly coarse, dry, and over-leavened. Until you become an expert at adjusting the amounts of sugar, shortening and baking powder, one or all, it is advisable to use recipes developed for the different altitudes.

Mixers and Methods. Included in this section are recipes for *hand-mixing*, sometimes called the *conventional* method; and some *hurry-up* or *one-bowl* method.

If you have a mechanical mixer, be sure to read the directions for its particular use. In general, when using the *conventional* method, softened shortening, sugar, eggs or egg yolks and flavoring are combined and beaten 5 minutes at high speed—until light and fluffy. Dry and liquid ingredients are added alternately at medium speed—beginning and ending with flour, and beating not more than 2 minutes. Beaten egg whites are folded in by hand. When using the *one-bowl* method, softened shortening, dry ingredients, ⅔ of the liquid and flavoring are beaten for 2 minutes at medium speed. Then the eggs and remaining liquid are added and beating is continued at medium speed for 2 more minutes. Be careful not to over-beat batter as this will dry out cake.

Baking Powder. There are 3 types of baking powder—*tartrate*, *phosphate* and *combination type* (SAS-phosphate) or *double-action*. Read the label on your baking powder tin to see what kind of baking powder you are going to use. Recipes in this book use *double-action* baking powder, allowing approximately 1 teaspoon per cup of flour. If you use *tartrate* or *phosphate* baking powder, you will need to increase *phosphate* baking powder to 1 ½ teaspoons per cup of flour; *tartrate* to 2 teaspoons per cup of flour.

Tests for Doneness. Although the time and temperature directions in each cake recipe are accurate, it is wise to learn the signs of a well-baked cake and to know how to test for doneness. When done, a cake shrinks slightly from the sides of the pan; pressed lightly, the crust springs back; and a tester inserted into the center comes out clean.

It is well to let a butter cake remain in the pan and on the rack for 10 minutes, before turning it out on the rack to cool.

TWO-EGG CAKE

(Delicate and feathery—easy to make)

Utensils Needed

Cake pans—2 layers, 1 square or 2 muffin pans; bowls; flour sifter, measuring cup and spoons; spatula, wooden spoon; rotary beater; rubber scraper

Makes 2 (8-inch) layers; 1 (9-inch) square; 12 to 20 cup cakes.

RECIPE

2 cups sifted cake flour
2 teaspoons double-action baking powder
½ teaspoon salt
½ cup soft shortening (at least ½ butter or margarine)
1 cup sugar
1 teaspoon flavoring
2 eggs, well beaten, or 2 eggs, unbeaten

¾ cup milk

Frosting (*pages* 188 *to* 193)

Order of Work

1. Assemble utensils and ingredients.
2. Prepare cake pans (*page* 171); use butter. Cup cakes hold shape best if baked in paper cup liners.
3. Light oven or turn on heat.
4. Mix batter. Fill pans. Bake.
5. Cool on cake rack. Frost as desired.

Sift flour, then measure 2 cups into sifter. Add baking powder and salt. Mix well, then sift on paper or into pan.

Cream shortening until soft and smooth. Add sugar gradually, beating until fluffy after each addition. Add flavoring.

Beat eggs until light and thick; then beat into butter-sugar mixture. Or add eggs, unbeaten, beating in thoroughly one at a time.

Divide flour in four piles. Beginning and ending with flour, add these piles alternately with milk, stirring, then beating until smooth after each addition of flour or milk.

Pour into prepared pans or pan. Tap pans sharply to break bubbles. Bake until cake tests done.

Bake layers in 375° F. (moderate) oven 20 to 30 minutes; cup cakes in 375° F. (moderate) oven 15 to 25 minutes; square cake in 350° F. (moderate) oven for 45 to 60 minutes. Cool in pan on rack 10 minutes. Turn onto rack and complete cooling. Frost as desired.

SPICE CAKE

Follow recipe for Two-Egg Cake, only omit flavoring. Add 1 teaspoon cinnamon, ½ teaspoon cloves, ½ teaspoon nutmeg and a dash of all spice to flour mixture. *Makes 2 (8-inch) layers; 1 (9-inch) square; 12 to 20 cup cakes.*

PINK AND YELLOW CAKE

Follow recipe for Two-Egg Cake. Divide batter into 2 parts. Blend a few drops of red food coloring into 1 part of batter. Spoon batters alternately into prepared pan. Pull spoon through batter to blend color and give marbled effect. *Makes 1 (9-inch) square.*

SILVER CAKE

(See Two-Egg Cake, *page* 173)

2 cups sifted cake flour
2¼ teaspoons double-action baking powder
½ teaspoon salt
½ cup soft shortening
1⅓ cups sugar
1 teaspoon vanilla
1 cup thin milk (½ water)
3 egg whites, stiffly beaten

Sift flour, then measure 2 cups into sifter. Add baking powder and salt. Mix well and sift.

Cream shortening until soft and smooth. Add 1 cup sugar gradually, beating until very fluffy. Add vanilla. Add flour, alternately with milk, beating until smooth after each addition, beginning and ending with flour.

Beat egg whites until just stiff but not dry. Beat in remaining ⅓ cup sugar gradually. Fold into cake batter, thoroughly and quickly. Turn into prepared layer pans, tube pan or square pan. Tap pans sharply to break bubbles.

Lady Baltimore Frosting (*page* 191), **Divinity Frosting** (*page* 191), **or Coconut Seven Minute Frosting** (*page* 190)

Makes 2 (8-inch) layers, or (8-inch) tube or (9-inch) square cake.

Bake layers in 375° F. (moderate) oven 20 to 30 minutes; tube or square pan in 350° F. (moderate) oven 45 to 60 minutes. Cool in pan on cake rack 10 minutes. Turn onto cake rack to complete cooling. Frost, as desired.

CHOCOLATE CAKE

(See Two-Egg Cake, *page* 173)

2 cups sifted cake flour
½ teaspoon double-action baking powder
½ teaspoon baking soda
½ teaspoon salt
3 squares chocolate, melted and cooled
½ cup soft shortening
1 cup sugar
1 egg   2 egg yolks
1 teaspoon vanilla
1 cup sour milk or buttermilk
Nougat Filling (*page* 193)
Seven Minute Frosting (*page* 190)

Makes 2 (8-inch) layers.

Sift flour, measure 2 cups into sifter. Add baking powder, soda and salt. Sift 3 times.

Melt chocolate over hot water. Cool slightly. Cream shortening, add sugar gradually, beating until fluffy after each addition. Beat in egg, egg yolks, vanilla and chocolate.

Add flour, alternately with sour milk, beating until smooth after each addition, beginning and ending with flour. Turn into 2 prepared (8-inch) layer pans. Tap pans sharply to break bubbles. Bake in 375° F. (moderate) oven 20 to 30 minutes. Cool in pans on cake rack 10 minutes. Then turn onto racks to complete cooling. Spread filling between layers. Spread frosting on top and sides.

CHOCOLATE ICICLE CAKE

1 recipe Chocolate Cake (*see above*)

Seven Minute Frosting (*page* 190)

2 squares chocolate, melted
1½ teaspoons butter

Makes 1 (2-layer) cake.

Make cake batter. Bake in 2 (8-inch) layer pans. Cool on cake rack.

Make frosting and spread between layers and over top and sides of cake. Let stand until set.

Melt chocolate over hot water. Stir in butter. Cool. When slightly cool, pour over top of frosted cake, permitting chocolate to run over edge and down sides of cake.

CHOCOLATE FUDGE CAKE

3 squares chocolate
¼ cup sugar
½ cup milk   1 egg yolk
1¾ cup sifted cake flour
**1 teaspoon double-action baking
   powder**
½ teaspoon baking soda
½ teaspoon salt
⅓ cup soft shortening
1 cup sugar   1 egg
1 teaspoon vanilla
¾ cup milk
Chocolate Butter Frosting (*page
   189*), **Fudge Frosting** (*page 191*),
   or Seven Minute Frosting (*page
   190*)

Place chocolate, sugar and milk over hot water, and heat until chocolate is melted, stirring occasionally. Stir slowly into slightly beaten egg yolk. Cool.

Sift flour, measure 1¾ cups into sifter. Add baking powder, soda and salt. Sift 3 times.

Cream shortening. Add sugar gradually, beating until fluffy after each addition. Beat in egg and vanilla thoroughly. Add cooled chocolate mixture.

Add flour, alternately with milk, beating until smooth after each addition beginning and ending with flour. Turn into prepared layer pans. Tap pans sharply to break bubbles.

Makes 2 (8-inch) layers.

Bake in 375° F. (moderate) oven 20 to 30 minutes. Cool in pans on rack 10 minutes. Turn onto racks to complete cooling. Spread frosting between layers and over cake.

GINGERBREAD

2 cups sifted flour
1 teaspoon baking soda
½ teaspoon salt
1½ teaspoons ginger
1 teaspoon cinnamon
2 eggs, beaten   ½ cup sugar
½ cup molasses
1 cup sour milk or buttermilk
½ cup soft shortening
**½ cup heavy cream, whipped, or
   applesauce or cheese whip**

*Makes 9 (3-inch) squares, or 9-inch
cake.*

Sift flour, measure 2 cups into sifter. Add soda, salt, spices and sugar. Mix, then sift 3 times.

Beat eggs until foamy. Stir in molasses, sour milk and shortening. Stir gradually into flour-sugar mixture, beating until smooth. Turn into greased square pan. Bake in 350° F. (moderate) oven for 40 to 50 minutes. Cut in squares and serve warm with whipped cream, applesauce, or cream cheese moistened with cream, then whipped until light.

The never-fail Two-Egg Cake (*page* 173), delicate and feathery, being expertly frosted according to directions (*Helps in frosting, page* 188).

ONE-EGG QUICK CAKE

(See Two-Egg Cake, *page* 173)

1½ cups sifted cake flour
1 cup sugar
2 teaspoons double-action baking powder
½ teaspoon salt
⅓ cup softened shortening
⅔ cup milk
1 teaspoon vanilla
1 large egg

Makes 2 thin (8-inch) layers;
1 (8-inch) square; 12 to 16 cup cakes.

Sift flour, then measure 1½ cups into sifter. Add sugar, baking powder and salt. Sift together into mixing bowl. Add shortening. Pour in a little more than half of milk and vanilla.

Beat in electric mixer at medium speed for 2 minutes, scraping down bowl constantly to make sure that ingredients are thoroughly blended (300 strokes if beaten by hand).

Add remaining milk and egg. Beat mixture 2 minutes (300 strokes if beaten by hand). Pour into prepared pans. Tap pans sharply to break bubbles. Bake until cake tests done.

Bake layers in 375° F (moderate) oven 20 to 30 minutes; cup cakes in 375° F. (moderate) oven 15 to 25 minutes; square cake in 350° F. (moderate) oven 45 to 60 minutes. Cool in pans on rack 10 minutes. Turn onto rack and complete cooling. Frost as desired.

BOSTON CREAM PIE

Follow recipe for One-Egg Quick Cake, baking batter in layers. Spread 1 recipe Cream Filling (*page* 192) between layers. Sift confectioner's sugar over top. *Makes* 1 *thin* (8-inch) *layer cake.*

PINEAPPLE UPSIDE-DOWN CAKE

½ cup firmly packed brown sugar
¼ cup butter or margarine
3 tablespoons water
1 can (No. 2½) sliced pineapple, halved
¼ cup walnut or pecan halves
8 maraschino cherries
1 recipe One-Egg Cake (*see above*)
½ cup heavy cream, whipped, if desired

Makes about 8 *portions.*

Put brown sugar, butter and water in heavy, 9-inch square cake pan, or in large, heavy frying pan. Heat until sugar is dissolved and butter melted. Arrange pineapple halves, nut halves and cherries, in sugar mixture.

Make cake batter. Turn out over the fruit. Bake in 350° (moderate) oven about 50 minutes. Loosen cake from sides and invert on large serving plate. Serve warm.

QUICK CUP CAKES

1½ cups sifted cake flour
¼ teaspoon baking soda
¼ teaspoon salt
1 cup sugar
2 eggs
sour heavy cream
½ teaspoon vanilla
¼ cup currants, seedless raisins, chopped nuts, or coconut

Makes about 14 *cup cakes.*

Sift flour, measure 1½ cups into sifter. Add soda, salt and sugar. Mix well, then sift into large bowl. Make deep well in center of mixture.

Break eggs into measuring cup, fill with cream. Pour into well, add vanilla and stir until mixed. Then beat vigorously 1 minute (150 strokes), or until smooth. Turn into muffin pans, buttered, or lined with paper cups, filling them ⅔ full. Sprinkle currants over tops.

Bake in 375° F. (moderate) oven 15 to 25 minutes. Cool on cake rack. Eat while warm or fresh.

GOLD CUP CAKES

1 cup sifted cake flour
1 ¼ teaspoons double-action
  baking powder
¼ teaspoon salt
¼ cup soft butter or margarine
½ cup sugar
1 ½ teaspoons grated orange rind
4 egg yolks, well beaten
1 tablespoon orange juice
¼ cup milk

Orange Butter Frosting (*page* 189)

Makes about 12 cup cakes.

Sift flour, then measure 1 cup into sifter. Add baking powder and salt. Mix well and sift.

Cream butter until soft. Add sugar gradually, beating until fluffy after each addition. Add orange rind.

Beat egg yolks until very thick and lemon-colored. Beat in orange juice. Add to butter-sugar mixture, beating thoroughly. Add flour, alternately with milk, beating until smooth after each addition, beginning and ending with flour. Turn into muffin pans, greased or lined with paper cups, filling them ⅔ full.

Bake in 375° F. (moderate) oven 15 to 25 minutes. Frost cold cakes.

ANGEL FOOD CAKE

Good angel food and sponge cakes are very light; symmetrical in shape, flat on top or only slightly rounded, and covered with a golden brown, porous and tender crust. The inside is somewhat porous but even grained, moist and springy, so tender that it is easily broken, and delicately flavored. For best results, make the day before use to allow for "ripening" of texture and flavor.

Utensils Needed

10-inch tube pan, 4-inches deep; large mixing bowl; flour sifter, measuring cup and spoons; spatula, metal spoon; flat wire whisk (or rotary beater); rubber scraper, cake rack

Order of Work

1. Take eggs out of refrigerator ahead of time.
2. Assemble utensils and ingredients. Do not grease tube pan.
3. Sift flour and sugar.
4. Light oven or turn on heat and adjust for 350° F. (moderate) oven.
5. Mix batter. Fill pan. Bake.
6. Hang cake upside-down on a funnel or jar until completely cold. Run spatula along edge and remove on rack.

RECIPE

1 cup sifted cake flour
¾ cup sifted dessert sugar (extra fine grained)
1 cup egg whites (8 to 9)
¼ teaspoon salt
1 teaspoon cream of tartar
1 teaspoon vanilla
½ teaspoon almond extract
½ cup sifted dessert sugar

Sift flour, then measure 1 cup into sifter. Sift 4 times with ¾ cup sifted sugar. Set aside. Put egg whites, salt, cream of tartar and flavorings in large bowl. With wire whisk, beat until just stiff enough to form peaks.

Beat in remaining ½ cup sifted sugar, 2 tablespoons at a time, beating about 10 seconds after each addition. (Medium speed on mixer.) Continue beating until meringue is very stiff and forms peaks when whisk is pulled up. (High speed on mixer.) Turn bowl slowly with left hand during beating process.

Sift flour-sugar mixture, 3 tablespoons at a time, over meringue. Fold in gently with rubber scraper or spatula, until addition disappears each time. Turn into un-buttered, dry tube pan. Run knife through batter to cut bubbles.

Bake in 350° F. (moderate) oven 30 to 45 minutes, or until firm to touch. (Don't worry about cracks on top.) Invert until completely cold.

Makes 1 (10-inch) tube cake.

COCOA ANGEL FOOD CAKE

Follow recipe for Angel Food Cake, only substitute ¼ cup cocoa for ¼ cup cake flour. Sift together 4 times. *Makes 1 (10-inch) tube cake.*

PEPPERMINT ANGEL FOOD CAKE

Follow recipe for Angel Food Cake, only omit flavorings and use 1 teaspoon peppermint extract with a few drops red food coloring. *Makes 1 (10-inch) tube cake.*

COCONUT ANGEL FOOD CAKE

Follow recipe for Angel Food Cake, only omit almond extract and use ¾ teaspoon lemon extract. At very last, gently fold in ¼ cup shredded coconut. *Makes 1 (10-inch) tube cake.*

LEMON CHIFFON CAKE

(See Angel Food Cake, *page* 179)

This cake is as light as angel food and rich enough to satisfy any sweet tooth.

2¼ cups sifted cake flour
1½ cups sugar
3 teaspoons double-action baking powder
1 teaspoon salt
½ cup cooking oil
5 egg yolks, unbeaten
¾ cup cold water
2 teaspoons vanilla
2 teaspoons grated lemon rind
1 cup egg whites (8 or 9)
½ teaspoon cream of tartar

Sift flour, then measure 2¼ cups into sifter. Add sugar, baking powder and salt. Sift 3 times.

Make well in the center of mixture and add in order: cooking oil, unbeaten egg yolks, water, vanilla and grated lemon rind. Beat with spoon until smooth or with electric mixer on medium speed 1 minute. Measure into a large mixing bowl egg whites and cream of tartar. Beat until whites form firm, *stiff* peaks. Do not underbeat. Egg whites are stiff enough when a rubber scraper drawn through them leaves a clean path.

Pour egg yolk mixture gradually over egg whites, gently folding with rubber scraper just until blended. Do not stir.

Pour into ungreased 10-inch tube pan, 4-inches deep. Bake in 325° F. (slow) oven for 55 minutes, then at 350° F. (moderate) oven for 10 to 15 minutes, or until cake is firm to touch. Hang upside down on funnel or jar until cold. Loosen from sides of pan with spatula. Turn pan over and hit edges sharply to free cake from pan. Frost as desired.

Makes 1 (10-inch) tube cake.

SPONGE CAKE

(See Angel Food Cake, *page* 179)

5 egg whites   ¼ cup sugar
1 teaspoons grated lemon rind
1½ teaspoons lemon juice
5 egg yolks   ¾ cup sugar

With a wire whisk, beat egg whites until foamy, but not dry. Beat in gradually ¼ cup sugar. Set aside.

With unwashed whisk, beat lemon rind, lemon juice and egg yolks. Continue to beat until thick and lemon-colored (5 to 10 minutes; high speed if mixer is used). Beat in ¾ cup sugar. Pour yolk mixture over entire surface of beaten egg whites, carefully folding with whisk or rubber scraper until completely blended.

1 cup sifted cake flour
¼ teaspoon salt

Mix and sift flour and salt 4 times. Sift over top of batter in small amounts and fold in gently. Do not beat after adding flour-salt mixture to avoid breaking small air bubbles.

Turn into ungreased tube pan, layer pans or muffin pans. Cut through mixture gently with knife to break any large air bubbles. Bake in 350° F. (moderate) oven 30 to 45 minutes for tube cake; 20 to 25 minutes for layer or cup cakes, or until firm to touch.

Hang tube cake upside-down over a funnel or jar until completely cold. Loosen from pan with spatula or shake sharply out of pan. Invert layers or cup cakes and rest one edge against rack until almost cold. Loosen with spatula and coax cakes free, before they are cold, to prevent breaking. Layer and cup cakes are not easily removed when cold.

Makes 1 (10-inch) *tube cake;* 2 (9-inch) *layers;* 12 *to* 18 *cup cakes.*

COOKIES

FLAKE MACAROONS

2 egg whites
½ teaspoon salt   1 cup sugar
½ teaspoon vanilla
1 cup shredded coconut
2 cups cornflakes or flaked cereal,
   or prepared rice cereal
seedless raisins or cinnamon drops

Makes about 36 cookies.

Beat egg whites until frothy. Sprinkle salt over top and beat until stiff. Beat in sugar gradually. Fold in vanilla, coconut, flakes. Drop from teaspoon in mounds on buttered baking sheet. Place raisin or candy in center of each.

Bake in 350° F. (moderate) oven about 15 minutes. Remove while warm.

DROP COOKIES

1½ cups sifted cake flour
1½ teaspoons double-action baking powder
¼ teaspoon salt
6 tablespoons soft butter or margarine
¾ cup sugar
1 egg
½ teaspoon vanilla, or 1 teaspoon grated orange rind
2 tablespoons milk or orange juice

For variation, add one of the following:
⅓ cup chopped nuts
½ cup raisins
½ cup coconut

Makes about 2 dozen cookies.

Sift flour, measure 1½ cups into sifter. Add baking powder and salt, mix, then sift.

Cream butter, beat in sugar, then egg and flavoring. Add flour, alternately with milk, beating until smooth after each addition.

Drop from teaspoon in mounds on buttered baking sheet, about 2 inches apart, using another spoon or rubber scraper to empty spoon.

Bake in 375° F. (moderate) oven for 8 to 12 minutes.

ORANGE COCONUT COOKIES

Follow recipe for Drop Cookies with the following changes: substitute 1 teaspoon each grated orange and lemon rind for vanilla; substitute orange juice for milk, and coconut for walnuts.

CHOCOLATE OR COCONUT TEA STRIPS

1 recipe Drop Cookies (*see page* 183)
1 square chocolate, melted and cooled
1 tablespoon sugar
½ teaspoon grated orange rind
¼ cup chopped pecans
⅔ cup shredded coconut *
1 tablespoon sugar
½ teaspoon grated orange rind

*For variety, use:
   plain batter and topping of—
   ¼ cup chopped almonds
   ¼ cup currants
   2 tablespoons crushed loaf sugar

Each pan makes 16 *strips.*

Make batter for cookies, flavoring with orange rind. Remove ½ to second bowl.

Stir chocolate into one batter. Turn into buttered 8-inch square pan and spread evenly. Sprinkle mixture of sugar, orange rind and nuts over top.

Stir ⅓ cup coconut into second batter. Spread evenly in buttered 8-inch pan. Sprinkle remaining coconut over top, then mixture of sugar and orange rind.

Bake in 350° F. (moderate) oven about 15 minutes. Cool in pans. Cut in 1-inch strips, then cut across in halves.

FRUIT DROPS

1 cup sweetened condensed milk
¼ teaspoon salt
1 teaspoon vanilla
1 cup cornflakes
2 cups shredded coconut
1 cup chopped dates, figs, dried prunes or apricots, raisins or currants

Makes about 30 *cookies.*

Measure ingredients into large bowl and stir enough to mix well.

Drop from teaspoon in mounds on buttered baking sheet, about 2 inches apart, using another spoon or rubber scraper to empty spoon.

Bake in 350° F. (moderate) oven 8 to 15 minutes, or until delicately browned. Remove carefully while warm.

MARGUERITES

½ recipe Seven-Minute Frosting
   (*page* 190)
3 tablespoons marshmallows, cut in small pieces
¼ cup shredded coconut
½ cup chopped nuts
24 crisp wafers

Makes 24 *marguerites.*

Make frosting and beat in marshmallows while still warm. Fold in coconut and nuts. Spread on wafers.

Bake in 350° F. (moderate) oven about 15 minutes, or until delicately browned.

BROWNIES

¾ cup sifted flour
½ teaspoon double-action baking
   powder
½ teaspoon salt
½ cup or more broken nut meats *
2 squares chocolate, melted
⅓ cup soft shortening
1 cup sugar
2 eggs
1 teaspoon vanilla

* For variety add:
   ½ cup nuts and ½ cup raisins or
   chopped dates

Makes 16 (2-inch) squares.

Sift flour, measure ¾ cup into sifter. Add baking powder and salt. Mix well, then sift into bowl. Stir in nuts.

Melt chocolate over hot water. Cream shortening until soft. Beat in sugar gradually, then eggs, one at a time, vanilla and chocolate. Stir in flour-nut mixture. Turn into buttered, 8-inch square pan.

Bake in 350° F. (moderate) oven 30 to 40 minutes until top has dull crust. (For chewy Brownies, bake in 300° F. (slow) oven 50 minutes.) Cool slightly, then cut in squares. Remove from pan.

SUGAR COOKIES

2 cups sifted flour (about)
1½ teaspoons double-action baking powder
½ teaspoon salt
½ cup soft butter or margarine
1 cup granulated sugar, or 1 cup
   firmly packed brown sugar
1 egg
1 teaspoon vanilla, or grated lemon
   or orange rind
1 tablespoon cream or fruit juice
flour for rolling

Makes about 36 small cookies.

Sift flour, measure 2 cups into sifter. Add baking powder and salt. Mix well, then sift.

Cream butter. Beat in sugar gradually, then egg, vanilla and cream. Stir in flour gradually, adding more if not stiff enough to roll. Chill thoroughly.

Remove part of dough to lightly floured board and shape into ball. Place remaining dough in refrigerator. With floured rolling pin, roll dough ⅛ inch thick. Cut with floured cooky cutter. With spatula remove to ungreased baking sheet. Sprinkle tops with sugar.

Bake in 375° F. (moderate) oven for 8 to 10 minutes, or until browned.

ROLLED COOKIES

Chill mixture in covered bowl or wrapped tightly in wax paper. To roll dough, dust board lightly with flour or powdered sugar. Work with small amounts of dough—never more than a cupful at a time. A canvas cover for rolling board and stockinette for rolling pin make rolling of dough easier.

DECORATED COOKIES FOR SPECIAL OCCASIONS

Cut rolled cooky dough with fancy cutters or special cut-outs as desired. Decorate with colored sugar or candies; raisins, currants or nuts; candied cherries, angelica or citron. Or decorate refrigerator slices or drop cookies as desired.

CHOCOLATE COOKIES

Follow recipe for Sugar Cookies, only add 2 squares chocolate, melted, to butter-sugar-egg mixture. Add more flour, if needed.

SPICED SUGAR COOKIES

Follow recipe for Sugar Cookies, only mix and sift $\frac{1}{4}$ teaspoon each cinnamon, allspice and cloves with flour. Omit vanilla.

SAND TARTS

Make dough for Sugar Cookies. Roll thin and cut in fancy shapes. Brush tops with slightly beaten egg white. Sprinkle with mixture of $\frac{1}{4}$ cup sugar and 1 teaspoon cinnamon. Garnish with sliced candied cherries and blanched almonds. Bake.

FILLED REFRIGERATOR COOKIES

Follow recipe for Butterscotch Slices with following changes: omit dates and nut meats. Cut in thin slices. Put 1 teaspoon firm marmalade (*page 219*) in centers of half of slices. Cover with remaining slices and press edges together. Bake in 375° F. (moderate) oven 10 minutes. Makes 4 to 5 dozen filled cookies.

BUTTERSCOTCH SLICES

3 ¼ cups sifted flour (about)
3 teaspoons double-action baking
  powder
½ teaspoon salt
1 cup chopped dates or raisins
1 cup finely chopped nut meats
1 cup soft shortening
1 ½ cups firmly packed brown
  sugar
½ teaspoon vanilla
2 eggs
Filbert Slices, omit: dates and nuts; sprinkle chopped filberts over un-baked slices.

Makes 8 to 10 dozen cookies.

Sift flour, measure 3 ¼ cups into sifter. Add baking powder and salt. Mix well, then sift into bowl. Stir in fruit and nuts. Cream shortening. Beat in sugar gradually, then vanilla and eggs, one at a time. Stir in flour. Shape into rolls, about 2 inches thick. Wrap each in waxed paper. Chill in refrigerator until hard.

Bake as needed, cutting rolls in ⅛-inch slices. Place on ungreased baking sheet and bake in 375° F. (moderate) oven 8 to 10 minutes.

DOUGHNUTS OR FRIED CAKES

(See Helps in Deep-Fat Frying, *page 57*)

4 cups sifted flour
¾ teaspoon baking soda
½ teaspoon cream of tartar
1 teaspoon salt
½ teaspoon nutmeg
¼ teaspoon cinnamon
2 eggs
1 egg yolk
1 cup sour milk
¾ cup sugar
2 tablespoons shortening, melted
flour for rolling

Makes about 3 dozen.

Sift flour, measure 4 cups into sifter. Add soda, cream of tartar, salt and spices. Mix, then sift.

Beat eggs and egg yolk until foamy. Add sour milk, sugar and shortening, and stir enough to mix. Stir in flour mixture, stirring until almost smooth.

Roll a small portion at a time on floured board or canvas. Shape lightly into ball. Roll ¼ inch thick. Cut with floured cutter. Fry in hot, deep fat (365° F.) for 2 to 3 minutes, or until golden brown, turning them when they rise to top and several times during cooking. Drain on paper.

Frostings and Fillings

Do Things for Cakes

Given one good cake recipe, and a collection of three or four frostings and fillings, a young cook has the makings of a number of cakes, of various shapes and sizes, color and flavor combinations. Begin with the never-fail and adaptable Two-Egg Cake recipe on *page* 173. It can be baked in cup-cake shapes, in layers, in a square or oblong sheet. Learn to make a few simple frostings and fillings, and very soon you may consider yourself a good cake maker.

Helps in Frosting. Brush off the loose crumbs from any cake with your hand before spreading on the frosting. If your cup cakes have little crisp rims around the top edge, trim them with kitchen scissors before frosting. If a cake or cup cake seems a little too peaked or lopsided, when you turn it out on the rack, turn it top-side down. That will help to make it flatter and better looking when frosted. If layers have baked unevenly, with a sharp knife slice off the too-rounded part. If layers slide, anchor them with toothpicks or a wire cake tester.

Be sure your frosting is thick enough to pile onto cake without sliding, even if you have to add a little extra confectioners' sugar. If frosting should be too thick, beat in a few drops of hot water. A sweet topping, baked or broiled on cake, is the simplest way to frost a cake, but confectioners' sugar icings are easy to make, too. Twirl cup cakes right in the frosting bowl. Cooked frostings, particularly the fudge type, must be made carefully. Use a candy thermometer for uniform success. If you want to glamorize your cake, add a sprinkling of coconut, nuts or colored sugar. See suggestions on *page* 188 for helpful suggestions on frosting.

Fillings and frostings add beauty and help to keep cakes moist. But special cakes, like pound cake or angel food, are often best unfrosted.

BUTTER FROSTING

¼ **cup butter**
2 cups confectioners' sugar
2 tablespoons cream (about)
1 teaspoon vanilla or ½ teaspoon
  almond extract
dash of salt

Makes frosting for tops and sides of 2 (8-inch) layers, tops of 2 (9-inch) layers, or 2 dozen cup cakes.

Cream butter until soft. Stir in 1 cup sugar gradually, mixing thoroughly. Then stir in remaining sugar, alternately with cream, until just right to spread. Add flavoring and salt, and beat well.

CHOCOLATE BUTTER FROSTING

Follow recipe for Butter Frosting with following changes: add 2 squares chocolate, melted, to butter-sugar mixture after ½ cup sugar has been added; flavor with ½ teaspoon vanilla or 1 teaspoon grated orange rind; add sugar to make a creamy frosting.

ORANGE BUTTER FROSTING

Follow recipe for Butter Frosting with following changes: substitute orange juice for cream; omit vanilla and flavor with 1 ½ teaspoons grated orange rind. For *Golden Orange Frosting,* add 1 egg yolk when half of sugar has been added.

LEMON OR ORANGE ICING

1 egg white
1 teaspoon lemon or orange juice
¼ **teaspoon grated lemon rind**
1 cup powdered sugar (about)

Makes icing for 8-inch square cake.

Beat egg white until frothy. Sprinkle juice over top. Then beat in sugar gradually until stiff enough to spread. Add rind.

BUTTERSCOTCH FROSTING

1 egg white
¾ cup dark brown sugar
dash of salt
2 teaspoons lemon juice
⅓ cup broken nut meats

Beat egg white until stiff. Gradually beat in sugar, salt and lemon juice. Spread on hot cake as soon as it is taken from oven. Sprinkle with nuts.

Makes frosting for 9-inch square cake.

COCONUT-LEMON FROSTING

Follow recipe for Butterscotch Frosting, only substitute ½ cup coconut for nut meats. Add 1 tablespoon grated lemon rind.

SEVEN MINUTE FROSTING

2 egg whites
½ cup sugar
dash of cream of tartar
2 teaspoons light corn syrup
1 teaspoon vanilla

Mix egg whites, sugar, cream of tartar and corn syrup in top part of double boiler until sugar is dissolved.

Place over boiling water and beat mixture until it holds its shape and stands in peaks (6 to 7 minutes with rotary beater; about 4 minutes with electric beater). Remove from boiling water. Fold in vanilla. Spread on cake.

Makes frosting for 2 (8-inch) layers, or 1 (9-inch) square, or 24 cup cakes.

In all variations, fold in additions carefully and at very last unless otherwise directed.

MARSHMALLOW FROSTING

To warm Seven Minute Frosting, add ½ cup diced marshmallows and beat thoroughly.

COCONUT SEVEN MINUTE FROSTING

Sprinkle 1 to 1 ½ cups shredded coconut over cake covered with Seven Minute Frosting, while frosting is soft.

ORANGE SEVEN MINUTE FROSTING

Follow recipe for Seven Minute Frosting with following changes: omit corn syrup and vanilla. Substitute 1 tablespoon orange juice for vanilla. Add 1 teaspoon grated orange rind.

DIVINITY FROSTING

To Seven Minute Frosting, add ¼ cup maraschino cherries and ¼ cup chopped nuts.

LADY BALTIMORE FROSTING

To Seven Minute Frosting, add ½ cup each chopped raisins and figs, and ¼ cup each chopped, blanched almonds and walnuts.

FUDGE FROSTING

1 recipe Chocolate Fudge (*page* 249)
1 cup broken nuts, or pecan, almond or walnut halves for decoration

Makes enough frosting for 2-layer cake.

Make fudge, cooking to very soft-ball stage (234° F.). When lukewarm, beat until thick enough to spread. If it gets too stiff while spreading, place pan over hot water to keep soft or add a little cream. Stir nuts into frosting, or sprinkle over frosted cake.

CARAMEL FUDGE FROSTING

(See Chocolate Fudge, *page* 249)

1⅓ cups firmly packed brown sugar
½ cup granulated sugar
dash of salt
1 cup rich milk, or 1½ cups sour cream
2 to 3 tablespoons butter ★
½ teaspoon vanilla
1 cup nut meats

★ Omit butter with cream

Makes frosting for 2-layer cake.

Boil sugars, salt and milk to soft-ball stage (234°–236° F.). Add butter and vanilla. Cool until lukewarm (110° F.).

Beat until creamy and thick. Sprinkle chopped nuts over frosted cake, or decorate with nut halves before frosting is firm.

DE LUXE BROILED TOPPING

¼ cup soft butter
½ cup brown sugar
3 tablespoons cream
½ cup coconut

Makes frosting for 9-inch square cake.

Mix ingredients. Spread over warm cake.

Place under broiler (about 3 inches from burner) until mixture bubbles and lightly browns.

DELICATE JELLY TOPPING

½ cup tart jelly: currant, grape,
    wild plum, or gooseberry
1 egg white   dash of salt

Makes enough topping for square cake.

Place jelly in top of double boiler and beat with rotary beater to break up slightly. Add egg white and salt, and beat until free from lumps.

Turn off heat and continue beating until stiff enough to peak. Spread on cold cake.

APPLE-MARMALADE TOPPING OR FILLING

½ cup thick applesauce, sweetened
2 tablespoons orange or kumquat
    marmalade*
½ cup heavy cream, whipped

* **Apple-Ginger Filling,** use:
    chopped preserved ginger

Makes topping for 9-inch square cake; makes enough filling for 2 (9-inch) layers.

Mix together applesauce and marmalade. Fold into whipped cream.

Spread between layers just before serving, or use as topping for square cake.

CREAM FILLING

¼ cup granulated sugar, or ½ cup
    firmly packed brown sugar
2 tablespoons cake flour, or 1 table-
    spoon cornstarch
dash of salt
2 egg yolks, slightly beaten
1 cup milk
1 tablespoon butter
1 teaspoon vanilla

Makes enough filling to spread be-tween 2 cake layers.

Mix together sugar, flour and salt in top of double boiler. Stir in egg yolks, then milk gradually. Place over boiling water and cook flour mixture 10 minutes, or cornstarch mixture 15 minutes. Stir constantly until thickened, then occasionally. Stir in butter and vanilla. Cool.

CHOCOLATE CREAM FILLING

Follow recipe for Cream Filling, only add 1 square chocolate to ingredients; place over boiling water, and stir constantly until chocolate is melted and mixture smooth and thickened. Or use 4 tablespoons cocoa, mixing it thoroughly with sugar, flour and salt.

NOUGAT CREAM FILLING

Follow recipe for Chocolate Cream Filling, only add ½ cup chopped nut meats, stirring them thoroughly into mixture.

LEMON FILLING

¾ cup sugar
2 tablespoons cornstarch
dash of salt
2 egg yolks, slightly beaten
½ cup water
1 teaspoon grated lemon rind
3 tablespoons lemon juice
2 tablespoons butter

Makes enough filling to spread between 2 layers, or on 14- × 10-inch cake roll.

Mix together sugar, cornstarch and salt. Stir in egg yolks, then water. Cook over boiling water 15 minutes, stirring constantly until thickened, then occasionally. Stir in grated lemon rind, juice and butter. Cool.

ORANGE FILLING

Follow recipe for Lemon Filling with following changes: reduce sugar to ½ cup; substitute orange juice for water, and 1 ½ teaspoons grated orange rind for lemon rind. Add ¼ cup shredded coconut to cooked filling, if desired.

The Ever Popular Sandwich

The first sandwich, so tradition tells us, was the invention of the Fourth Earl of Sandwich, a convivial fellow, too impatient to stop watching the races, who preferred to eat afoot. However, that substantial slice of good old English beef or mutton was a simple snack compared with its numerous namesakes today.

Nowadays, there are almost as many shapes, kinds and sizes of sandwiches as there are people to eat them. From picnics to high teas, graduation parties to wedding receptions, the sandwich graces the occasion and exactly fills the bill.

The purpose of this section is not to give you countless sandwich recipes, but rather to suggest how many kinds you can make, how adaptable and versatile the sandwich is, and how easy it is to figure out new fillings and combinations.

TEA OR PARTY SANDWICHES

Any dainty sandwich may be served for tea or special occasions. They may be: open or closed and cut in fancy shapes such as rounds, crescents, triangles, diamonds, squares, oblongs, stars or strips; rolled, then toasted or served plain, or cut in thin slices. They may be more elaborate in design, such as pinwheels, checkerboard or ribbon slices. Use thin slices of dark or white bread, nut or fruit bread or steamed bread; remove crusts and spread thin with a Butter Spread (*page* 195) or with softened butter or margarine and a Cream Cheese Filling (*page* 196) or any other desired filling. Garnish simply with parsley leaves, sliced stuffed olives or pimiento, candied cherries, ginger, citron and the like. *One slice white bread makes about 4 open sandwiches.*

BUTTER SPREADS

4 tablespoons butter seasoning

Makes enough for about 12 dainty sandwiches or canapés.

Cream butter until soft and smooth, then stir in ingredients given in one of the following butters. Use for dainty sandwiches and canapés.

ANCHOVY BUTTER

To creamed butter, add 1 tablespoon anchovy paste, ½ teaspoon lemon juice and dash of paprika.

CHEESE BUTTER

To creamed butter, add ½ package (1 ½ oz.) cream cheese, dash each of salt and paprika, and ¼ teaspoon Worcestershire sauce.

GOLDEN BUTTER

To creamed butter, add 2 hard-cooked egg yolks put through a sieve, ½ teaspoon lemon juice and dash each of tabasco sauce, salt and cayenne.

GREEN BUTTER

To creamed butter, add 2 tablespoons spinach purée, 1 tablespoon chopped parsley and ½ teaspoon lemon juice.

LEMON BUTTER

To creamed butter, add a few gratings lemon rind and 2 teaspoons lemon juice. Lime or orange rind and juice may be substituted for lemon.

OLIVE BUTTER

To creamed butter, add 2 tablespoons chopped stuffed olives and 1 teaspoon lemon juice. For *Nut Butter*, substitute nuts for olives.

ONION OR CHIVES BUTTER

To creamed butter, add 1 teaspoon finely chopped onion, or onion juice, or chives.

PARSLEY OR WATERCRESS BUTTER

To creamed butter, add 2 tablespoons chopped parsley or watercress and 1 teaspoon lemon juice.

PEANUT BUTTER SPREAD

To creamed butter, add 4 tablespoons peanut butter, 1 teaspoon honey and ⅛ teaspoon salt.

PIMIENTO BUTTER

To creamed butter, add 2 tablespoons mashed pimiento and 1 teaspoon finely chopped pickle.

DEVILED EGGS

Follow recipe for Deviled Egg Salad (*page* 143). Put two filled halves together. Wrap in waxed paper and chill. Or moisten mashed egg yolks with mayonnaise and season with salt and paprika.

CREAM CHEESE FILLINGS

2 tablespoons cream, mayonnaise, or other liquid (about)
1 package (3 oz.) cream cheese
seasonings below

Makes enough for about 2 dozen open-faced, dainty sandwiches, or 6 large hearty sandwiches.

Stir liquid into cheese until it is soft enough to spread easily. Mix well with ingredients given in one of the following spreads.

Spread thin for tea or dainty sandwiches or canapés, or more generously for luncheon or hearty sandwiches.

CHEESE AND ANCHOVY SPREAD

Moisten cheese with cream and add 1 to 3 teaspoons anchovy paste.

CHEESE AND JELLY SPREAD

Moisten cheese with cream; add your favorite tart jelly, jam, marmalade or honey, using 2 to 4 tablespoons.

CHEESE AND MARASCHINO SPREAD

Moisten cheese with maraschino cherry liquor and add 1 to 2 tablespoons finely chopped maraschino cherries.

CHEESE AND MINT SPREAD

Moisten cheese with cream and add 1 to 2 teaspoons finely chopped fresh mint.

CHEESE AND NUT OR DATE SPREAD

Moisten cheese with mayonnaise or cream and add 2 to 4 table-spoons finely chopped nuts or dates. Raisins, figs or prunes may be substituted for nuts or dates.

CHEESE AND ONION SPREAD

Moisten cheese with cream and add 1 tablespoon minced onion and a dash each of salt and paprika.

CHEESE AND PINEAPPLE SPREAD

Moisten cheese with pineapple juice and add 1 cup drained crushed pineapple, 1 tablespoon grated carrot and $\frac{1}{8}$ teaspoon salt. Makes about 1 $\frac{1}{2}$ cups filling.

CHEESE AND VEGETABLE SPREAD

Moisten cheese with mayonnaise and add 1 to 3 tablespoons chopped cucumbers, radishes, peppers or scallions, or a mixture of all.

CHEESE AND HAM SANDWICH

Put sliced American or Swiss cheese and boiled or baked ham between slices of buttered, whole wheat or white bread.

PINWHEEL SANDWICHES

fresh, fine-grained bread, white, whole wheat or graham*—part or whole loaf

Butter Spreads (*page* 195), Cream Cheese Fillings (*page* 196), or any other spread or filling contrasting in color with bread

small sweet pickles, stuffed olives or pimiento

* Bread may be sliced thin, then made thinner and easier to handle by rolling with rolling pin before spreading with butter.

One small slice makes about 8 and one lengthwise slice about 24 pinwheels.

Trim off crusts with sharp thin knife. Cut in thin slices, about $\frac{1}{4}$ inch thick, either in usual manner or lengthwise. For small slice, spread first before cutting; for large slice, cut and place between dampened cloths before spreading.

Lay pickles, olives or pimiento strips, end to end, along edge to be rolled. Roll tightly, fasten with toothpicks and wrap in waxed paper. Chill in refrigerator $\frac{1}{2}$ hour or longer. Just before serving, cut in $\frac{1}{4}$-inch slices and arrange on sandwich plate.

TOASTED ROLLED SANDWICHES

Use fresh white bread, a whole or part of loaf, as needed, and trim off crusts. Spread bread with Cheese and Anchovy Spread (*page* 196) or other Cheese or Butter Spreads (*page* 195) before cutting in ¼-inch slices. Roll each tightly and fasten with toothpicks. Wrap in waxed paper and chill 1 hour or longer. Just before serving, remove rolls from paper and cut each in half. Toast quickly under broiler, turning to brown evenly. Remove toothpicks and serve hot. *One slice makes 2 small sandwiches.*

PARTY SANDWICH LOAF

1 loaf white bread
5 tablespoons butter, creamed

Trim crusts from loaf, and cut lengthwise in slices, about ⅓ inch thick, spreading each slice with butter before cutting. Place 1 slice on platter to rebuild loaf.

1 bunch watercress
6 tablespoons mayonnaise

Mince watercress and mix with mayonnaise. Spread ½ over bread on platter, and cover with second slice.

3 hard-cooked eggs
2 tablespoons cream
salt and pepper

Mince eggs, moisten with cream, and season to taste. Spread on second slice, and cover with third slice.

2 pimientos
2 tablespoons relish spread

Chop pimientos very fine and mix with relish spread. Spread on third slice, and cover with fourth slice. Spread remaining watercress and mayonnaise mixture over top and cover with last slice.

2 packages (3 oz. each) cream cheese
¼ cup light cream

Mix cheese with cream, and beat until light. Spread over sides and top of loaf and chill 1 hour or longer.

2 tablespoons minced parsley
Radish Roses (*page* 138)
parsley sprigs

Sprinkle parsley over loaf and garnish platter with Radish Roses and sprigs of parsley. Slice at table.

Makes about 16 (*⅓-inch*) *slices.*

CUCUMBER SANDWICHES

Trim off crusts from part of loaf of white bread to be used. Cut in very thin slices, spreading bread each time with Lemon Butter (*page 195*) before slicing. Put thin slices of crisp cucumber between pieces of bread and cut in small triangles, squares or strips. Arrange attractively on sandwich plate and serve at once. They may be covered with waxed paper, then wrapped in a damp cloth, and stored in refrigerator for 1 hour before serving. *Two slices make about 4 small sandwiches.*

GINGERBREAD SANDWICHES

Cut gingerbread in thin slices and put 2 together with cream cheese moistened with cream. Cut each in half or in triangles.

PEANUT BUTTER SANDWICHES

Cut whole wheat bread in thin slices, spreading bread with mixture of equal amounts of peanut butter and cherry jam before slicing. Put 2 slices together and cut in dainty shapes. For hearty sandwiches, cut in ⅓-inch slices and spread generously with mixture. For variety, use honey with peanut butter.

EGG SANDWICH FILLINGS

**1 hard-cooked egg, chopped or
  minced
2 to 3 tablespoons mayonnaise, or
  other dressings
salt and pepper**

Makes enough filling for about 8 dainty sandwiches or 1 large sandwich.

Mix egg with dressing until soft enough to spread. Season to taste. Mix with one of combinations given below.

Spread thin for tea or dainty sandwiches, or generously for lunch box or picnic or other hearty sandwiches.

SAVORY EGG FILLING

Add ⅛ to ½ teaspoon minced onion and dash of dry mustard to egg base.

EGG AND VEGETABLE FILLING

Add 1 to 2 tablespoons of one of the following; chopped celery, cucumber, green pepper, parsley, radishes, fresh spinach, tomatoes, watercress, cooked beets or broiled mushrooms to egg base.

EGG AND PICKLE OR OLIVE FILLING

Add 1 to 2 tablespoons finely chopped pickle or stuffed olives, or pimiento and celery to egg base.

EGG AND ALMOND FILLING

Add 1 tablespoon each chopped almonds and celery to egg base.

EGG AND LIVER OR HAM FILLING

Add chopped chicken liver or giblet; or add 2 to 4 tablespoons finely chopped cooked liver, 1 teaspoon chopped parsley, and 4 drops onion juice; or ham or bacon to egg base.

EGG AND ANCHOVY OR SARDINE FILLING

Add 1 to 2 tablespoons chopped anchovies or sardines, and ½ teaspoon lemon juice to egg base.

FRIED HAM SANDWICHES

Toast bread quickly, spread with softened butter and place hot Fried Ham (*page* 40), topped with thinly sliced Bermuda onion, between 2 slices.

HOT VIRGINIA HAM SANDWICHES

Split hot baking powder biscuits in halves, spread with softened butter and place sliced hot Virginia ham between each. For Sunday night supper, place plates of buttered hot biscuits, hot baked ham and a bowl of coleslaw on buffet and let each one serve himself.

CLUB SANDWICHES

3 slices bread
softened butter
crisp lettuce or other greens
meat, fish, cheese or hard-cooked
  egg, sliced or chopped
salad dressing
sliced vegetables   garnish

Toast bread quickly and spread with butter. Cover 1 slice with lettuce, place meat, fish, or cheese on top and spread with dressing. Cover with second piece of toast, top with lettuce, if desired, and sliced vegetable; spread with dressing. Place third piece on top. Cut in triangles and garnish with parsley, pickles or olives.

CHICKEN CLUB SANDWICH

Use crisp lettuce, sliced chicken meat, sliced tomato, crisp bacon and mayonnaise. Any sliced meat may be substituted for chicken.

TONGUE CLUB SANDWICH

Use crisp watercress, sliced tongue, sliced crisp cucumbers and Horseradish Sour Cream Dressing (*page* 135).

CHOPPED HAM CLUB SANDWICH

Use crisp lettuce, chopped cooked ham, piccalilli, thinly sliced mild onion and Cooked Salad Dressing (*page* 136).

TUNA FISH CLUB SANDWICH

Use crisp lettuce, tuna fish mixed with mayonnaise, and sliced crisp cucumbers. Any fish or shellfish may be substituted for tuna fish.

VEGETABLE CLUB SANDWICH

Use crisp lettuce, sliced tomatoes, cream cheese mixed with diced cucumber and moistened with cream, and mayonnaise.

GRILLED SARDINE SANDWICHES

1 can (No. ¼ key) tiny sardines, or
    18 to 22 fish
sliced bread, ⅓ inch thick
lemon juice
softened butter
olives and pickles

Bone sardines and lay 5 to 6 on slice of bread. Sprinkle with lemon juice and cover with second slice. Butter outside of each slice and fry slowly in sandwich grill or heavy frying pan, turning to brown both sides. Place on hot plate, cut in half, garnish as desired and serve hot.

HOT MEAT SANDWICHES

Heat slices of roast beef, veal, lamb, pork, poultry or turkey in left-over gravy. Serve on buttered hot toast with tomato or cucumber slices, radishes, scallions, pickles or olives.

CHOPPED MEAT SANDWICHES

Use chopped or ground cooked beef, veal, lamb, ham, corned beef, chicken, liver or tongue. Moisten with mayonnaise and season with salt, pepper, horseradish, ketchup, Worcestershire or chili sauce, pickle relish, piccalilli, chopped pickles, pimiento, celery, tomatoes, green peppers, parsley or watercress, as desired. Or use sliced meats.

FLAKED FISH SANDWICHES

Use flaked cooked fresh fish, tuna, salmon, sardines, lobster, crabmeat or shrimp. Moisten with mayonnaise; add chopped celery, tomatoes, green peppers, pimiento, cucumbers, radishes, chives or onions, as desired.

MEAT OR FISH SANDWICHES

For lunch box, picnic or luncheon sandwiches, use white, whole wheat, rye, pumpernickel, cereal or brown bread. Cut in ¼ to ⅓ inch thick slices and spread with softened butter. Place filling between slices and cut in halves.

MEAL-IN-A-SANDWICH

5 cubed thin steaks (1 lb.)
5 tablespoons butter
salt and pepper
2½ large tomatoes, halved crosswise
5 large mushroom caps, washed
melted butter
5 slices white bread

Sauté steaks in butter 1 minute on 1 side. Turn and cook 1 minute on the other side. Season; remove and keep hot.

Butter tomato halves and mushroom caps and sprinkle lightly with salt and pepper. Place with bread under broiler. Toast bread on one side only; then dip slices, untoasted side down, in drippings in pan. Place toast, gravy side up, on hot plates and lay one steak on each. Put grilled tomato half on steak. Top with mushroom.

SPORT MODEL SANDWICHES

American cheese, sliced
sliced white bread, ⅓ inch thick
softened butter
parsley or watercress for garnish

Place cheese between 2 slices of bread, then butter outside of each slice. Place in center of medium-hot waffle iron, close tightly and bake about 2 minutes, or until browned. Divide in sections or serve whole on hot plate. Garnish.

These sandwiches may be fried in sandwich grill or heavy frying pan.

Refreshing Beverages

Although we may think of cold drinks as refreshing and hot drinks as cheering, it is well to remember that beverages may supply real food to meals. A frosty homemade ice cream soda as a luncheon-dessert on a summer day, when appetites are lagging, supplies good honest nourishment, unawares. By the same token, a pitcher of hot chocolate on a winter supper table when, perhaps, the meal is a bit slim, gives that satisfied feeling.

A bowl of delicious and colorful punch gives a party look. See the festive table on *page* 208. The cakes, sandwiches, candies and all are lovely, but it is the punch bowl that catches the eye.

Fruit drinks and egg drinks, sour drinks and sweet drinks, tall drinks and short, the good cook knows them all. So does the good host and hostess.

ICED CHOCOLATE

4 cups cold milk *
½ cup Chocolate Syrup * (*page* 204)

* Iced Chocolate for One:
  1 cup milk
  2 tablespoons syrup

Makes 4 tall glasses.

Stir milk into chocolate syrup. Then beat with rotary beater in bowl, or shake in shaker until frothy.

Pour into tall glasses, about one-third filled with cracked ice; and serve at once. Top each with 2 tablespoons whipped cream and dust with cinnamon, if desired.

ICED COCOA

Follow recipe for Iced Chocolate, only use Cocoa Syrup (*page* 204) instead of Chocolate Syrup.

CHOCOLATE SYRUP

4 squares chocolate
1 cup hot water

Put chocolate and water in saucepan, and heat slowly until chocolate is melted, stirring occasionally.

1 cup sugar *
⅛ teaspoon salt

Stir in sugar and salt, and cook about 5 minutes, stirring until smooth.

1 teaspoon vanilla

* For a sweeter syrup use:
   1¼ to 1½ cups sugar

Makes about 1 ½ cups syrup, or enough for 12 chocolate drinks.

Remove from heat, cool, then add vanilla. Pour into pint jar and cover tightly. Store syrup in refrigerator. It will keep several weeks. For chocolate drinks, use 2 tablespoons syrup for 1 cup milk.

COCOA SYRUP

Use recipe for Chocolate Syrup, only substitute ½ to ¾ cup cocoa in place of chocolate. Mix together cocoa, sugar and salt before adding hot water. Makes about 1 ½ cups syrup.

Cocoa Syrup and Chocolate Syrup may be used interchangeably. For ice cream or dessert sauce, reheat syrup, add 1 tablespoon butter and serve hot.

CHOCOLATE FLOAT

1 recipe Iced Chocolate (*page* 203)
½ pint chocolate ice cream

Makes 4 tall glasses.

Make Iced Chocolate and pour into tall glasses (without ice). Add scoop of ice cream to each glass.

ICE CREAM SODA

2 tablespoons Chocolate Syrup
   (*above*)
½ cup cold milk
½ cup carbonated water or ginger ale
ice cream

Makes 1 tall glass.

Measure syrup into tall glass, and stir in milk until well mixed.

Add carbonated water and small scoop of ice cream, and stir slightly with spoon. Serve at once. Vanilla, chocolate, caramel, coffee or peppermint ice cream may be used.

CHOCOLATE MALTED MILK

1 recipe Iced Chocolate (*page* 203)
½ cup malted milk powder

Makes 4 tall glasses.

Follow recipe for Iced Chocolate, only stir malted milk powder into chocolate syrup before adding milk.

EGGNOG

1 egg
2 teaspoons sugar

1 cup cold top milk, or rich milk
¼ teaspoon vanilla

Makes 1 glass.

Beat egg in small deep bowl with rotary beater until light and thick, then beat in sugar.

Stir milk and vanilla into egg, and beat or shake well in shaker.

Pour into tall glass. Sprinkle nutmeg or cinnamon over top as desired

FLUFFY EGGNOG

Follow recipe for Eggnog, only beat egg yolk and white separately, and fold stiffly beaten white into yolk and milk mixture. *Makes 1 glass.*

FRUIT EGGNOG

1 recipe Eggnog (*above*)
1 tablespoon fruit juice

Makes 1 glass.

Make Eggnog, only omit vanilla, and flavor with fruit juice such as orange, grape or cherry. Crushed or homogenized fruit may be used.

CHOCOLATE EGGNOG

4 eggs, separated
dash of salt
4 cups cold milk
½ cup Chocolate Syrup (*page* 204)

Makes 4 tall glasses.

Beat egg whites until stiff. Then beat egg yolks with salt until thick and light.

Stir milk into chocolate syrup. Add to egg yolks, and beat well. Fold in stiffly beaten egg whites. Serve in tall glasses.

NEW ENGLAND SHAKE

2 tablespoons Sugar Syrup (*below*)
2 tablespoons lemon juice
2 tablespoons pineapple or grape
  juice
1 egg   milk

Makes 1 large glass.

Measure syrup and juices into tall glass. Add egg, then milk to fill glass. Pour into shaker or bowl and shake or beat with cracked ice until well mixed.

ROOTBEER EGG SHAKE

3 cups cold milk
1/2 cup orange juice
1/2 cup light cream
3 tablespoons sugar
1/8 teaspoon salt
1 1/2 teaspoons rootbeer extract
2 eggs

Makes 4 tall glasses.

Measure ingredients in order listed into large shaker or bowl. Shake or beat well with cracked ice, pour into tall glasses.

SUGAR SYRUP

1 cup sugar   1 cup water

Makes about 1 1/3 cups syrup.

Bring sugar and water to a boil, stirring until sugar is dissolved. Boil 10 minutes. Pour into sterilized jar, cover tightly. Store in refrigerator. Use in beverages.

LEMONADE

4 lemons (3/4 cup juice)
2/3 to 3/4 cup Sugar Syrup (*above*)
2 1/2 cups water   cracked ice

Makes 4 glasses.

Squeeze juice from lemons into pitcher or bowl. Add sugar syrup and water, and mix well. Chill with cracked ice.

QUICK LEMONADE

4 lemons (3/4 cup juice)
1/2 to 3/4 cup sugar
3 cups water

Makes 4 glasses.

Mix lemon juice, sugar and water, stirring to dissolve sugar. Chill with ice.

FROSTED CRANBERRY CREAM

½ pint vanilla ice cream
2 cups cold cranberry juice
1 pint carbonated water

Makes 4 tall glasses.

Put a small scoop of ice cream in each of 4 tall glasses. Add ½ cup each cranberry juice and carbonated water to each, and mix slightly.

SUMMER PUNCH

⅔ cup sugar
2 cups water
2 tablespoons grated lemon rind

½ cup lemon juice
⅔ cup raspberry juice
1 pint ginger ale (about)
fresh mint

Makes 4 tall glasses.

Boil sugar, 1 cup water and lemon rind for 5 minutes. Add remaining cup water and cool.

Add fruit juices and pour into 4 tall glasses, one-third filled with cracked ice. Then fill glasses with ginger ale, garnish with mint, and serve at once.

MINT JULEP PUNCH

1 bunch fresh mint
3 whole cloves
2 cups hot strong tea
½ cup lemon juice
1 cup orange juice
¾ cup sugar

1 orange, sections diced
¼ cup diced pineapple
¼ cup maraschino cherries, diced
1 pint white grape juice
1 quart carbonated water

Makes about 20 punch-cup portions, or 10 tall glasses.

Chop mint, add with cloves to hot tea. Let stand until cold. Strain into large pitcher.

Add fruit juices and sugar to minted tea and stir until sugar is dissolved. Chill several hours.

When ready to serve, add fruits, juice and carbonated water to tea. Pour over large piece of ice in punch bowl; or pour into tall glasses, half-filled with cracked ice. Garnish with small sprigs of mint, if desired.

A festive table for friends should be set with your very best. Get out your prettiest service, linens, silver, candles, flowers. Serve choice small cakes, savory and dainty sandwiches, arrange candies and nuts here and there and serve Orange Ice Punch (*page* 209).

FROZEN FRUIT SHRUB

1 cup sugar
1 cup water
4 whole cloves
1 stick cinnamon
4 cups canned pineapple juice
4 cups strained orange juice
¾ cup strained lemon juice
1 quart orange sherbet or ice

Makes about 20 punch-cup portions.

Boil sugar, water and spices for 5 minutes. Strain and cool.

Add fruit juices to syrup and chill. A few drops of green vegetable coloring may be added, if desired.

Just before serving, put orange sherbet in chilled punch bowl. Add fruit mixture.

ORANGE ICE PUNCH

5 small oranges

2 quarts orange ice
4 quarts ginger ale, chilled

Makes about 20 punch-cup portions.

Squeeze and strain juice from oranges permitting pulp to pass through strainer.

Put orange ice in chilled punch bowl and add orange pulp, juice and ginger ale.

GOBLIN PUNCH

½ cup sugar   2 cups water
1½ teaspoons grated lemon rind
½ teaspoon cinnamon
2½ cups orange juice
1 cup pineapple juice
6 cups chilled cider
orange slices
whole cloves

Makes about 24 punch-cup portions.

Heat sugar and water to boiling point, stirring to dissolve sugar. Cool.

Add lemon rind, cinnamon and juices to syrup, and let stand in refrigerator for about 3 hours. Strain.

Stir cider into fruit mixture, pour into small punch bowl and place in large Jack-o'-lantern. Serve with orange slices studded with cloves.

BROWN FROST COCKTAIL

1 gallon cider, chilled
2 quarts orange ice

Makes about 25 glasses.

Pour cider into glasses and add a scoop of orange ice to each. Serve at once.

Summer Time
Is Preserving Time

So few things we cook last more than a meal or two. But put up a few boxes of strawberries one warm June day—and in December, there they are in shining glasses on the cupboard shelf, ready to add to a pudding, or to make a whole meal gay. There's no doubt about it, cooks who preserve, pickle and can " have the edge" on those less provident. They "put sunshine away for a rainy day."

In canning, the object should be to preserve, as nearly as possible, the flavor, aroma, shape, color, and food value of the fresh food. All food to be canned must be sterilized and sealed completely. Fruits, rhubarb and tomatoes, are easily sterilized by cooking at the boiling temperature. Non-acid vegetables, and all meats, poultry and fish, contain heat-resisting bacteria (spores) and always should be cooked under pressure in a pressure cooker. *The cooking period in all canning is called processing*.

In this connection, a warning: always examine canned foods for spoilage before using. Discard any that has a foreign odor, cloudiness or softening of the product. It is wise to cook home-canned meats and non-acid vegetables fifteen minutes before using. With either the home-canned or commercially-canned foods, there should be no leakage, no bulging, no flattening of cans nor bulging of rubbers on glass jars.

Before opening tin cans, always wash tops, and use a clean can opener. Food will not spoil if left in open can in refrigerator. However, some foods react slightly with tin after the cans are opened, changing the color and imparting a slight metal taste. Unless the cans are enamel lined, it is advisable to empty berries, corn, meats and fish from the can soon after opening.

Household Methods of Canning

Open-Kettle Method—In this method, food is cooked in an open pan until sterile and done, then packed into hot, *sterilized* jars and sealed immediately. This method requires extreme care in canning to prevent contamination, and is not recommended for fruits, tomatoes or tomato juice because spoilage organisms may get into the jar when the food is transferred from the kettle to jar. *It may be used, however, in preserving, pickling and for fruit juices other than tomato. Fruit juice jars must be inverted immediately after sealing.*

Boiling-Water-Bath Method—In this method, jars are completely covered with boiling water throughout the processing. Put food, precooked or not according to directions, into hot, *clean* jars. Pack loosely. Pour boiling liquid (according to kind of food to be processed) over food being canned. Cover well with liquid, but leave space at top as directed. The food is then processed in boiling water. *This method is used for fruits, tomatoes, tomato juice, rhubarb, pickled vegetables and for acid-canning of vegetables.*

Pressure Cooker Method—This method is used for foods containing heat-resisting bacteria (spores) that take temperatures higher than that of boiling water to make them safe to use. To get these high temperatures, steam under pressure—a pressure cooker—must be used. The food to be canned is packed in hot, *clean* jars as in the Boiling-Water-Bath Method, only processing is done in pressure cooker rather than in boiling water. *This method is the only method recommended for all vegetables (except tomatoes and vegetables canned in acid solution), meats, poultry and fish.*

Canning Equipment and Its Use

Clean Jars for all Canning Methods—Use glass jars and lids, free from cracks and nicks, and new rubbers which are soft, pliable and elastic. Wash in hot soapy water, rinse well. Let stand in hot water until ready to use. Use new lids each time metal lids with sealing compound are used. When ready to fill jars, remove one jar at a time and drain. Adjust rubber before filling jar. Use in boiling-water-bath and pressure cooker methods of canning.

Sterilize Jars for Open-Kettle Method—Place clean, perfect jars and glass covers in water in large pan. Bring to a boil and boil about 20 minutes. Leave jars entirely immersed in water until ready to fill. Remove one jar at a time and drain. Dip new rubbers in boiling water, then adjust on jar just before filling jar. For self-sealing covers, follow directions given with each type.

Water Bath (for fruits, tomato juice and tomatoes)—Any large kettle or wash boiler with tightly fitting cover, deep enough to allow jars to be completely submerged, may be used. Fit bottom with metal or wooden rack to permit water to circulate freely around jars. Special canning kettles, equipped with racks which are used in lowering and raising the jars, are convenient to use. Fill bath with very hot water, about ¾ full. With jar tongs lower hot, filled jars on rack, allowing space between each for water to circulate. Add boiling water to extend 1 or 2 inches above jars. Cover tightly and when water boils vigorously, begin to count time. When time is up lift jars from water. Do not set on cold surface. Seal completely, if necessary.

Pressure Cooker (for non-acid vegetables, meat and poultry)—Several types of steam cookers may be used; always follow manufacturer's directions for operation and care. Each cooker comes equipped with a rack. Add hot water to come just below rack. Place filled jars on rack, allowing space between each for circulation of steam. Adjust cover and fasten securely. Keep petcock open until steam escapes (at least 10 minutes) and all air is exhausted from cooker. Then close petcock and allow pressure to rise until gauge registers the desired point. Begin counting time at this point, adjusting heat to keep constant pressure. When time is up, remove cooker from heat and let stand until gauge registers zero. Then open petcock gradually to allow escape of steam. Allow cooker to cool 15 minutes after petcock has been opened. Then remove cover, opening it away from you. Lift out jars with jar tongs or can lifter and seal completely, if necessary. Leave clamps on self-sealing jars until jars are cold. If pressure fluctuates during processing, some liquid is lost; do not, however, open jars to add liquid. Do not let draft strike jars. If cans are used, follow the steps outlined above, and plunge cans into cold water.

DIRECTIONS FOR CANNING

(Boiling-Water-Bath Method)

FRUITS, TOMATOES, TOMATO JUICE AND VEGETABLES
PROCESSED IN ACID SOLUTION

Wash jars, rubbers and covers (*page* 212).

Prepare canning syrup (*page* 214) or heat water

Prepare just enough material to be canned each time. Select only fresh, sound, ripe fruit or vegetables. Wash in running water, peel or pare, stem or pit, as needed. Dip pared fruits that discolor into a solution made of 2 quarts water and 1 tablespoon each of salt and vinegar.

Drop prepared fruit into syrup and heat to boiling. Drop vegetables into boiling water and reheat to boiling. Save water to fill jars.

Remove one jar at a time from hot water, drain and adjust rubber. Pack food attractively into jar. Fill with hot liquid: with glass cover, fill to within $\frac{1}{2}$ inch of top; with self-sealing cover, fill to within $1\frac{1}{2}$ inches of top. *For vegetables*, add $\frac{1}{2}$ teaspoon salt to each pint jar.

Wipe jars and adjust tops: with screw tops, screw tight, then turn back ½ inch; with glass-topped jars, snap top clamps in place and leave side clamps up; with self-seal covers, screw bands tight or adjust clamps.

With jar tongs place hot jars in water bath or pressure cooker and process (*pages 211–212*) the required time specified for each food. *The processing times given are for altitudes of* 1000 *feet or less*. Increase processing time in boiling-water-bath method 1 minute for each 1000 feet above sea level, if the time is 20 minutes or less, and 2

minutes per 1000 feet if processing time is more than 20 minutes. Add ½ pound to the gauge pressure for each additional 1000 feet in altitude.

Remove jars from cooker, and seal completely, if necessary. Do not remove screw bands or clamps from self-sealing jars until jars are cold. Invert all but self-sealing jars, and cool away from draft. If can leaks, repack in new container and process again.

Store in cool, dry place, protected from strong light.

SUGAR SYRUPS FOR CANNING FRUITS

Bring sugar and water or fruit juice to a boil, stirring until sugar is dissolved. Then boil 5 minutes. For peaches or apricots, add several cracked pits to sugar solution. Boil, then strain. Allow ½ to ¾ cup syrup for each pint jar.

Very Thin Syrup—Use ½ cup sugar to 2 cups water.

Thin Syrup—Use 1 cup sugar to 2 cups water.

Medium Syrup—Use 1 ½ cups sugar to 2 cups water.

Heavy Syrup—Use 2 cups sugar to 2 cups water.

CANNED BERRIES

(Directions for Canning, *pages* 213–214)

1 ½ quarts firm berries: blackberries, blueberries, dewberries, loganberries, raspberries washed, stemmed or capped

¾ cup sugar

Makes about 2 (pint) jars.

Put berries and sugar in layers in kettle, using sugar according to sweetness of fruit. If necessary, add 2 tablespoons water. Cover pan.

Heat slowly to boiling, shaking pan to prevent them from sticking. Pack into hot jars. Cover with hot liquid. Process in boiling-water-bath 15 minutes.

CANNED PEACHES OR APRICOTS

(Directions for Canning, *pages* 213–214)

2½ pounds fruit: about 10 large, sound, ripe peaches; or 20 large, sound, ripe apricots

1½ cups Medium Syrup (*page* 214), **for apricots; Medium or Heavy Syrup** (*page* 214) **for peaches, boiling hot**

Drop fruit (except clingstone peaches) into boiling water about 1 minute to loosen skins, then plunge into cold water. Peel, cut in halves or slices and remove pits. Dip in salt and vinegar solution (*page* 213) to prevent discoloration.

Heat fruit through in syrup, then pack into jars, arranging halves in overlapping layers. Cover with boiling syrup. Process in boiling-water-bath 20 minutes for halved apricots and peaches; 25 minutes for clingstone peaches.

Makes about 2 (pint) jars.

CANNED TOMATOES

(Directions for Canning, *pages* 213–214)

3 pounds or 8 medium-sized, firm, ripe tomatoes

1½ cups tomato juice, boiling hot

1 teaspoon salt

Wash, sort and drop tomatoes into boiling water 1 minute to loosen skins. Plunge into cold water. Peel and remove core. Save any juice to heat with tomato juice.

Pack into hot jars, pressing lightly. Fill with tomato juice and add ½ teaspoon salt to each pint jar. Process in boiling-water-bath 35 minutes.

Makes about 2 (pint) jars.

Pears and tomatoes being prepared according to directions for Boiling - Water - Bath Method (*page* 213).

CANNED KERNEL CORN
(Canning in Pressure Cooker, *page* 211)

10 to 12 small ears of corn: Golden Bantam, Evergreen, Country Gentleman—tender and in milky stage
1 cup boiling water
1 teaspoon salt
2 teaspoons sugar

Can corn immediately after picking. Shuck and remove silk. With sharp knife, cut kernels from cob to ⅔ of their total depth, cutting from tip to butt. Do not scrape cob.

Heat corn, water, salt and sugar to boiling. Pack into hot pint jars to within 1 inch of top. Place in pressure cooker. Exhaust air from cooker 10 minutes, close petcock and process at 10 pounds pressure for 55 minutes.

Makes about 2 (pint) jars.

THE JAM, JELLY AND PICKLE KETTLE

It is the large amount of sugar in preserves and jellies which is responsible for their long keeping qualities. Several terms are used to designate the results obtained from cooking fruit with a large amount of sugar.

Mixtures made of whole small fruits, or chopped or sliced larger fruits, and sugar are called *preserves*, *marmalades*, and *conserves*. Conserves are made of two or more fruits and usually have nuts or raisins added. When fruit is crushed before cooking the result is *jam*.

Fruit butters are made of sieved, cooked fruit; spice is frequently added. And when only the juice of pectin and acid-rich fruit is cooked with sugar, the result is *jelly*. Jellies can also be made of fruits low in acid and pectin, with the use of commercial pectin in liquid or powdered form. Definite directions are given with each commercial product and must be followed.

Pickles and relishes add zest and interest to the simplest meal. Although markets have many different brands and kinds of each, still who would deny that the homemade variety is in a class all by itself?

DIRECTIONS FOR JAM AND JELLY MAKING

Wash glasses and jars. Sterilize and leave in water (*page* 212).

Use sound fresh fruit. It need not be uniform in size or free from blemishes, but discard all damaged parts: for preserves, use ripe fruit; for jellies, use slightly underripe fruit, but with a commercial pectin, use ripe fruit.

Use small amounts of fruit at a time: 2 to 3 quarts berries, or 2 or 3 pounds larger fruit. Prepare fruit for jams; extract juice (*page* 222) for jelly.

Measure prepared fruit or juice and sugar into large saucepan or kettle, and bring to a boil, stirring gently (juice may be boiled 5 minutes before adding sugar). Then boil rapidly to the desired stage. Stir jams as needed to prevent sticking on bottom or burning. If cooked slowly and for a long time, fruit becomes dark and strong in flavor. Remove scum as it collects. A small piece of butter added to juice before it boils will tend to keep the juice from boiling over and will reduce the amount of scum. Test frequently for doneness, especially when bubbles become large and break with a crackling sound and a puff of steam. Use spoon or sheet test, or a thermometer.

Spoon or Sheet Test—Dip spoon into mixture, lift it about 1 foot above kettle and pour contents back into kettle over side of spoon. The final drops form a single stream when mixture is thin; as it becomes thicker, 2 drops appear and form 2 streams; at jellying point, the drops flatten into a sheet and shear away from spoon.

Thermometer Test at Sea Level— Use a candy thermometer, or a chemical one, easily read, and take frequent readings. For preserves or soft jellies, cook to 218° F. to 220° F.; for jellies, cook to 221° F. Always place chemical thermometer on damp cloth on removing from kettle to prevent breaking.

With ladle or large spoon dip mixture into sterilized glasses or jars, filling them to 1/4 inch of tops. Pour hot jelly directly into sterilized glasses.

Seal thin mixtures at once, pouring hot melted paraffin over tops to make a thin layer. When cold and set, cover with another thin layer, turning glass to bring paraffin well up on sides. Seal jars as in canning. For jellies and stiff mixtures, lay clean paper over tops and allow to set. Then cover with paraffin as above.

When cold, adjust metal covers, label and store in cool, dark, dry place.

STRAWBERRY PRESERVES

(Jam and Jelly Making, *pages* 216–217)

2 quarts ripe, large strawberries, washed and hulled
2 pounds or 4½ cups sugar

Arrange berries and sugar in layers in kettle. Let stand for several hours.

Heat to boiling, stirring gently. Boil rapidly 10 minutes. Let stand overnight to plump berries.

Pack berries in hot, sterilized jars or glasses. Reheat syrup to boiling and pour over berries. Seal at once.

Makes about 4 (6-oz.) *glasses.*

RHUBARB AND STRAWBERRY PRESERVES

(Jam and Jelly Making, *pages* 216–217)

1 pound rhubarb, cut in ½-inch lengths
1 quart strawberries, washed and hulled
4 cups sugar

Arrange rhubarb, strawberries and sugar in layers in kettle. Let stand several hours. Heat slowly to boiling, stirring gently. Boil rapidly about 20 minutes, or until thick (218° F.). Turn into glasses. Seal.

Makes about 7 (6-oz.) *glasses.*

Fresh cranberries, lemon, orange and sugar—the makings of a delicious Cranberry Relish (*page* 225).

CITRUS FRUIT MARMALADES

Orange Marmalade:
  4 medium-sized seedless oranges
  2 lemons
Amber Marmalade:
  1 large seedless orange
  1 medium-sized grapefruit
  1 lemon
Kumquat Marmalade:
  1 quart kumquats
  2 lemons
Grapefruit Marmalade:
  2 medium-sized grapefruit
  1 lemon
water   sugar

Makes 12 to 16 (6-oz.) glasses.

Select one combination of fruits. Scrub citrus fruits thorughly, remove all blemishes and discard ends. Cut in very thin slices, stack and cut in halves. Measure into large kettle; for each cup, add 3 cups water. Let stand overnight.

In morning, bring to a boil and boil gently 30 to 40 minutes, or until skins are tender; cover and let stand again overnight.

The next day measure fruit and liquid; for each cup, add ¾ cup sugar. Bring slowly to a boil, then boil rapidly 15 to 25 minutes, or until syrup sheets like jelly (221° F.). Cool 10 minutes, stirring frequently to distribute fruit. Then turn into glasses. Paraffin when cold.

Mint jelly made with mint leaves from your garden—a fresh taste to preserve (*page* 224).

CARROT MARMALADE

3 medium-sized seedless oranges
1 lemon
water
6 medium-sized carrots, scraped
and ground
sugar

Makes about 14 (6-oz.) glasses.

Prepare and cook oranges and lemons as for Citrus Fruit Marmalades.

After standing overnight, add carrots. Then measure fruit and liquid. For each cup of mixture, add ⅔ cup sugar. Proceed as for marmalade.

GRAPE CONSERVE

(Jam and Jelly Making, *pages* 216–217)

4 pounds Concord grapes, washed
and pulped, keeping pulp and
skins separate
sugar
1 seedless orange, scrubbed, thinly
sliced and quartered, discarding
end slices
1 cup seedless raisins
1 cup broken nut meats

Makes about 9 (6-oz.) glasses.

Cook grape pulp 10 minutes. Force through colander to remove seeds. Add pulp and juice to skins.

Measure mixture of skins and pulp into kettle. For each cup, add ⅔ cup sugar.

Add oranges and raisins, and bring to a boil, stirring to dissolve sugar. Boil rapidly 15 minutes, or until thick (219° F.). Add nut meats and boil 3 minutes longer. Turn into glasses. Paraffin when cold.

PEACH CONSERVE

(Jam and Jelly Making, *pages* 216–217)

3 seedless oranges, scrubbed, thinly
sliced and quartered, discarding
end slices
water
8 medium-sized ripe peaches,
peeled and diced (about 2½
cups)
1½ cups diced pineapple, canned
or fresh
4 cups sugar
1 cup blanched almonds

Makes about 6 (6-oz.) glasses.

Stack orange slices, then quarter. Measure into kettle, and for each cup, add 2 cups water. Let stand overnight.

Boil orange mixture rapidly 30 minutes. Add peaches, pineapple and sugar, and bring to a boil, stirring gently. Then boil rapidly about 15 minutes, or until thick (219° F.). Add almonds and boil 5 minutes longer. Turn into glasses. Paraffin when cold.

PLUM OR PEACH BUTTER

(Jam and Jelly Making, *pages* 216–217)

2 pounds red plums, or peaches, washed and stoned
1 cup water   sugar

Makes about 4 (6-*oz.*) *glasses.*

Cook in water until soft. Rub through colander or sieve. For each cup pulp, add ⅔ cup sugar. Boil until thick, stirring frequently. Turn into glasses. Paraffin when cold.

SPICED APPLE BUTTER

(Jam and Jelly Making, *pages* 216–217)

1 quart apples, washed, pared, quartered, cored
1 quart cider vinegar
¾ cup sugar
¾ teaspoon cinnamon
¼ teaspoon cloves
¼ teaspoon allspice

Makes about 4 (6-*oz.*) *glasses.*

Cook apples slowly in vinegar about 1 hour, or until mushy. Do not sieve. Add sugar and spices, and cook until thick, stirring constantly. Turn into glasses. Paraffin when cold.

BERRY JAM

(Jam and Jelly Making, *pages* 216–217)

3 quarts berries: blackberries, dewberries, loganberries, raspberries, or strawberries—washed, stemmed or hulled
sugar

Makes about 10 (6-*oz.*) *glasses.*

Bring berries slowly to a boil, and boil 10 minutes, stirring frequently. For a less seedy jam, rub ½ or more through colander.

Measure pulp and juice into kettle; for each cup, add ⅔ cup sugar. Heat, stirring until sugar is dissolved. Boil rapidly 10 minutes, or until thick (218° F.). Turn into glasses. Seal at once.

RASPBERRY AND CURRANT JAM

(Jam and Jelly Making, *pages* 216–217)

1 quart red currants, washed and stemmed
½ cup water
2 quarts red raspberries, washed and drained
sugar

Makes about 12 (6-oz.) *glasses.*

Mash currants. Add water and bring mixture to a boil. Boil 10 minutes. Force through colander or sieve to remove seeds.

Crush raspberries. Add currant juice and pulp; then measure into kettle. Add ¾ cup sugar for each cup of mixture. Bring to a boil and boil rapidly 10 minutes, or until at jellying stage (221° F.). Turn into glasses. Paraffin when cold.

JELLIES

Good jellies are clear or transparent, free from pulpy particles, scum or bubbles. When turned out on plates, they hold their shape and quiver when moved. They are tender, not sticky nor tough. They cut with sharp lines. They have a fruity flavor and are neither too sweet nor too sour.

JELLY-MAKING FRUITS

Tart apples, crab apples and quinces, blackberries, cranberries, currants and gooseberries, blue grapes and tart plums contain sufficient pectin and acid to make jelly. Select sound, firm fruit, underripe rather than overripe. Wash fruit and remove all damaged or spoiled parts. Remove blossom end from apples and quinces. Cut all hard fruits in pieces; crush soft fruits.

EXTRACTION OF JUICES FOR JELLY

For each pound of prepared fruit, add the following amount of water and cook until soft:

Apples, crab apples, quinces or wild grapes—1 cup water or enough to cover. Cook apples and crab apples, 15 to 20 minutes; quinces, 20 to 30 minutes; wild grapes, 10 to 15 minutes.

Blackberries, currants, gooseberries, Concord grapes—¼ cup water or none. Crush berries and currants to start the flow of juice. Cook each 15 minutes.

Plums—½ cup water. Cook 15 to 20 minutes.

Turn fruit and juice into a jelly bag made of canton flannel or several thicknesses of cheesecloth, dipping bag first in hot water, then wringing it dry. Allow juice to drain into a kettle. Shift pulp occasionally to keep juice flowing. If pressed, juice is likely to be cloudy. Drain cloudy juice again through several thicknesses of cheesecloth, repeating until clear. In pectin-rich fruits, such as currants, berries and sour apples, pulp can be cooked a second and even third time to extract more pectin. Barely cover residue each time with water and cook slowly 30 minutes, stirring occasionally. Drain as for first extract. Keep second and third extracts separate and make into jelly. (See recipes for jellies, *pages* 223 *and* 224.)

TESTING FOR PECTIN

The amount of pectin varies in fruits. To determine the amount in a juice, pour about 1 tablespoon fruit juice and 3 to 5 tablespoons alcohol (ethyl or denatured) into small glass. Turn glass slowly so that all of the fruit juice will come in contact with the alcohol. If pectin comes down in solid, jelly-like mass, juice is rich in pectin. If it is flocculent or light, pectin is scant, so boil down juice to concentrate pectin. Always discard residue in making chemical test.

CURRANT, CRAB APPLE OR GOOSEBERRY JELLY

(Jam and Jelly Making, *pages* 216–217)

2 cups currant, crab apple, * **or gooseberry juice** (*page* 222)
2 cups sugar
* Add 2 tablespoons lemon juice if fruit is ripe

Makes about 6 (6-*oz.*) *glasses.*

Boil juice 5 minutes. Add sugar and stir until juice boils. Boil rapidly to jellying point (221° F.). Long, slow cooking gives a dark, tough jelly, strong in flavor. Remove scum as it collects. Pour into glasses. Paraffin when cold and set.

APPLE, BLACKBERRY, CRANBERRY, PLUM OR QUINCE JELLY

Follow recipe for Currant Jelly (*see above*), only use 1½ cups sugar instead of 2 cups. Add 2 tablespoons lemon juice to both apple and quince juices if extracted from ripe fruits. Makes about 6 (6-oz.) glasses.

MINT JELLY
(Jam and Jelly Making, *pages 216–217*)

2 cups apple juice (*page 222*)
1 cup mint leaves and stems,
   washed
2 tablespoons lemon juice
1 ½ cups sugar
green vegetable coloring

Makes about 5 (6-oz.) glasses.

Prepare apple juice. Crush mint in saucepan with wooden masher. Add applejuice and boil 5 minutes. Then add lemon juice, sugar and small amount of green coloring to tint a delicate shade. Bring to a boil and boil rapidly until syrup sheets like jelly (221° F.). Remove scum. Pour through fine sieve into glasses. Paraffin when cold.

PINEAPPLE MINT JELLY

1 cup unsweetened, canned pine-
   apple juice
¼ cup lemon juice
1 ¾ cups sugar
green vegetable coloring
½ cup commercial liquid pectin
1 tablespoon spearmint extract

Makes about 4 (6-oz.) glasses.

Measure juices and sugar into saucepan; add small amount of green coloring and bring to a rapid boil. Stir in pectin and boil hard ½ minute, stirring constantly.

Remove from heat, add extract, skim and pour into glasses. Paraffin when cold.

CRANBERRY JELLY

1 pound (4 cups) cranberries—
   sort, stem, wash, drain
2 cups water   2 cups sugar

Makes 1 mold or 5 (6-oz.) glasses.

Bring cranberries and water to a boil. Boil, covered, 20 minutes, or until skins are broken. Force through sieve.

Bring pulp to a boil, stir in sugar and boil 4 minutes. Skim. Turn into large mold or glasses. Paraffin glasses when cold.

JELLIED CRANBERRY SAUCE

Follow recipe for Cranberry Jelly, only boil cranberries, water and sugar together 20 minutes; do not force through sieve. *Makes 1 large mold.*

PICKLED PEACHES, PEARS OR CRAB APPLES

1 stick (3-inch) cinnamon
1 teaspoon whole cloves
1 cup vinegar   ½ cup water
2¼ cups granulated sugar or 1
   pound brown sugar
12 to 18 ripe peaches (clingstone),
   or pears, or 2 pounds ripe, red
   crab apples, uniform in size

Makes about 2 (pint) jars.

Tie spices in cheesecloth and drop into kettle with vinegar, water and sugar. Boil 10 minutes.

Prepare ½ of fruit at a time and cook until tender or transparent. Pack in sterilized jars, fill with syrup and seal at once. Remove skins from peaches, leave whole, or cut large ones in halves. Remove stones. Remove blossom ends from pears and peel. Leave stems on small pears. Cut large pears in halves and core.

Remove blossom ends from crab apples. Do not pare. Leave stems on.

CRANBERRY RELISH

1 pound or 1 quart cranberries,
   washed and sorted
1 seedless orange, scrubbed and
   sliced
1 lemon, scrubbed and sliced
2 cups sugar

Makes about 1 quart relish.

Put cranberries through food chopper, using fine knife. Then grind orange and lemon slices, removing all seeds first. Stir in sugar. Chill several hours.

CHERRY OLIVES

1 quart large, sour cherries, perfect and with stems
1 tablespoon salt
1 cup vinegar
cold water

Makes about 2 (pint) jars.

Wash cherries. Pack closely in sterilized pint glass jars. To each pint, add 1 ½ teaspoons salt and ½ cup vinegar. Fill jar with cold water. Seal and turn upside down several times to mix thoroughly. Cherries should stand 2 weeks or longer.

PICKLED MELON RINDS

2 pounds prepared rind: cantaloupe,   watermelon,   citron,
cucumber
brine (2 tablespoons salt to 1 quart
water)
fresh water
1 stick (3-inch) cinnamon
1 teaspoon whole cloves
1 teaspoon whole allspice
4½ cups sugar
2 cups water
2 cups vinegar
1 lemon, scrubbed and sliced

Makes about 2 (pint) jars.

Pare rind and cut off inside flesh and cut
into medium-thin slices, or fancy shapes.
Soak in brine overnight. In morning,
drain, rinse and cook in fresh water about
1 hour, or until tender.

Tie spices in cheesecloth and drop into
kettle with sugar, water, vinegar, and lemon. Boil 5 minutes. Add tender rinds and
cook slowly about 1 ½ hours, or until clear
and syrup is thick. Pack into sterilized
jars and seal at once.

SPICED ORANGE SLICES

5 large seedless oranges, scrubbed
and cut in ¼-inch slices
water
2 sticks (3-inch) cinnamon
1 tablespoon whole cloves
4 cups sugar
1 cup vinegar

Makes about 3 (pint) jars.

Cover orange slices with water and bring
to a boil. Simmer, covered, about 1 ½
hours, or until tender; drain.

Tie spices in cheesecloth. Drop into sugar
and vinegar, boil 5 minutes. Add orange
slices, about ½ at a time. Cover and cook
gently, ½ hour, or until clear, removing
slices carefully after each cooking. Let
slices stand in syrup overnight or 8 hours.
In morning, drain. Cook syrup until thick.
Add orange slices, bring to a boil. Then
transfer carefully to sterilized jars. Seal.

The Home Freezer

With a freezer, you can have food at the peak of perfection. Fruits and vegetables are frozen as soon after harvesting as possible; meats, poultry and fish can be bought at bargain prices for later use. What's more, you can have out-of-season delicacies every month of the year at in-season prices.

A freezer stretches the food dollar in many ways. Certainly it cuts down waste because leftovers can be stored for future use. Scraps of meat can be saved until you have enough for a meat-vegetable casserole. Leftover vegetables and juices can be frozen and made into cream soups on a cold, wintry day. Leftovers can be combined and put through the food grinder, then used as sandwich fillers.

The freezer is a time-saver, too. Sandwiches can be assembly-made and packaged in small quantities for two or three weeks in advance. Casseroles can be made for later use—packaged in 4-ounce containers for the school lunch box. T.V. dinners can be prepared and items individually packaged —all ready to heat as directed and serve on trays. For special times, such as Christmas and Thanksgiving, the home freezer can be your most willing helper. The turkey can be prepared days or weeks in advance— ditto for the stuffing, but *do not stuff any fowl until time of use*. Cookies, cakes and pies can be made and decorated ahead of time. And if you are going to give food goodies for Christmas gifts, not only can you prepare the delicacies at your convenience, but you can pre-wrap them.

These are just a few of the plus values of a home freezer. Freezing food is much easier than canning. And frozen food retains the fresh flavor, color and texture better than your canned ones. There is little vitamin loss in the freezing process, and fruits and vegetables may have a higher vitamin content than the not-always-so-fresh fruits and vegetables

227

available in the market. With a freezer, you can have at all times a supply of the best-tasting, most nutritious and varied fresh and prepared foods at the least cost and effort to you in terms of time, money and labor.

THINGS TO REMEMBER

The quality of food to be frozen should be top grade. Freezing may slightly improve the flavor of some foods, but it can't put into them flavor that never was there. Do not waste freezer space on inferior foods or on ready-cooked foods that do not freeze well.

Freezing does not sterilize food. Foods cooked before freezing are often more subject to spoilage when thawed than are fresh foods. Your home freezer should register 0° F. before you attempt to use it for any freezing of foods.

Food must be thoroughly chilled before putting into freezer. The method of chilling varies for different foods, so read directions carefully for each food to be frozen. Better safe than poor eating or spoiled food later!

Proper packaging is a must.

Label carefully and keep a handy inventory of frozen foods. The label should include name of food, with weight (for meats, vegetables, and so forth), number of servings, date of freezing and last date when food may be used with safety.

Follow reheating directions. This is important in keeping the original flavor, texture and nutritional value of the food.

TIPS ON FREEZING PRECOOKED AND PREPARED FOODS

It is not wise to freeze precooked and prepared food unless you have some plan for its use. Freezing will not help its quality and prolonged storage will lead to deterioration. When food is reheated, there may be some loss in food value. In other words, precooked foods—casseroles and other prepared dishes—should be used within a reasonable length of time.

Spices and seasoning change the flavor of the made dish when frozen—the stronger ones, such as onion and garlic, get stronger; the milder ones, such as salt, tend to fade. Use double-action baking powder for frozen batters. Use only pure extracts; synthetic ones get bitter.

In general, do not freeze a combination of foods on a tray. Rather, package individual servings and place them in a carton. When you are ready to use your combination, the relishes and desserts can be thawing while meat and vegetables are being heated.

WHAT TO FREEZE

BREADS—YEAST AND BAKING POWDER

Breads (with the exception of Steamed Brown Bread) are baked before freezing. They should be baked to light brown and cooled to room temperature before freezing. The most satisfactory breads for freezing are:

Yeast Rolls—Standard Rolls, *page 72*, Parker House, *page 71*, Clover Leaf, *page 71*, Coffee Bread, *page 73*, Christmas Bread, *page 275*.

Baking Powder Biscuits, *page 66*, Butterscotch Rolls, *page 68*, Cornbread, *page 65*.

Date-Nut Bread, *page 69*, Nut Bread, *page 69*, Orange Bread, *page 69*.

Steamed Brown Bread, *page 68*.

Griddlecakes, *page 40*, Waffles, *page 42*.

See page 230 for Packaging, Storing and Reheating Bread and Rolls.

CAKES—ANGEL, BUTTER, CHIFFON, FRUIT AND SPONGE

The air-leavened cakes, such as Angel Food Cake, *page 179*, Sponge Cake, *page 182*, and Chiffon Cake, *page 181*, freeze particularly well, whole or in meal-size portions. Fruit Cake, *page 272*, improves with freezing and will not crumble when sliced after it is thawed. All cakes must be completely cool before freezing. They may be frozen frosted or unfrosted. If frosted, use confectioners' sugar or fudge-type frosting, the corn syrup or honey recipes and fruit fillings. Don't use frosting containing egg white or cream fillings. Frosted cakes should be frozen before wrapping to prevent damaging the soft icing. Put in freezing compartment for a couple of hours, then wrap.

See page 231 for Packaging, Storing and Thawing Cakes.

PACKAGING, STORING AND REHEATING BREAD AND ROLLS

Food	How Packaged	Storage Time	To Prepare for Table
Bread, Yeast	Freezer aluminum foil is excellent for packaging all breads and rolls.	Not more than 6 months	Thaw in wrapping at room temperature for 1 hour, or warm in preheated 400° F. (hot) oven if wrapped in aluminum foil, or in 300° F. (slow) oven if wrapped in cellophane, 10 to 25 minutes.
Steamed Brown Bread	See Yeast Bread.	Not more than 6 months	Thaw at room temperature for about 1 hour, then reheat in wrappings as above.
Baking Powder Biscuit	See Yeast Bread.	2 to 4 months	Do not thaw. Heat in foil in 375° F. (moderate) oven 30 to 40 minutes.
Rolls, Yeast (all varieties)	See Yeast Bread.	Not more than 6 months	Do not thaw. Heat in foil in 375° F. (moderate) oven 30 to 40 minutes
Griddlecakes and Waffles	Freezer aluminum foil, separated by heavy waxed paper.	1 month	Remove wrapping. Heat, unthawed, in pop-up toaster set on "light" degree. Put through toasting twice to heat thoroughly. Or set on cooky sheet and heat in 300° F. (slow) oven 15 minutes.

PACKAGING, STORING AND THAWING CAKES

Food	How Packaged	Storage Time	To Prepare for Table
Butter Cakes	Polyethylene laminated or aluminum foil, or polyethylene bags. Seal carefully. Store whole cakes in box or carton after wrapping to avoid crushing.	Not more than 4 months	Remove wrappings if iced so frosting will not soften and stick to paper. Let stand at room temperature for about 2 hours for whole cake. Serve at once.
Angel, Chiffon and Sponge Cakes	See Butter Cakes.	4 to 6 months	Thaw in wrapping on a rack at room temperature for 2 to 4 hours. Allow cake to come to room temperature and serve at once.
Fruit Cake	See Butter Cakes.	1 year	Thaw in wrappings. Requires about 2 hours for 2 pounds of cake.

Parties from your freezer. See directions for freezing cakes (*page* 229) and table above for packaging, storing and thawing.

DESSERTS—FROZEN PIES AND PUDDINGS

Here you will find your freezer a real convenience with a yield of delicious desserts for every occasion. Frozen desserts keep in good condition for 2 to 3 months. Whipped, dry skimmed milk may be substituted for heavy cream in ice cream and mousse recipes. Pies may be frozen before or after baking, but most tasters vote for after baking. Do not freeze pies baked with frozen fruit filling. In making fruit pies for storing, add thickening up to 4 tablespoons of cornstarch as the freezing process increases the "runniness" of the pie. Do not freeze pies made with custard or with meringue topping. Some of the most satisfactory desserts for freezing are:

Frozen Desserts—Ice cream, *page* 159, Mousse, *page* 161, and Sherbet, *page* 161.

Pies (without whipped cream)—Orange Chiffon, *page* 167, Fruit, *pages* 167–168, and Pumpkin, *page* 168.

Puddings—Plum, *page* 271, Rice, *page* 151, Tapioca, *page* 151.

CASSEROLES: READY-COOKED MEATS, FISH AND POULTRY

When you make your favorite casserole for freezing, use as little fat as possible. You may add ¼ teaspoon gelatin to each quart of white sauce if you decrease butter. Cool rapidly by setting pan in ice water. Stir, but do not beat. Omit hard-cooked eggs and cooked potatoes from your casserole dishes. Vegetables should be slightly under-cooked. Remove salt pork or bacon, if used. Where thawing is called for, do this in refrigerator. *Do not refreeze these products.* Some of your choices can be:

Casseroles—Shrimp and Rice, *page* 56, Baked Macaroni and Cheese, *page* 57, Spaghetti Mélange, *page* 57, Chicken Pot Pie, *page* 101, Chop Suey, *page* 264, Chili Con Carne, *page* 284, Rabbit Casserole, *page* 301, Hungarian Goulash, *page* 282, Beef Stew, *page* 90

Meats—Kebabs, *page* 292, Meat Loaf, *page* 88, Ham, *page* 93

Poultry—Roasted, *page* 100

Fish—Baked or Broiled, *page* 104, Baked Mackerel, *page* 105, Salmon Loaf, *page* 110.

See pages 234–235 for Packaging, Storing and Thawing Casseroles, Meats, Fish and Poultry.

PACKAGING, STORING AND THAWING DESSERTS

Food	How Packaged	Storage Time	To Prepare for Table
Ice Cream, Mousse and Sherbet (Crank-type gives best results)	Rigid container or individual covered cups. Store in an overwrap or plastic bag. Mix Mousse and pour into container.	1 to 2 months	Let stand in refrigerator until soft enough to cut or scoop. Do not refreeze.
Pies	Polyethylene or freezer-weight foil; polyethylene and stockinette; or in laminated paper.	Baked, 4 months. Unbaked, 2 months	Place, unwrapped, in 375° F. (moderate) oven about 45 minutes. For unbaked, remove wrappings and cut vent holes in upper crust. Bake without thawing, 15 to 20 minutes in 475° F. (very hot) oven, then at 375° F. (moderate) oven 20 to 30 minutes, or until done.
Rice and Tapioca Puddings	Rigid container. Leave ½-inch head space. Cover surface with waxed paper cut to fit. Or use individual covered cups.	2 weeks	Thaw in container in refrigerator.
Plum Pudding	Container as above. Wrap in plastic bag.	6 to 8 months	Reheat in steam.

PACKAGING, STORING AND THAWING CASSEROLES, MEATS, FISH AND POULTRY

Food	How Packaged	Storage Time	To Prepare for Table
Creamed meat, poultry and fish	Use rigid wide-mouth container or glass jars made for freezing. Package in layers (if large amount) in casserole. Separate layers with double fold locker paper. Cover with single thickness paper cut to fit top. Leave ½-inch top space in carton. If casserole is used, seal tightly.	Not more than 4 to 6 months	Heat from frozen state in top of double boiler or in casserole in 350° F. (moderate) oven 25 to 45 minutes. Do not let stand at room temperature.
Baked Beans, Spaghetti, Macaroni, Stew and Chop Suey	Glass jars or casseroles, polyethylene bags, or rigid containers.	Not more than 6 months	If packaged in jars, set in cold water until soft enough to move. Place in covered saucepan, add potatoes (if called for) and heat. Or bake in casserole in 350° F. (moderate) oven 1 hour. Do not let stand at room temperature.

Food	How Packaged	Storage Time	To Prepare for Table
Baked and broiled meat, fish and poultry	Freezer-weight aluminum foil or plastic bag; or rigid container. (Remove roasted meat and poultry from bones.)	2 to 4 months	Thaw in refrigerator 5 to 6 hours. Then make into meat pie, hash; or heat chunks in broth, thicken gravy and add freshly cooked vegetables. Allow 20 minutes per pound in 350° F. (moderate) oven for reheating solid piece.
Meat and fish loaves	Aluminum foil or polyethylene bags.	1 to 2 months	Thaw in refrigerator, wrapped, for 1 to 2 hours. Bake in 450° F. (very hot) oven 15 minutes, then 350° F. (moderate) oven until done.

Proper packaging is a must: freezer weight aluminum foil, heavy waxed paper, rigid wide-mouthed plastic containers, glass jars, polyethylene bags, freezer trays.

POTATOES

Baked and Stuffed, *page* 122, Scalloped, *below*, or Shoe String Potatoes, *page* 123, freeze well, so you can always have a supply of ready-to-serve potatoes on hand in your freezer for an extra or unexpected guest. Potatoes in combination dishes do not freeze well. Add potatoes to these dishes when preparing to serve them. For scalloped potatoes, prepare and bake until not quite done and pale in color. Leave in baking dish and cool before freezing.

PACKAGING, STORING AND THAWING POTATOES

Food	How Packaged	Storage Time	To Prepare for Table
Baked and Stuffed	Plastic bags if halves are put together.	7 to 10 days	Bake from frozen state in 375° F. (moderate) oven until thoroughly heated and lightly browned.
French Fried	Rigid container or plastic bag.	1 month	Spread on cooky sheet. Heat in 475° F. (very hot) oven 10 to 20 minutes. Watch carefully.
Scalloped	Casserole or wide-necked jar.	2 weeks	Place in cold oven. Set heat at 350° F. (moderate) oven and bake 45 to 60 minutes until thoroughly heated and top is lightly browned.
Sweet, mashed	Plastic bag or rigid container.	6 to 8 months	Heat in saucepan or double boiler.

SOUPS AND SAUCES

Soups with milk base do not freeze satisfactorily. Do not add pastes or rice before freezing. Make these additions when you reheat to serve. Whenever possible, concentrate soups as much as possible by adding less liquid in preparing, or by cooking down to less volume. Don't overseason for freezing. Bouillon, *page* 80, Chicken Broth, *page* 305, Dried Lima Bean Soup, *page* 280, Split Pea Soup, *page* 280, and Leek and Potato Soup, *page* 52, are good starters for you.

Either dessert or meat sauces freeze satisfactorily. Fluffy Berry Sauce, *page* 164, Butterscotch Sauce, *page* 163, Chocolate Fudge Sauce, *page* 163, Barbecue Sauce, *page* 265, and Cocktail Sauce, *page* 78, are fine when frozen. But don't try Cucumber Sauce or sauces heavy with mayonnaise for your freezing projects.

All soups and sauces must be thoroughly chilled before freezing. Freeze in ice cube tray and then put cubes in carton or plastic bag; or use glass jars, leaving top space for expansion. Do not keep more than 4 months. Heat from frozen state. If concentrated soup, add hot liquid to reconstitute.

SANDWICHES—LUNCH BOX TYPE

Sandwiches may be stored for 2 to 4 weeks. For best results, use day-old bread. Spread with softened butter or butter spread, *page* 195. Omit crisp vegetables and hard-cooked eggs unless chopped *very* fine. Wrap individually or in pairs in polyethylene or freezer foil. Do not crush or pack too tightly. If you wrap individually, all you will have to do for your school lunch box, is pick out an assortment of your choice and place in the box. Sandwiches thaw in 3 to 4 hours—and will be thawed to eating perfection by noon.

OPEN-FACE SANDWICHES

The canapés made with only one piece of bread and no topping—must be made on very thin pieces of day-old bread cut in desired shape with cooky cutter. Spread butter to very edge of bread. (Save bread and crusts for bread crumbs for casseroles or croquettes.) Place buttered shapes on cooky sheet, turn oven to 250° F. (very slow) and toast bread until golden brown. Watch carefully. Top with sandwich filling of your choice. Pinwheel Sandwiches, *page* 197, and Toasted Rolled Sandwiches, *page* 198, are two good starters for canapé freezing. Spread out and freeze. Pack in layers in top-opening box. Separate layers with heavy waxed paper cut to size of container. (Save cake boxes or rigid containers for this.) Place an assortment ready for serving in each container. To serve, arrange on trays ½ to 1 hour in advance of serving. Storage time for these sandwiches is 1 to 2 weeks.

TIPS ON PREPARING FRESH FOODS

Meats, Fish and Poultry. Select a good quality of fresh meat, fish or poultry. Meat should be firm, of good color and not too fat. Fish should be fresh, cleaned, scaled, dressed and washed. Wash oysters in water for 5 to 10 minutes; do not cook. Remove and discard heads of shrimps. Package and freeze shrimp meat in the shells without cooking. Poultry should be plump with well-fleshed breasts and legs (the new broad-breasted varieties are excellent). Or if you butcher your own meat and fowl, consult manufacturer or local farm adviser for preparation directions.

If laminated paper is used for wrapping, place waxed side next to meat, and use 2 sheets. In stacking steaks or chops in a package, be sure to use a piece of locker paper or freezer foil between each one for easy separation. Place the meat in the center of the paper and match edges, folding toward center. Make a drugstore wrap of at least 3 folds. If cellophane or pliofilm is used for the first wrap, an outer wrap of heavier paper or stockinette must be used to prevent freezer burn. Fasten securely with twine or freezer tape. Label and give date of freezing and last date of safe use, type of meat and number of servings.

To prepare poultry for freezing, see Dressing of Poultry, *page 95*. Wrap giblets separately. Omit liver or wrap separately and use within 3 months. Chill meat rapidly.

Long storage impairs quality so plan to use *first* food that has been stored longest. Be sure to note that the storage time of most cooked and prepared foods is much shorter than that of uncooked foods. The following storage times are a guide only and should be checked against the directions for your particular home freezer:

Ground meats	1 to	3 months
Pork, fish and lamb	3 to	6 months
Beef, veal and chicken	9 to	12 months
Turkeys	3 to	6 months

Fruits and Vegetables. Select only fresh, firm, fully mature, colorful and flavorsome fruits for freezing. All fruits and berries, except rhubarb and strawberries, require special treatment before freezing. This is necessary to hold the color, flavor and nutritive value during the storage period. Wash fruit in cold water and use syrup, dry sugar or pectin pack according to manufacturer's directions. Most fruits have the best color and flavor if served just before they are completely defrosted. They should be thawed in the sealed container as contact with air will change their color. To thaw a 1-pound package, leave in refrigerator 6 to 8 hours; or leave at room temperature 2 to 3 hours; or place in pan of cold water ½ to 1 hour.

All vegetables, except peppers and pimientos, should be blanched or cooked before freezing for the same reasons. Select young, barely mature vegetables, harvested if possible the morning you are to freeze. Wash in cold water, cut and sort for size. Blanch, being sure that water is at a rolling boil and that you have enough water to cover vegetable. For nonleafy vegetables, use about 2 quarts of water per pound; for leafy vegetables, use about 3 quarts per pound. Work in small amounts—not more than 2 pounds of vegetable at one time. Start counting time for blanching when the

water comes to a boil again. Chill quickly and thoroughly in iced water or cold running water. *Do not pack while warm.* (Break or cut beans in center to test for coldness.) Remove from water, drain and pat dry. Then package.

If you want to purée a vegetable, blanch the vegetable according to directions, cool and put through a puréer or food chopper. (Heat tomatoes to 165° F. either before or after puréeing.) Chill quickly and package for freezing.

Vegetables lose quality if allowed to thaw before cooking (except corn on cob and some blocks of frozen greens). Read Vegetable Cookery, *page* 113. Allow ¼ to ⅓ cup boiling water for a 12-ounce package of vegetables.

For your purposes, it would be well to freeze fruits and vegetables in amounts for one family serving—2 to 4 portions. Be sure to check the vegetable blanching time listed below with the manufacturer's directions for your freezer.

See pages 240–242 for directions for Freezing Fruit and Vegetables.

DIRECTIONS FOR FREEZING FRUITS

Fruit	Preparation	Sugar
Apples	Peel, core and slice. Make into applesauce, or syrup scald for 2 minutes.	Syrup scald: 1 cup sugar to 1 quart water. Bring to a boil.
Berries (except strawberries)	Wash. Pick over.	Cold syrup: 2 cups sugar to 1 quart water. Dry sugar as desired, or freeze without sugar.
Cantaloupe	Cut in pieces and remove seeds. Pack in cold syrup.	Cold syrup: 2 cups sugar to 1 quart water.
Cherries, sweet	Wash. Pit if desired. Pack in cold syrup.	Cold syrup: 2 to 3 cups sugar to 1 quart water.
Peaches	Peel without scalding. Cut into quarters, halves or slices directly into syrup.	Cold syrup: 2 to 3 cups sugar to 1 quart water.
Strawberries	Wash. Pick over. Remove hulls. Crush with sugar or slice. Place a few whole berries in carton for garnish.	Dry sugar: 1 pound sugar to 4 to 6 pounds berries.
Mixed Fruits	Use any combination. Prepare each fruit separately according to directions. Mix. Pack in cold syrup.	Cold syrup: 2 to 3 cups sugar to 1 quart water.

DIRECTIONS FOR FREEZING VEGETABLES

Vegetable	Preparation	Blanching Time
Artichokes	Pull off outer leaves and trim stem. Wash.	8 to 10 minutes in boiling citric acid solution (3 teaspoons citric acid crystals to 2 quarts water).
Asparagus	Wash and sort for size.	Small stalks, 2 minutes; medium stalks, 3 minutes; large stalks, 4 minutes.
Beans, snap, green or wax	Wash and string. Cut or break into 1-inch pieces, or French-cut.	3 minutes.
Broccoli, flowerets 1 ½-inches in diameter	Wash and cut to size.	3 minutes.
Brussels sprouts	Trim off outer leaves. Wash and sort for size.	Small heads, 3 minutes; medium heads, 4 minutes; large heads, 5 minutes.
Carrots	Wash and cut into desired size.	Whole small, 5 minutes; diced or sliced, 2 minutes; lengthwise strips, 2 minutes.
Cauliflower, flowerets 1-inch in diameter	Wash and break to size.	3 minutes.
Corn, sweet, on the cob.	Husk and de-silk.	Small ears (1 ¼-inch or less in diameter), 7 minutes; medium ears (1 ¼ to 1 ½-inches in diameter), 9 minutes; large ears (over 1 ½-inches in diameter), 11 minutes

DIRECTIONS FOR FREEZING VEGETABLES

Vegetables	Preparation	Blanching Time
Corn, sweet, yellow, cut	Husk and de-silk. Blanch and chill. Cut from cob.	1 ½ minutes (on cob).
Peas, green	Remove pods. Sort for size.	1 ½ minutes.
Squash, summer	Wash and cut into ½-inch pieces.	3 minutes.

The Home
Candy Maker

Candy making is fascinating work. A seemingly simple sugar and liquid mixture can be transformed into a soft, creamy fondant or fudge, a chewy caramel a "pully" taffy, or shining, crisp brittle. And the beauty of it is that the home candy maker can manage every one of them, fudge to brittle, "with the greatest of ease." Better start with the simpler ones, however!

Of course, the interesting thing about all of the different types of candies is that, although they appear to be so very different after they are made, the real difference lies largely in the degree to which they were cooked. You can determine these differences in degree either by the old and more commonly used cold-water test, or by the modern, accurate, and simpler thermometer test. A combination of both is ideal.

Equipment for candy making includes: a 2-quart, deep saucepan with cover, so deep that the mixture does not boil over; a fork wrapped with cloth and moistened slightly, for washing down the sides of pan as crystals form; a candy thermometer, with adjustable clip, or a chemical thermometer measuring degrees of temperature as high as 350° to 450° F.; a cup, spoon and cold water for the cold-water test; a wooden spoon for beating, measuring cup and spoons, spatula, platter or pans.

PROCEDURE FOR MAKING CANDY

1. Stir until mixture boils and sugar is dissolved.
2. Boil, covered, 2 to 3 minutes to dissolve crystals on sides of pan.
3. Attach thermometer to side of saucepan. The bulb must be covered in the syrup, but it must not touch the bottom of the pan.
4. Boil, uncovered, to the desired degree. Use combination thermometer and cold-water test.
5. Keep syrup boiling or bubbling over surface. If it boils too slowly, the candy is likely to be sticky; if it boils too fast, the candy is apt to be sugary.
6. Do not stir fondant or most fudge candies, or the syrup for divinity.
7. Stir thicker candies such as caramels, taffies and hard candies occasionally at first, then constantly.
8. On a rainy or humid day, boil mixture to higher degree than on a clear, dry day. With corn syrup, molasses, or honey, cook mixture to a slightly higher temperature than you would a straight sugar solution.
9. Pour fondant from pan. Do not scrape sides or bottom.
10. Cool fudge quickly to 110° F. before beating. It is more likely to sugar if beaten at once.

TEMPERATURES AND TESTS FOR COOKING CANDIES

Thermometer test: take reading by having the eye on a level with the degree indicated on the scale.

Cold-water test: remove pan from fire. Drop about ½ teaspoon syrup to be tested into small cup or bowl of very cold water. Pick up cooled mass with fingers, and bring it out of the water—and judge consistency according to chart following.

Candy	Temperature Degrees F.	Cold-Water Test
Syrup	230–234	Spins 2-inch thread
Fudge	234–240	Very soft to soft ball
Fondant	234–240	Medium-soft ball
Caramels	244–248	Firm ball, holds shape
Divinity	250–266	Hard ball, plastic, chewy
Pulled Candies	270–290	Crack, heavy threads
Brittle	300–310	Hard crack, brittle
Caramel	338	Very hard—liquid becomes brown

Don't forget about altitude: The boiling points of water and candy go down as altitude increases, so that they are lower at high altitudes than at sea level. Cook the syrup about 1 degree F. lower for each increase of 500 feet in elevation.

TUTTI-FRUTTI SLICES

1 cup seedless raisins
1 cup pitted dates
1 cup figs
½ cup nut meats
½ cup candied orange peel
1 cup cornflakes
1 tablespoon lemon juice

Wash and dry fruit. Put through food chopper with nuts, orange peel and cornflakes. Add lemon juice and knead well. Shape into rolls, 1 ½ inches thick. Chill. Cut in ⅓-inch slices. Or make into small balls.

Makes about 48 slices or balls.

FONDANT

Plain fondant is a snowy white, creamy candy with sugar crystals, so small that they are not perceptible on the tongue or palate. Fondant is moist, soft, pliable and easily molded—not dry and crumbly. It is rather sweet when eaten plain. It is used as the foundation for many candies such as bonbons, centers, kisses, fruit and nut loaves, patties and fondant-covered candies.

Utensils Needed	*Order of Work*
Two-quart saucepan; large platter; measuring cup and spoon; tablespoon, wooden spoon, spatula, shallow cup or small bowl; candy thermometer, if possible; cheesecloth strip for swab, fork; cake rack.	1. Assemble the utensils and ingredients. Wind cheesecloth strip around fork to make swab. Dip in water, then squeeze.
	2. Measure ingredients into saucepan, stirring until sugar is dissolved.
	3. Adjust thermometer to pan, if used, when removing cover from pan.
	4. Boil to soft-ball stage, testing with ice water and taking thermometer readings frequently. Wipe off all crystals.
	5. Pour into platter and cool to lukewarm.
	6. Beat, then knead.
Makes about 1 pound fondant.	7. Store, covered, for several days to ripen.

RECIPE

2 cups sugar
1 cup water
2 tablespoons light corn syrup, or ⅛ teaspoon cream of tartar

Bring sugar, water and syrup to a boil in saucepan, stirring constantly until sugar dissolves. Boil, covered, 3 minutes to dissolve crystals that may collect on sides.

Boil, uncovered, without stirring, to soft-ball stage (238° F.), wiping sides of pan with damp cloth as crystals appear. Pour out on rinsed platter. Cool on rack.

½ teaspoon vanilla or other flavoring

When platter can be held in hand or when syrup is lukewarm (110° F.), stir with wooden spoon until mass becomes snowy white and creamy, and is cool enough to handle. Add flavoring and work in hands until fondant is smooth.

COCONUT, NUT OR FRUIT KISSES

1 cup Fondant (*page* 246)
1 teaspoon grated orange rind, or
   ¼ teaspoon almond extract
1 to 2 drops vegetable coloring, if
   desired
⅓ cup shredded coconut, chopped
   nuts, or candied fruit

Makes about ⅔ pound candy.

Melt fondant over hot water (185° F.). Add flavoring and coloring to tint a delicate shade, if desired. Stir in coconut, nuts or fruit.

If thin, cool slightly. Drop from tip of teaspoon in mounds on waxed paper.

COCONUT FONDANT BALLS

1 cup Fondant (*page* 246)
½ teaspoon vanilla
⅓ cup shredded coconut
⅔ cup green tinted coconut, or
   toasted coconut

Makes about 22 balls.

Knead vanilla and white coconut into fondant. Shape into small balls.

Roll balls in coconut, tinted delicate green, or in toasted coconut.

TINTED COCONUT

To tint coconut, use vegetable coloring (paste, powder or liquid). Dilute a small amount in a small amount of water (2 to 4 tablespoons) to the desired shade. Sprinkle over coconut, scattered on paper. With fingers rub coloring carefully and evenly into coconut. Always tint a delicate shade. Use for decorative purposes in candies and on cakes.

TOASTED COCONUT

To toast coconut, scatter it in a thin layer over baking sheet. Place in 400° F. (hot) oven until delicately browned, stirring frequently to brown evenly. Use in candies, frostings, puddings and ice creams.

STUFFED DATES AND PRUNES

dates
prunes

Fondant (*page* 246)
walnuts   powdered sugar

Wash fruit. Steam prunes about 5 minutes in strainer over hot water. Remove pits by cutting length of fruit. Dry.

Stuff with fondant or nuts. Pat into shape and roll in sugar. Store in covered container.

DIVINITY CANDY

(Making Candy, *pages 244–245*)

2 cups sugar
dash of salt
½ cup corn syrup
½ cup water

Combine sugar, salt, syrup and water in saucepan. Bring to boiling point, stirring constantly until sugar is dissolved.

Cover and boil slowly about 3 minutes to dissolve any crystals on sides of pan. Then boil, uncovered and without stirring, to hard-ball stage (266° F.), washing away with damp cloth any crystals that collect.

2 egg whites, stiffly beaten
¾ teaspoon vanilla
1 cup chopped nut meats

Just before syrup is done, beat egg whites until stiff. Then pour hot syrup slowly over egg whites, beating constantly. Add vanilla and continue beating until candy holds its shape when dropped from spoon.

Coconut-Cherry Divinity,
  substitute for nuts:
1 cup shredded coconut
½ cup candied cherries, sliced

Makes about 25 (1 ½-inch) squares.

Stir in nuts and turn into slightly buttered 8-inch square pan. Cut in squares when cold. Or drop fondant from teaspoon on waxed paper.

PANOCHA

(Chocolate Fudge, *page 249*)

2 cups firmly packed brown sugar
dash of salt
¾ cup rich milk
1 tablespoon butter
½ teaspoon vanilla
½ to ¾ cup broken pecans, English or black walnuts, or peanuts, shredded coconut, cut marshmallows, or chopped raisins or dates

Makes about 18 large pieces.

Boil brown sugar, salt and milk to soft-ball stage (238° F.). The temperature is higher than for fudge. Add butter and vanilla, but do not stir. Cool to lukewarm (110° F.).

Beat until creamy. Stir in nuts, coconut, marshmallows or fruit, one or a combination of several. Turn at once into buttered loaf pan. Cut in squares when firm. Or drop creamy candy from spoon in mounds on waxed paper.

CHOCOLATE FUDGE

2 squares chocolate
2 cups granulated sugar, or 1 cup
  firmly packed brown sugar and
  1 cup granulated sugar
1 tablespoon light corn syrup *
dash of salt
¾ cup milk
2 tablespoons butter
1 teaspoon vanilla

* Omit syrup with brown sugar

Makes about 18 (1 ½-inch) squares.

Heat chocolate, sugar, syrup, salt and milk in saucepan, stirring constantly until chocolate melts, sugar dissolves and mixture boils. Boil, covered, 3 minutes Then boil, uncovered, to soft-ball stage (234°–240° F.), stirring occasionally. Add butter and vanilla. Set pan in cold water until fudge is lukewarm (110° F.), or pan feels warm.

Beat until creamy and fudge loses its gloss. Turn into buttered loaf pan. When firm, cut in squares.

NUT, MARSHMALLOW, COCONUT OR FRUIT FUDGE

Add ½ to ¾ cup of one of the following to creamy fudge just before turning out into buttered pan: broken nut meats; marshmallows, cut in pieces; shredded coconut; seedless raisins, or chopped dates or figs.

Let's make fudge! Rich, creamy chocolate fudge with nuts can be party entertainment and party food as well.

MOLASSES TAFFY

(Making Candy, *pages 244–245*)

1 cup granulated sugar
½ cup firmly packed brown sugar
2 cups molasses
¾ cup water
¼ cup butter
⅛ teaspoon baking soda
¼ teaspoon salt

Bring sugars, molasses and water to a boil in deep saucepan, stirring constantly.

Boil until a small amount of mixture dropped into cold water is hard, cracks, almost brittle (270° F.), stirring frequently.

Remove from heat, and stir in butter, soda and salt until just mixed. Pour into buttered large pan, let stand until cold enough to handle.

With fingers, oiled slightly, pick up taffy into ball and pull with fingers until it becomes firm and light in color. Stretch out into long rope, twist slightly and cut with scissors into 1-inch lengths, dipping scissors in cold water.

NOTE: For a party, divide cooled taffy into several parts for pulling. For storing, keep cut pieces separate and wrap each in waxed paper.

Makes about 50 pieces or 2 pounds.

POPCORN-PEANUT BALLS

5 cups salted popped corn
2 cups salted peanuts
½ cup light molasses
½ cup light corn syrup
1½ tablespoons vinegar
2 tablespoons butter

Put popped corn in large bowl. Sprinkle lightly with salt and stir in peanuts.

Boil molasses, syrup and vinegar to very hard-ball or crack stage (270° F.), stirring occasionally to prevent burning.

Remove from heat. Stir in butter, and pour over corn and peanuts. Cool slightly. With lightly buttered fingers shape into balls. Cool on waxed paper.

Makes 8 to 10 balls.

NUT BRITTLE

1 cup broken nuts, or chopped, roasted peanuts
dash of salt   2 cups sugar

Makes about 1 pound brittle.

Put nuts in well-buttered 9-inch square pan and sprinkle with salt.

Melt sugar in heavy frying pan over low heat, stirring constantly until golden brown. Pour over nuts. Mark in squares while warm; or break when brittle.

ROCKY ROAD CANDY

12 marshmallows, cut in quarters
½ cup broken nut meats

½ pound sweet or dipping chocolate, melted
Makes about 16 pieces.

Cut marshmallows, wetting scissors between cuts. Scatter, with nut meats, on bottom of buttered pan.

Melt chocolate over hot water. Then pour over nuts and marshmallows. When cool, cut in squares.

SALTED NUTS

1 pound almonds,* cashews, pecans, walnuts or peanuts *
2 teaspoons melted butter or salad oil
salt

* Blanch, if desired

Sprinkle nuts with butter or oil, then salt. Mix well, then spread in shallow pan.

Bake in 400° F. (hot) oven 10 minutes, stirring frequently. Drain on paper.

All Alone
for the Day

Let us suppose that your mother has taken a full day off, that you are in charge of a younger brother or sister, and that everybody, including your father, will be home for meals, as usual. Here is your opportunity to demonstrate all you have learned of cooking, meal planning and management, up to date.

The following proposed schedule of work with menus may help you with your task of meal planning and preparation, as well as with the working in of the daily chores.

Breakfast–Luncheon

Orange Juice
Scrambled Eggs, 37   Crisp Bacon, 40
Toasted Raisin Bread   Butter
Coffee, 33   Milk

★

One-Dish Soup, 253
Assorted Vegetable Straws, 136
Rich Meringue Pudding, 254
Milk or Chocolate, 35

Dinner

Stuffed Flank Steak, 254
Brown Gravy, 86
Baked Potatoes, 122   Butter
Buttered String Beans
Green Salad Bowl, 139   Pickles
Rye Bread   Butter
Strawberry Shortcake, 255
Whipped Cream
Tea, 34   Fruit Juice

SCHEDULE OF WORK FOR MORNING

1. Set the breakfast table (*page* 24).
2. Prepare breakfast and serve it.
3. Telephone market order early.

4. Wash dishes, sweep kitchen and dining room, dust. Pick up and dust other parts of the house.

5. Make beds which have been airing, dust.
6. Clean bathroom.
7. Put away groceries: wash and prepare vegetables, cover and put all but potatoes in refrigerator to crisp.
8. Make dressing, stuff flank steak, put in refrigerator.
9. Preheat oven to 350° F. (moderate). Prepare Rice Meringue Pudding, *page 254*, and bake for luncheon.

10. Set table 45 minutes before luncheon is served and get out supplies for soup.
11. Make soup and beverage. Heat soup bowls (and tureen if used).
12. Serve luncheon (*page 49*).
13. Wash dishes (*page 22*) and leave kitchen in order. Pick up dining room if meal has been served there.
14. Time for leisure—at least 2 hours.

SCHEDULE OF WORK FOR AFTERNOON

1. Start meat 3 hours before dinner.
2. Prepare berries, sweeten, crush slightly, all but ½ cup.
3. Set dinner table (*page 6*).
4. Start potatoes 1 hour before dinner.
5. Prepare shortcake biscuits, store in refrigerator until ready to bake.
6. Prepare salad 20 minutes before serving, chill. Start beans.
7. Put dishes for hot food on warm oven or warming oven.
8. Whip cream, sweeten. Chill in bowl.

9. Remove meat, keep hot. Make gravy. Start beverage.
10. Fill glasses, place bread, butter, salad bowl and pickles on table. Adjust oven to 450° F. (very hot). Put shortcake in oven.
11. Serve dinner (*page 7*). Remove shortcake when baked and keep hot. While some one clears table, put finishing touches on shortcake.
12. Wash dishes. Tidy kitchen and dining room (*page 22*).

ONE-DISH SOUP

1 can (No. 1) **cream of spinach soup**
1 can (No. 1) **cream of mushroom soup**
rich milk
1 can (No. ½, flat) **crabmeat, flaked pumpernickel, crisp crackers or Melba toast**

Makes about 4 generous portions.

Empty contents of soup cans into saucepan. Add from ½ to an equal quantity of rich milk, and heat to just below boiling point, stirring until smooth.

Add flaked crabmeat and heat thoroughly. Serve in hot soup bowls with bread.

RICE MERINGUE PUDDING

1 cup cooked rice (*page* 54)
½ cup raisins, or chopped dates or
 figs
2 cups milk
2 eggs, separated
½ cup sugar
¼ teaspoon salt
⅛ teaspoon nutmeg or cinnamon
cream

Makes 6 portions.

Heat rice, raisins and milk in double boiler. Beat egg yolks with 6 tablespoons sugar, salt and nutmeg. Stir slowly into rice-milk mixture. Turn into baking dish.

Beat egg whites until stiff. Beat in gradually remaining 2 tablespoons sugar. Pile on pudding. Bake in 350° F. (moderate) oven 15 minutes. Serve with cream.

STUFFED FLANK STEAK

1 flank steak (2–2½ lb.)
salt and pepper
⅛ teaspoon ginger

2 cups Bread Stuffing (*page* 102)
flour
3 tablespoons chopped suet
½ cup boiling water

Have butcher score steak. Wipe meat with damp cloth and sprinkle with salt, pepper and ginger.

Spread stuffing evenly over steak and roll with fiber. Sew edges together and sprinkle roll with salt, pepper and flour.

Sauté roll in suet in heavy frying pan 20 minutes, or until well browned. Then add water, cover and simmer about 2½ hours, or until very tender, turning occasionally.

parsley or watercress
Brown Gravy (*page* 86)

Makes about 6 portions.

Remove thread and place roll on hot platter. Garnish and serve with bowl of gravy. Slice, cutting across fiber.

Preparing Stuffed Flank Steaks (see recipe above).

FRUIT SHORTCAKE

Fresh, frozen or canned fruits may be used to make this quick and yummy shortcake.

2 cups sifted flour
2½ teaspoons double-action bak-ing powder
½ teaspoon salt
2 tablespoons sugar
⅓ cup shortening
1 egg, well beaten
½ cup milk
butter, softened
3 cups strawberries or raspber-ries, crushed slightly and sweet-ened; or
6 large peaches or 18 apricots, sliced and sweetened; or
3 large bananas, sliced, sprinkled with lemon juice and sweetened
1 cup heavy cream, whipped and lightly sweetened

Makes about 6 portions.

Sift flour, measure 2 cups into sifter. Add baking powder, salt and sugar, and sift into bowl. Cut in shortening.

Beat egg, add milk. Stir quickly into flour mixture to form soft dough. Shape in ball on lightly floured board. Roll ¼ inch thick. Cut in 3-inch rounds. Place ½ in shallow pan, spread tops with butter. Cover with remaining rounds, butter tops well. Bake in 450° F. (very hot) 10 to 15 minutes.

Separate halves, spread soft sides with butter. Cover bottom halves with prepared fruit. Lay other halves on top, soft sides up, cover with fruit. Top with cream and fruit, whole or sliced.

BISCUIT SHORTCAKE

Use rich Baking Powder Biscuit dough, *page 67,* or your favorite ready-mix.

The School Lunch Box

Whether you have a dainty appetite, or a husky one, your school lunch should be as carefully thought out as your other two meals of the day. Remember, your noon-day lunch should supply almost one-third of your day's quota of food. That means it should have a starch, a fat, a sweet; meat, eggs or fish; a vegetable and a fruit. And you must never forget your ration of milk. Always plan to have milk—plain, in a chocolate drink, a creamy soup or dessert, like custard or tapioca. Fortunately, many schools sell milk at cost.

Plan your school lunch in advance. Plan to have leftovers to use. Get permission to slice off some of the baked or boiled ham the family has one night for dinner, and put it away. Set aside, ahead, some of a day's luncheon fish or meat, to be made into a salad to carry to school. Just a little cream cheese saved out from a salad will make a good sandwich, alone, or with nuts, dried fruits, chopped vegetables or jelly. Break off some raw flowerets from the cauliflower you cook for supper. They will make a crisp delicious bite next day at school. Cut a wedge from a firm head of lettuce; next morning put it into the lunch box, wrapped in waxed paper, and at school eat it with salt. A whole tomato you will find a refreshing bite, eaten with either salt or sugar; and raw carrots are crunchy bites good to chew on and good for you.

Variety is hard to get into your lunch box every day, but one way to be sure of it is not to have too many different things in one day's box.

SUGGESTED SCHOOL LUNCH BOX MENUS

Egg-Olive Sandwich, 200
Cheddar Corn Muffin, 66   Tomato
Baked Apple, 26   Milk (School)

★

Chicken Leg   Watermelon Pickle, 226
Whole Wheat Bread and Butter
Cheese-Onion Sandwich, 197
Fruit Salad, 146   Carrot Cooky, 257
Cocoa

★

Celery Soup, 51   Cheese Crackers
Salami Sandwich   Carrot Straws
Fruit Drops, 184   Milk (School)

Chili Con Carne, 284 Lettuce Wedge
Cucumber Sandwich   Dill Pickle
Meringue Coconut Tart, 169
Milk (School)

★

Potato Salad, 142
Sardine Sandwich, 202
Rye Bread and Butter
Radishes and Celery, 126-138
Applesauce Cake, 258 Lemonade, 206

★

Cream of Pea Soup, 52   Crackers
Egg-Bacon Sandwich
Spiced Pears, 225
Brownies, 185   Milk (School)

CARROT COOKIES

2 cups sifted flour
3 teaspoons double-action baking
   powder
¼ teaspoon salt
½ teaspoon cinnamon
½ teaspoon nutmeg
2 cups quick-cooking oatmeal
1 cup raisins
1 cup chopped nuts
⅓ cup shortening
1 cup grated raw carrots
1 cup honey
2 eggs, well beaten

Makes about 36 small cookies.

Sift flour, measure 2 cups into sifter. Add baking powder, salt and spices. Mix and sift. Stir in oatmeal, raisins and nuts.

Cream fat. Stir in carrots, honey and eggs. Stir in flour-nut mixture. Drop from teaspoon on buttered sheet. Flatten slightly.

Bake in 350° F. (moderate) oven for 25 to 30 minutes.

APPLESAUCE CAKE

1½ cups sifted flour
1 teaspoon baking soda
⅛ teaspoon salt
1 teaspoon cinnamon
½ teaspoon cloves
1 cup chopped nuts (optional)
1½ cups seedless raisins
¼ cup shortening
⅓ cup firmly packed brown sugar
1 egg
1 cup thick applesauce (*page 25*)

Makes 6 × 3-inch loaf.

Sift flour, measure 1½ cups into sifter. Add soda, salt and spices. Mix well, then sift. Stir in nuts and fruit.

Cream fat. Beat in sugar, then egg. Stir in flour-fruit mixture, alternately with sauce, beating well after each addition.

Turn into buttered, small loaf pan. Bake in 350° F. (moderate) oven 45 to 60 minutes.

It's Fun to Entertain

One very soon learns that certain people and certain homes radiate hospitality. The habit of hospitality is worth cultivating for it gives pleasure both ways—to the host even more than to the guest.

Any gathering can be a success. An impromptu fudge making or taffy pull with everybody helping in the kitchen can be as much fun as an elaborate supper. No one need be denied the pleasure of entertaining friends because of expense or lack of space. If you cannot have a dinner ask the crowd in one Friday night after skating or the school game and have "Sport Model Sandwiches" (*page* 202) and hot chocolate. They will love that simple snack, if the sandwiches are good and the chocolate, rich and hot—and you're honestly glad to have your friends at your house.

You want something different? Give an Italian supper or luncheon. Serve Antipasto (*page* 78), Spaghetti with Marinara Sauce (*page* 57)— lots of both—and a ripe, yellow pear or red apple to be eaten with sharp cheese. If, along about St. Patrick's Day, you feel the urge to have a party, have the simplest menu—but good—and pretty decorations to establish the mood. A few dimes will provide you with materials to dress up the dining room; but be wary—let simplicity guide you with decorations, always, for too many spoil the effect.

Sometimes a co-operative party is just the thing, gay and informal. Several young people can "go in" together. One provides the home, the china, the silver and the first course. The others bring the other dishes, all made. A progressive dinner is fun.

Make use of your household electric equipment in entertaining. Electric toasters, waffle irons, grills or chafing dishes can give an "air" to a gathering.

A waffle party is very amusing if you are having only a few guests. Make up the batter ahead of time and bake the waffles at the table. With creamed chicken or creamed dried beef, they're very good.

Toast for sandwiches can be made at the table. Have the fillings all ready, ahead. Electric sandwich grills make two large sandwiches at a time. They are extra good sandwiches, too, for the grilling gives delicious flavor to the buttery bread.

Make Welsh Rabbit (*page* 62) or Tomato Rabbit (*page* 62) at the table in the electric chafing dish. Make creamed mushrooms, or scrambled eggs. Use the electric chafing dish for serving buffet style, at a "brunch" or supper. It will keep the food warm and guests can help themselves. Electric equipment makes all entertaining simpler.

CHICKEN À LA KING

(Chafing dish)

2 cups **Medium White Sauce** (*page* 109)
1 cup **light cream**
1 cup **sliced mushrooms**
1 **green pepper, chopped**
3 tablespoons **butter**
1 **pimiento, cut in thin strips**
2 cups **diced cooked chicken**
salt and pepper
2 **egg yolks, slightly beaten**
toast, English muffins, or patty shells

Makes about 8 portions.

Make sauce, using 1 cup each milk and chicken stock. Add cream. Heat, keep hot.

Sauté mushrooms and green pepper in butter 5 minutes, stirring frequently. Add to sauce. Add pimiento and chicken. Season to taste, and simmer 5 minutes. Stir in egg yolks slowly, then cook 1 minute, stirring constantly.

Serve on hot toast, toasted English muffins, or in patty shells. Or serve on hot waffles.

There are endless possibilities for all kinds of entertaining when you make use of electrical equipment.

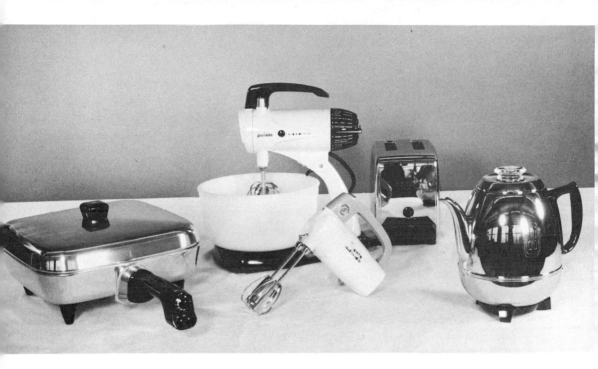

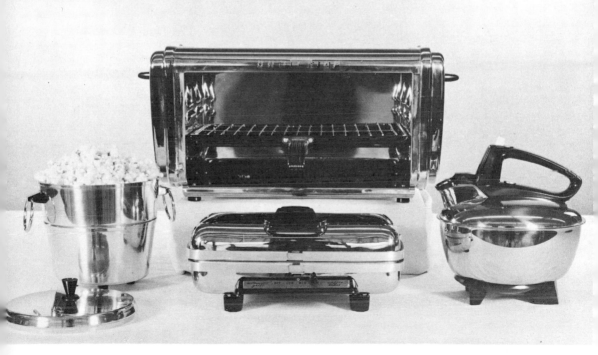

SPECIAL PARTY MENUS

Barbecued Dinner

Cider   Potato Chips, 123
Barbecued Spareribs, or Chicken, 265
Crusty Bread   Barbecue Sauce, 265
Coleslaw, 140   Small Tomatoes
Apple Dumplings, 156   Beverage

★

After the Football Game

Chop Suey, 264,   Boiled Rice, 55
Watermelon Pickle, 226
Toasted French Bread
Green Salad Bowl, Italian Style, 139
Upside-Down Cup Cake, 266
Beverage

★

Hot Bites at Winter Sports

(Cooked before an open fire)
Grilled Frankfurters, 292   Rolls
Mustard   Dills   Apples
Toasted Marshmallows   Cocoa

★

T.V. Snacks

Grilled Sandwiches   Pickles
Marble Layer Cake, 266
Quick Lemonade, 206

Open House New Year's Day

Broiled Tiny Sausages on Toothpicks
Baked Ham, 94
Small Hot Biscuits, 66
Fruitcake, 272 Almond Wreaths, 274
Salted Nuts, 251 Candies Punch, 209

★

Birthday Party

Chicken à la King, 260
Broiled Peach, 129
Sliced Tomato Salad
Stuffed Celery, 138
Currant Muffins, 64
Birthday Silver Cake, 174
Ice Cream, 159   Beverage

★

Tea Dance

Chipped Beef Pinwheels, 269
Toasted Rolled Sandwiches, 198
Tiny Frosted Cakes, 179
Salted Nuts, 251 Summer Punch, 207

★

T.V. Supper

Fruit Salad Bowl, 146
Cheese Muffins, 65
Veal Aspic, 263   Potato Chips, 123
Pickles   Radishes   Olives
Gingerbread, 176   Whipped Cream
Beverage

Family Christmas Dinner

Grape Juice—Ginger Ale Cup, 77
Popcorn
Roast Goose or Turkey, 100
Gravy, 86
Mashed Potatoes, 123   Peas
Cranberry Relish 225 Olives Celery
Pineapple Coleslaw, 140   Rolls, 72
Jellied Raspberry Grapefruit, 153 or
Plum Pudding, 271   Beverage

St. Patrick's Progressive Dinner

(To be served at four houses)
Potato Leek Soup, 52 Crisp Crackers
Schnitzel, 92   Spinach   Carrots
Scone Biscuits, 67   Mint Jelly, 224
Molded Vegetable Salad, 143
(Lime Gelatin)
Cheese Niblets
Pistachio Ice Cream Shamrock Cakes
(Two-Egg Cake baked in sheet, 173,
cut into shamrock shapes—frosted
green and white) Beverage

VEAL ASPIC

**5 pounds shoulder of veal: or 1 veal
shank and 2 pounds lean veal
(remove fat and crack bones)**
water
1 small onion, sliced
2 teaspoons salt
¼ teaspoon pepper
1 teaspoon celery seeds
1 bay leaf
1 package aspic gelatin

Wipe meat, place in large kettle and cover with water. Add onions and seasonings. Boil 5 minutes. Skim and simmer, covered, about 3 hours, or until meat falls off bones. Remove meat. Strain stock through cheesecloth.

Stock should measure 3 cups; if too much, boil rapidly to reduce it, or add water to make 3 cups. Add more seasoning, if necessary.

Dissolve aspic in stock, following directions on package. Remove all fat and gristle from meat. Cut meat fine and place in large loaf or shallow pan. Pour aspic over meat and chill until firm. To serve, unmold loaf on platter, garnish and cut in ½-inch slices. Cut shallow mold in squares.

Makes about 10 portions.

Use your rotisserie for Barbecued Chicken or Spareribs (*page* 265).

CHOP SUEY

1 chicken (3 lb.), or 3 cups shredded, cooked chicken
1 cup julienne green peppers, seeds
removed
2 cups julienne celery
1 cup thinly sliced onion
4 tablespoons butter
1 cup sliced mushrooms
2 cups chicken stock
1 teaspoon salt
⅛ teaspoon pepper
1 tablespoon cornstarch
2 tablespoons water
1 can (No. 2) bean sprouts
4 tablespoons soy sauce
1 cup toasted almonds, broken

Makes 6 to 8 portions.

Cook chicken (*page* 100); or remove skin from cooked chicken and cut in thin strips.

Sauté pepper, celery and onion in butter 5 minutes, stirring to brown evenly. Then add chicken and mushrooms, and cook 5 minutes, stirring to brown evenly. Add stock, salt and pepper, and bring to a boil.

Mix cornstarch and water to a smooth paste. Add to chicken mixture, stirring until smooth and thickened. Add bean sprouts and cook gently 10 minutes, stirring occasionally. Add soy sauce, almonds and more seasoning, if desired. Vegetables should be slightly crunchy, not mushy. Serve hot with hot, steamed rice and soy sauce.

CHOP SUEY VARIATIONS

One to 1 ½ pounds lean pork, veal, crab or lobster may be used instead of chicken. Cut raw meat in thin strips and sauté in butter until browned and cooked. Then proceed as with chicken.

BARBECUED CHICKEN OR SPARERIBS

Dig a trench about a foot deep and three feet long; or use an out-of-door fireplace, a charcoal grill or rotisserie. If hardwood is used, build fire about 3 hours before using to get a bed of glowing coals. With charcoal allow about ½ hour. Use an oven broiler to place across pit or fireplace for broiling meat. Follow manufacturer's directions for use of rotisserie. If meat browns too quickly, remove some of coals to reduce heat.

1 large onion, minced
1 clove garlic, minced
2 green peppers, minced
1 can tomato juice
1 cup water
1 cup vinegar
½ cup ketchup
½ cup Worcestershire sauce
¼ cup butter
1 teaspoon salt
½ teaspoon cayenne or red pepper pods
2 large broilers, cleaned, split down back and opened; or 6 to 8 pounds spareribs
crusty loaf bread, cut in slabs; or hard rolls, split

Allow ¼ large broiler, or ⅔ to 1 pound spareribs per portion.

Prepare barbecue sauce by boiling vegetables, liquids, butter and seasonings 15 minutes. Let cool.

Put washed and dried chicken in cold barbecue sauce for at least 1 hour so that flavor permeates chicken. Turn once. Follow same procedure for spareribs.

Put chickens, skin side down, on oven broiler; put spareribs, rounded side down, on broiler. Place across pit with bed of glowing coals and broil on both sides, turning with long toasting fork or tongs. Then brush with barbecue sauce, using a swab made by wrapping a clean cloth around end of a long stick, basting, then turning meat every 10 minutes until well browned and done. For broilers allow about 1 hour. Test for doneness by twisting a broiler leg; if joint breaks easily, chicken is done. For spareribs, allow about ½ hour. Serve remaining barbecue sauce, piping hot, in a bowl, with slabs of bread for dunking.

UPSIDE-DOWN CUP CAKES

1 recipe **Two-Egg Cake** (*page* 173)
butter
⅓ **cup firmly packed brown sugar,
 or 12 tablespoons**
18 canned peach or apricot halves
**18 marashino cherries, or walnut
 halves**
heavy cream, whipped, if desired

Make cake batter, using ½ teaspoon vanilla. Brush bottoms of medium-sized muffin pans heavily with butter, and put 2 teaspoons brown sugar in each. Place cherry in hollow of each fruit half, then drop one into each cup, hollow side down. Fill each cup ⅔ full with batter.

Bake in 375° F. (moderate) oven 15 to 25 minutes. Loosen cakes and turn out at once on cake rack, tapping bottoms if cakes stick. Serve warm or cold.

Makes about 12 to 16 cup cakes.

ORANGE-COCONUT-BLACK CAT CAKE

1 recipe **Two-Egg Cake** (*page* 173)

Make cake batter, substituting 1 ½ teaspoons grated orange rind for vanilla. Bake in buttered 9-inch square pan. Cool.

1 recipe **Orange Seven Minute
 Frosting** (*page* 190)
1 **cup shredded coconut**

Make frosting. Spread ⅔ of it over cake. Lay a cat cut-out of waxed paper on top center of cake. Sprinkle shredded coconut over frosting around pattern and on sides of cake. Remove waxed paper cat, then smooth frosting.

1 **square chocolate, melted**

Stir melted and cooled chocolate into remaining frosting. Pile lightly over cat shape in center of cake.

Makes 1 (9-inch) cake.

MARBLE LAYER CAKE

1 recipe **Silver Cake** (*page* 174)
2 **squares chocolate, melted**
Chocolate Butter Frosting (*page*
 189), **or Fudge Frosting** (*page*
 191)

Make cake batter. Remove half to other bowl. Stir melted chocolate into one half. Put by spoonfuls into 2 buttered layer pans, alternating light and dark mixtures. Bake.

Put layers together, with frosting, then cover.

Makes 1 (9-inch) layer cake.

Your First Party—
Something Different

What food to serve is the question which confronts every one giving a party, be it simple or elaborate. The meal must be interesting, not too expensive, easily prepared and served. An ideal way to serve is buffet style. For help in selecting attractive food combinations see *page* 3. Suggested menus for Buffet-Cafeteria Service are given on *page* 268.

Cafeteria-Buffet Service. A very novel buffet party is served cafeteria-style, in both kitchen and dining room—the main course from the kitchen, salad and dessert from the dining room. Kitchens are coming into their own as party rooms!

Appetizer in the Living Room. Enlist the services of a guest or two to help with the serving of the first course in the living room before you call everybody to the kitchen. Glasses and plates of appetizers can be arranged on a small table.

The Order of the Meal. You, the chef, will serve, assisted by a special friend. Guests come in from the dining room, each with a tray and silver, which are found lined up on the dining-room table or buffet. On the way back through the dining room guests are served salad and bread or biscuits. Later they will return there with their trays. A helper can carry the empty plates to the kitchen. Then all can be given dessert and beverage. Let someone who's shy preside at the buffet or table in the dining room. Being busy and useful compliments a guest, and breaks the ice for the most bashful.

Buffet-Cafeteria Service

Cranberry Juice   Cheesies, 268
    (Living Room)
Rabbit Casserole, 301
Brown Gravy,   86
Parsley Potatoes, 124
Asparagus or Green Beans, 118
Hot Rolls, 72   Jelly, 223
Lettuce Salad Russian Dressing, 135
Pickles
Lemon Ice Cream, 160
Brownies, 185
Beverage   Mint Candies

★

Tomato Juice with Lemon Wedges
Crackers
    (Living Room)
Planked Salmon Loaf, 132
Cream Sauce, 109
Candied Sweet Potatoes, 124
Braised Mushrooms
Celery, Club Style, 136
Carrot Straws, 136
Cranberry Relish, 225
Cornbread, 65   Butter
Fruit Salad Bowl, 146
Beverage   Salted Nuts, 251

Grape Juice-Ginger Ale Cup, 77
Chipped Beef Pinwheels, 269
    (Living Room)
West Indian Veal, 269
Buttered Peas
Baking Powder Biscuits, 66
Orange Marmalade, 219
Cabbage and Pineapple Salad, 144
Candy Apple Pie, 269   Beverage
Coconut Fondant Balls, 247

★

Melon-Mint Cup, 77
Cheesies, 268
    (Living Room)
Meat Loaf, 88   Devil Sauce, 111
Pickled Pears, 225
Potato Salad, 142
Sweet Carrots, 120
Radish Roses, 138
Blueberry Muffins, 65   Butter
Marble Layer Cake, 266
Beverage
Stuffed Dates and Prunes, 247

CHEESIES

1 package (3 oz.) snappy cheese
4 tablespoons butter
½ cup flour

Makes about 20 cheesies.

Mix ingredients into a paste, using the back of a spoon. With palms of hands shape into small balls, twice the size of small marbles, then flatten and place on ungreased baking sheet. Chill 3 to 4 hours.

Bake in 450° F. (very hot) oven for 7 to 10 minutes. Serve hot.

CHIPPED BEEF PINWHEELS

2 packages (3 oz. each) cream
  cheese
2 teaspoons scraped onion or chopped chives
3 tablespoons cream (about)
4 ounces dried beef, large, thin
  slices

Makes about 30 pinwheels.

Work cheese, onion and cream to a smooth paste, easy to spread.

Arrange beef in 8-inch square with pieces overlapping. Spread cheese over top. Then roll tight and wrap in waxed paper. Chill several hours. Just before serving, cut in thin slices.

WEST INDIAN VEAL

1 clove garlic, chopped
4 tablespoons bacon fat
2 pounds veal steak, ½ inch thick,
  cut in pieces for serving
¼ cup flour
1 teaspoon salt
⅛ teaspoon pepper
1 can (No. 303) or 2 cups tomatoes
1 small bottle stuffed olives with
  liquor
Candied Sweet Potatoes (*page* 124)

Makes 4 to 6 portions.

Sauté garlic in fat in heavy frying pan about 5 minutes, or until lightly browned. Remove garlic to plate.

Roll veal cutlets in seasoned flour and brown in fat on both sides.

Add browned garlic, tomatoes and olives. Bring to a boil, cover and simmer slowly about 1 ½ hours.

Place on hot platter with sauce poured over it, and serve with candied sweet potatoes.

CANDY APPLE PIE

4 tart apples, pared, cored and
  sliced
1 cup firmly packed brown sugar
dash of salt
1 cup sifted flour
½ to 1 cup ground nuts or 4 tablespoons peanut butter
½ cup butter, softened
½ cup heavy cream, whipped

Makes about 6 portions.

Slice 2 apples into greased baking dish, sprinkle with ½ cup brown sugar. Slice other apples on top and add salt.

For topping mix flour, remaining ½ cup brown sugar and nuts. Stir gradually into softened butter, mixing well. Pat into round the size of top of dish. Adjust crust on top of filling and cut several gashes for steam to escape.

Bake in 350° F. (moderate) oven about 1 hour, or until apples are tender. Serve warm with whipped cream.

Christmas

Is on the Way

The recipes in this section have been gathered with the generous giving and sharing of the Christmas season in mind. From these recipes you can contribute to the family feasts and make delicious gifts for friends. They are the most personal of all, these gifts you make yourself, particularly if they are dressed with the trappings and wrappings of the season.

Although you will find them in other sections of this book, remember homemade jellies, jams and conserves as Christmas gifts.

When you are preserving and jellying in the summer and fall, put aside some special glasses for Christmas giving. Use pretty and unusual little containers of glass or pottery. They are very inexpensive. Or, for a bride, buy a half-dozen tumblers or special beverage glasses, fill them with jelly or jam and save them until Christmas. You will be very glad that you have been forehanded. And if you have not been, remember that dried and canned fruits can be made into very good winter jams. Canned and bottled fruit juices make attractive jellies when used with commercial pectins. Mint Jelly (*page* 224) fits well into gift color schemes, and can be made at Christmas time, too. Cranberry Relish (*page* 225) is another colorful, seasonable and delicious homemade Christmas gift. Pour jam, jelly or conserve into regular jelly glasses and while the layers of paraffin on top are still soft, stick a sprig of holly or mistletoe into each. Or make designs in the soft paraffin with tiny red or silver candies, and citron or angelica.

Candies. Any kind of homemade candy makes a good Christmas gift. The fondants and divinity can be used to introduce pretty color; coconut, delicately tinted, brings color, too. Little crinkly paper cups for the candies give a professional look to the box. And no box of candy made at home is ever complete without fudge and panocha. See the pictures on *pages* 243 and 273 for suggestions as to the selection of gifts and the packing.

CHRISTMAS PLUM PUDDING

2 cups sifted flour
½ pound seedless raisins
¼ pound currants
¼ pound figs, chopped
2 ounces citron, chopped
2 ounces candied orange peel, chopped
1 cup nut meats
½ pound beef suet
2 teaspoons double-action baking powder
1 teaspoon salt
½ teaspoon nutmeg
½ teaspoon cinnamon
¼ teaspoon cloves
3 eggs, well beaten
1 cup firmly packed brown sugar
½ cup milk
½ cup boiled cider
Hard Sauce (*page* 161)

Makes about 3 (1 *lb.*) *molds.*

Prepare molds or tin cans with tight lids by greasing thoroughly and sprinkling with sugar.

Wash dried fruit and dry thoroughly. Dredge lightly with some of flour. Chop or slice figs, citron, peel and nuts. Mix well. Chop or grind suet.

Mix and sift remaining flour, baking powder, salt and spices into large bowl. Add prepared fruit and mix well.

Beat eggs until light in large bowl. Beat in sugar gradually. Stir in suet. Stir in flour-fruit mixture, alternately with milk. Add cider and stir well.

Turn into well-greased molds or coffee cans, filling them ⅔ full. Cover tightly. Heavy paper, spread with butter, may be tied around bowls.

Place molds in steamer; or on rack in large kettle, with hot water not more than half-way up around molds. Cover tightly and keep water boiling gently, adding boiling water as needed. Steam 2 ½ to 3 ½ hours, according to size.

Remove molds, uncover and invert on cake racks. When cold, return to molds, cover tightly and store in cold place. To reheat, steam ½ hour. Serve hot with hard sauce.

STEAMED FRUITCAKE

Cover filled pans with buttered heavy paper and tie securely. Place in steamer and steam 3 to 4 hours as for Plum Pudding (*page* 271); then uncover and bake in 250° F. (very slow) ½ to 1 hour to dry the tops. (Recipe for cake follows.)

HOLIDAY FRUITCAKE

1 pound seedless raisins
1 pound currants
1 pound pitted dates, sliced
½ pound each candied pineapple, cherries and orange peel, chopped
½ pound citron, sliced
½ pound walnut meats, chopped
4 cups sifted flour
½ teaspoon baking soda
1 teaspoon cinnamon
½ teaspoon cloves
½ teaspoon ground nutmeg
2 cups shortening
1 pound brown sugar
1 tablespoon grated lemon rind
10 eggs, well beaten
1 cup molasses   1 cup honey
½ cup cider

Makes about 10 *pounds fruitcake.*

Wash dried fruits, dry thoroughly. Chop or slice fruits, peel and nuts.

Prepare 5 small or 4 large loaf pans, or 2 tube pans; grease pans, line sides and bottoms with heavy waxed paper, then butter well.

Sift flour, measure 4 cups into sifter. Add soda and spices, and sift three times.

Cream shortening well. Beat in sugar gradually, then lemon rind and eggs. Stir in fruits, peel, nuts, molasses and honey. Stir in flour gradually, alternately with cider. Turn into prepared pans, filling them ¾ full. Cover and chill overnight.

Set pans in shallow pans of hot water; bake in 275° F. (very slow) oven until done, removing pans from hot water after 2 hours of baking. Bake large loaves about 4 hours; small loaves, about 3 hours. Cool in pans. Turn onto rack and remove waxed paper. Store in tightly covered cans in cool place.

Christmas gifts you've made yourself are always special. Here are crisp sugar cookies (*page* 185) cut in fancy shapes and packed in a gay tin. Include other cookies and cakes, and don't forget candies (*page* 243). They all say Merry Christmas.

ALMOND WREATHS (MANDELKRANSER)

4 cups sifted flour
1½ cups butter
1 cup finely chopped, blanched
almonds
2 eggs, well beaten
¾ cup sugar
1 teaspoon vanilla

Sift flour, measure 4 cups into sifter. Sift into bowl. Cut in butter. Stir in almonds. Beat eggs; beat in sugar, then vanilla. Stir in flour-butter mixture. Chill.

Pack dough into cooky press, using plate with star-shaped die. Force out in rolls. Cut in three-inch lengths. Bring ends together to form rings.

Bake on ungreased baking sheet in 375° F. (moderate) oven for 8 to 10 minutes.

NOTE: To shape dough without cooky press, roll, with hands, small amounts on lightly floured boards into ½ inch thick rolls. Run fork tines along length to rib top; cut, shape and bake.

Makes about 7 dozen cookies.

CZECHOSLOVAKIAN CHRISTMAS COOKIES

3¾ cups sifted cake flour
½ teaspoon baking soda
⅛ teaspoon salt
1 teaspoon cinnamon
½ teaspoon cloves
¾ teaspoon ginger
¼ teaspoon allspice
¼ teaspoon ground nutmeg
½ cup shortening, melted
1 cup molasses
⅓ cup firmly packed brown sugar
flour for rolling

Sift flour, then measure 3 ¾ cups into flour sifter. Add soda, salt and spices, mix well, then sift 3 times.

Melt shortening, add molasses and heat slightly. Stir in sugar, then flour mixture gradually, mixing well after each addition. Pack in bowl, cover tightly and store in refrigerator 1 week before rolling.

Place small amount of dough at a time on lightly floured board and roll very thin. Cut with floured, small cooky cutters in fancy shapes and place on greased sheets. Bake in 375° F. (moderate) oven for 8 to 10 minutes. Store in tightly covered containers. Cookies keep well.

Makes about 220 cookies.

CHRISTMAS BREAD (YEAST ROLLS, *page 70*)

2 cups milk, scalded
¼ cup sugar
1 to 2 cakes compressed yeast
8 cups sifted flour (about)
1½ teaspoons salt
½ cup butter, melted
3 eggs, beaten
1½ cups seedless raisins
¾ cup sliced citron
¼ cup sliced candied cherries
½ cup chopped, candied orange
  peel *

* For variety omit peel: add 1 teaspoon cardamom seed to sponge.

Makes 3 small or 2 large loaves.

Scald milk. Add sugar and cool. When lukewarm, add crumbled yeast cake and 3 cups flour, beating thoroughly. Cover and let rise in warm place until spongy.

Stir in salt, butter and beaten eggs. Stir in flour until stiff enough to knead. Knead until smooth, cover and let double.

Add raisins, citron, cherries and peel. Knead until mixed. Shape into loaves and place in greased loaf pans. Brush with melted butter, cover and let double.

Bake in 400° F. (hot) oven 30 to 40 minutes.

Vacationing at Camp or Cottage

In making plans for camp, remember that food is of first interest. "When do we eat?" is the all-important question. Activity out-of-doors has an amazing effect on appetites. Plan a whole week's menus ahead of time—and consult the others who will be with you. Everybody going to camp will have ideas and favorite dishes to contribute.

Supplies Available. Find out if there are farms near camp where you can get fresh milk, butter, eggs, fruit and vegetables. Scout around and learn if grocery, butcher or bakery wagons stop by on regular days. Can you get all the ice you need? What about storage for staples and perishables? Will you need to use some dehydrated foods?

Ranges, Equipment and Fuel. What about the stove at camp? Is the surface large enough to hold several good-sized pots? What about the oven? Will you be able to bake? That will have a bearing on how much flour and other staples you buy. Is there an out-of-door fireplace for a barbecue, or a bean-baking pit for bean-hole beans? A place where you can have a clam bake? Have you plenty of large-enough kettles and pots for generous stews and soups? So many things affect the buying of supplies. Incidentally, it may be wise to know what fuel is used in the stove— wood, gas, gasoline or kerosene. Learning something about the stove's operation will prevent delays in meal-getting, and is a safety-measure.

Plan to serve the main meal at noon. That makes evening work light. Plan to cook an occasional meal out-of-doors, even if you haven't a real fireplace there. An outdoor fire, especially at night, is friendly, the food cooked over it, extra good.

Prepared Mixes and Canned Foods. Make use of the prepared pie, pancake, biscuit, cake and pudding mixes on the market. They are most satisfactory. Canned fruits, vegetables and meats make good meals. Think how delicious canned corned beef hash is. You may wish, however, to use your own seasonings or to make your own hash from canned corned beef. Cook the hash over slow heat until it is brown and crisp; serve it with Devil Sauce (*page* 111) and you serve a feast. Split Pea Soup and Dried Lima Bean Soup (*page* 280) are delicious, hearty, and nourishing, made with canned corned beef in place of the usual ham bone. There you have a splendid and easily prepared supper.

Food Cooked Ahead and Leftovers. Keep plenty of potatoes boiled ahead and in the refrigerator, ready for creaming, frying or for use in salads. Other vegetables, washed or cooked ahead, can be creamed or used in salads. Plan to use leftovers. Cook a ham or good-sized roast ahead. Use what's left in good casseroles, loaves, salads.

One-Dish Meals. Have one-dish meals as often as you can. Good wholesome beef and kidney stew with dumplings is a meal for camp, if ever there was. Baked casserole dishes, with plenty of nourishment in them, are perfect camp fare, and provide whole meals in one container. They save fuel, also. Save yourself time one afternoon, when you are off on a hike, by having Bean-Hole Beans (*page* 301), cooking away in a sizzling stone pit.

Easy Serving. Serve meals cafeteria-style. It is easy and fun. The dining table can be set indoors or on the porch, with the silver, bread, butter and beverage. In the kitchen, pile the plates, and have the dishes of food arranged nearby. Let campers and guests troop in, and carry their filled plates to the dining table. Individual trays are handy for this cafeteria-serving.

Delegate the Work. To make sure all work is done, delegate tasks. There is always a good planner in the group. Let him—or her—outline each job, and determine who is to do it for a day. Of course, during the week, the various tasks will rotate among the members. Because meal-making is the biggest job, more should be assigned to it. One can be responsible for the getting of provisions (the daily provisions like milk, eggs, butter, vegetables and fruits). One can take care of the beverages of the day—from breakfast on through supper. The salads can be prepared by one, the desserts by another. Vegetables should be washed and prepared for cooking by someone with nothing else to do, and the main course will be the work of the Number One cook of the day.

Cleaning Up. Of course, the cooks will not be the dishwashers. That is someone else's work, and should be delegated for each day. The table clearing, the putting away of food and the dishwashing must also be provided for each day. When you change the crew every twenty-four hours, work is more interesting for everybody.

Menus for an entire week at camp are included in this section, together with easily managed recipes for twelve which fit into camp cookery. You will find, throughout this book, other recipes which can be easily prepared at camp. Just double or treble them.

SUGGESTED MENUS FOR A WEEK AT CAMP

	Breakfast	Dinner	Supper (or Lunch)
FRI.	Bananas and Prepared Cereal; Cream; Cooked Eggs, 36; Currant Muffins, 64; Beverage	Relishes; Salmon Roly-Poly, 281; Tomato Sauce, 111; String Beans; Baked Potatoes; Vegetable Salad; Bread; Butter; Prune Whip, 284; Milk	Consommé Potatoes, 282; Crisp Bacon, 40; Carrot Sticks; Cracked Wheat Bread; Butter; Preserves; Lemon Snow Pudding, 152 Milk
SAT.	Orange Juice; Cooked Farina, 30; Fluffy Jelly Omelet, 38; Buttered Toast; Milk; Coffee, 33	Chili Con Carne, 284; Brown Bread, 68; Beet Relish; Celery; Rolls; Butter; Sliced Peaches and Cream; Milk	Cream of Corn Soup, 51; Fruit Salad, 146; Raisin Bread and Butter; Lemonade, 206
SUN	Fresh Pineapple; Griddlecakes, 40; Sausage, 40; Café au Lait, 34; Milk	Fruit Juice; Baked Ham, 94; Candied Sweet Potatoes, 124; Spinach; Relishes; Rye Crisp; Chocolate Ice Cream, 160; Cake; Beverage	Creamed Frizzled Beef, 283; Coleslaw, 140; Fruit Sauce; Brownies, 185; Iced Tea, 35; Milk
MON.	Grapefruit Juice; Fried Mush, 31; Crisp Bacon, 40; Blueberry Muffins, 65; Cocoa, 35	Jellied Bouillon, 80; Hungarian Goulash, 282 Carrot Straws, 136; Fruit Salad Bowl, 146; Bread; Butter; Butterscotch Slices, 187; Milk	Potato-Frankfurter Salad, 142; Radishes; Scallions; Nut Bread, 69; Butter, Peach Dumplings, 156; Lemon Sauce, 162; Beverage
TUES.	Applesauce, 25; Poached Egg, 36; Quick Swedish Tea Ring, 283; Milk; Coffee, 33	Tomato Juice; Kebabs, 292; Roasted Sweet Corn, 293; Sliced Cucumber; Lemon Wedges; Assorted Fresh Fruit; Sugar Cooky, 185; Beverage	Cold Sliced Ham; Vegetable Salad, 140; Rye Bread and Butter; Baked Apple, 26; Iced Chocolate, 203
WED.	Sliced Oranges; Shirred Eggs, 37; Fried Leftover Ham; Toasted Cinnamon Rolls; Beverage	Fruit Cup, 146; Corned Beef Hash, 282; Sweet Carrots, 120; Sliced Tomatoes; Bread; Butter; Nut Fruit Pudding, 284; Milk	Cornbread Shortcake, 283; Celery; Olives; Watermelon; Cookies; Milk
THURS.	Stewed Prunes, 29; Scrambled Eggs, 37; Toast; Jelly; Milk; Coffee, 33	Pineapple Juice; Beef and Kidney Stew with Dumplings, 280; Green Peas; Celery and Scallions; Rolls; Crisscross Cherry Pie, 167; Milk	Split Pea Soup (hambone), 280; Vegetable Medley Salad with Tomatoes, 141; Rye Bread and Butter; Gingerbread, 176; Beverage

SPLIT PEA OR LIMA SOUP

1 pound or 4 cups split peas, or dried lima beans
1 smoked ham bone or bone from boiled or baked ham, or 1 can corned beef
5 quarts water
2 cloves garlic, minced, or 2 onions, minced
2 teaspoons salt
¼ teaspoon pepper
rye bread or pumpernickel

Makes about 12 portions.

Cover peas or beans with cold water. Soak several hours or overnight. Drain. Place in large kettle. Add bone or corned beef, water, garlic, salt and pepper. Bring to a boil and boil 10 minutes, removing any scum which may collect. Then cover and simmer 4 hours, stirring occasionally.

Remove bone and season with additional salt and pepper to taste. Turn into hot soup plates and serve with rye bread.

BEEF AND KIDNEY STEW WITH DUMPLINGS

3 beef kidneys
2 onions, chopped
4 tablespoons chopped suet
4 pounds stewing meat (chuck, flank, heel or round), cut in pieces for serving
3 quarts boiling water
3 teaspoons salt
½ teaspoon pepper
¾ cup flour
1½ cups cold water
2 recipes Dumplings (*below*)

Makes 12 portions.

Remove fat from kidneys, split in halves and cut out tubes. Wash and soak in cold salted water about ½ hour. Then drain and cut in pieces.

Sauté onions in suet in Dutch oven or large kettle until lightly browned. Remove onion. Then sauté meat in fat about 20 minutes, or until browned, turning frequently. Add hot water, kidneys, and browned onions. Simmer, covered, about 1 ½ hours, or until tender, adding seasonings ½ hour before meat is done.

Make a smooth paste of flour and water. Add slowly to hot stew, stirring constantly until thickened.

Make dumpling dough. Drop by small spoonfuls on top of meat, using a rubber scraper to empty spoon. Do not pile on top of each other or on liquid. Cook for 10 minutes uncovered. Cover tightly and cook 10 minutes longer. Serve at once.

DUMPLINGS FOR STEW

2 cups sifted flour
4 teaspoons double-action baking
   powder
1 teaspoon salt
1 tablespoon shortening
1 cup milk

Makes 12 dumplings, or 6 portions.

Mix and sift dry ingredients. Cut in fat. Stir in milk quickly to make a soft dough.

Drop by spoonfuls on top of meat or vegetables and cook uncovered 10 minutes. Cover tightly and cook 10 minutes longer. Serve at once.

STEAMED DUMPLING

Use only enough milk to make dough like baking powder biscuits. Pat, roll and cut with biscuit cutter. Arrange close together on buttered steamer or plate. Cover tightly and cook over rapidly boiling water, about 12 minutes. Serve at once.

SALMON ROLY-POLY

2 pounds fresh salmon, or 2 cans
   (No. 1) salmon
6 cups soft bread crumbs
1 cup warm water
1 cup milk
2 medium-sized onions, minced
2 tablespoons butter
4 tomatoes, chopped
1 ¼ teaspoons salt
⅛ teaspoon pepper
1 ½ teaspoons chili powder
1 recipe Baking Powder Biscuits
   (*page* 66) or biscuit ready-mix
1 egg, slightly beaten
Tomato Sauce (*page* 111)

Makes about 6 portions.

Cook fresh salmon 8 minutes in boiling salted water. Drain. Bone and flake fish. Mix bread, water and milk.

Sauté onion in butter until lightly browned. Add tomatoes, seasonings and bread mixture. Cook and stir 5 minutes.

Make biscuit dough. Roll out thin. Place half of bread mixture in center. Pile salmon on top and cover with remaining bread mixture. Fold dough over all, moisten edges with water and seal completely.

Place roll, seam down, in greased pan. Cut gashes in top and brush with egg.

Bake in 375° F. (moderate) oven for 40 to 50 minutes. Serve hot with sauce.

HUNGARIAN GOULASH

2 pounds lean beef: top round or
   chuck, or lamb, chuck
1 large onion, chopped
1 clove garlic, minced
¼ cup butter
2 large green peppers, minced
1 can (No. 2) tomatoes
1 teaspoon salt
1 teaspoon paprika
3 peppercorns
4 medium-sized potatoes
boiling water

Makes about 6 portions.

Wipe meat, trim and cut in cubes. Sauté onion and garlic in butter about 5 minutes, or until lightly browned, stirring well. Remove onion and garlic, then sauté meat about 10 minutes, or until browned, turning frequently. Add browned onion and garlic, green peppers, tomatoes and seasonings. Bring to a boil and simmer, covered, about 1 hour, or until almost tender.
Pare and cube potatoes and add to meat. Add hot water to almost cover them. Heat to boiling, then cover and cook slowly about 20 minutes, or until potatoes are soft. Turn into hot dish and serve hot.

CORNED BEEF HASH

3 cups chopped, cooked corned
   beef, or 2 cans (12 oz. each)
6 cups finely chopped or mashed,
   cooked potatoes
½ cup chopped onion
1 green pepper, finely chopped
⅔ cup stock, or rich milk
salt and pepper
4 tablespoons butter
parsley

Makes about 12 portions.

Prepare beef and vegetable, and mix well with stock or milk. Season to taste with salt and pepper.
Melt butter in heavy frying pan. Spread hash mixture evenly over bottom Cook over low heat until browned on bottom.
Fold over as for omelet. Put on hot platter and garnish with parsley. Serve with Devil Sauce (*page* 111), if desired.
NOTE: Reconstituted dehydrated potatoes may be used in place of fresh potatoes. See package for directions.

CONSOMMÉ POTATOES

5 medium-sized potatoes, pared
   and sliced thin
salt   pepper
1 can concentrated consommé

Makes about 4 portions.

For 12, make three times the recipe

Arrange potatoes in layers in buttered 1 ½-quart casserole, sprinkling salt and pepper lightly between layers. Pour consommé over top and bake in 350° F. (moderate) oven for 45 to 60 minutes. Serve hot or serve cold with meats in place of potato salad.

CORNBREAD SHORTCAKE

1 recipe Cornbread (*page* 65) **or** cornbread ready-mix
2 cups **Medium White Sauce** (*page* 109)
2 cups diced, cooked veal or chicken, or flaked tuna fish; or 2 cups cooked vegetable
6 tablespoons butter
pimiento or stuffed olives, sliced

Makes 6 portions.

Make cornbread. Bake in greased 8 × 12-inch pan.

Make white sauce. Add meat or fish and heat thoroughly. Season with additional salt and pepper if desired.

Cut hot cornbread in 4-inch squares and spread with butter. Put creamed meat or fish between pieces and on top of cornbread. Garnish with strips of pimiento or olive slices.

CREAMED FRIZZLED BEEF

4 ounces dried beef, shredded
4 tablespoons butter
4 tablespoons flour   2 cups milk
hot toast, buttered, or hot baked potatoes

Makes 4 to 6 portions.

Sauté beef in butter 5 minutes, or until edges curl. Then stir in flour and add milk slowly, stirring until mixture boils and thickens. Cook 3 minutes longer.

Serve on hot toast or with baked potatoes.

QUICK SWEDISH TEA RING

2 cups prepared biscuit mix
water or milk
$\frac{1}{3}$ cup butter, softened
$\frac{1}{4}$ cup firmly packed brown sugar
1 teaspoon cinnamon
$\frac{1}{2}$ cup currants, seedless raisins, chopped dates, or nuts

Makes about 12 slices.

Prepare biscuit dough, adding water or milk as directed on package.

Roll dough $\frac{1}{3}$ inch thick and spread with butter. Sprinkle with mixture of brown sugar, cinnamon, fruit or nuts. Roll lengthwise as for jelly roll, place on greased baking sheet and join ends to form ring.

With scissors cut $\frac{3}{4}$-inch slices almost to center, turning each slice over on flat side to show filling.

Bake in 425° F. oven about 25 minutes, or until browned.

NUT FRUIT PUDDING

3 cups fine, soft bread crumbs
2 cups chopped pecans or black
  walnuts
2 cups seedless raisins
4 medium-sized cooking apples
2 cups sugar
1 teaspoon cinnamon
1 teaspoon grated orange rind
1 cup milk
4 eggs, slightly beaten

Makes about 12 portions.

Crumble soft bread between hands into bowl. Add nuts and raisins, and mix well. Pare, quarter and core apples, then chop very fine. Stir in sugar, cinnamon and orange rind, and add to bread mixture. Beat eggs slightly, add milk. Stir into bread-apple mixture.

Turn into greased top part of double boiler and steam over boiling water 2 hours. Serve hot with any desired sauce.

CHILI CON CARNE

¼ cup finely chopped suet
1 large onion, minced
1 clove garlic, minced
1 green pepper, chopped
2 pounds round steak, ground
1 tablespoon chili powder
1 teaspoon salt
2 cups canned tomatoes or juice
2 cups canned red kidney beans,
  Mexican chili beans, or lima
  beans

Makes about 8 portions.

Try out suet in frying pan. Add onion, garlic and green pepper, and sauté slowly 10 minutes, stirring frequently. Remove vegetables.

Sauté meat in suet about 15 minutes, or until well browned, stirring frequently. Stir in chili powder, salt, and sautéed vegetables. Add tomatoes, bring to a boil, and simmer, covered, 1 hour.

Add beans and simmer 20 minutes, adding hot water, if mixture seems dry.

PRUNE OR FRUIT WHIP

¼ pound prunes, stewed (*page* 29),
  or 1½ cups fresh or cooked fruit
  pulp
2 egg whites
⅛ teaspoon salt
1 tablespoon lemon juice
¼ cup sugar

Makes about 4 portions.

Drain stewed prunes. Stone.

Beat egg whites until foamy. Add salt and lemon juice, and beat until stiff. Beat in sugar gradually. Add prunes and continue beating until they are broken up. Chill. Pile in sherbet dishes.

Making Outdoor Cooking Your Hobby

Almost everyone likes to cook and eat out-of-doors some of the time. It's informal, everyone pitches in to help and appetites are enormous—or so it seems to the cook-planner. But even if you are a novice cook, you will find that you can plan meals for outdoor enjoyment. Generally, such meals fall into one of the following classes:

The picnic in home garden, seashore or mountains, its only qualification being that it be eaten in the open. This may be as simple as the sandwich, fruit and cooky pack which hikers, hunters and fishermen carry in knapsacks or pockets, or the informal snack-type refreshment served after a swim or when gardening is finished. Or it may be a meal to which you will carry all or most of the food prepared. The family's lunch container can be used to advantage when this is the choice. It will store the "tools" for eating as well as the meal—salad, cold cuts, bread and butter, thermos and fruits—or whatever you may take. All you have to do is to lay out your "spread" when you arrive at your destination. There is another type of picnic meal which is gaining in importance—the outdoor meal at which you will do all or part of the cooking on the spot—at a park or roadside stop where grill and running water are available. And, of course, the picnic is a great favorite for home entertaining—in patio or garden when sandwich, casserole or grilled delicacy is to be featured.

The Barbecued Meal is known in many parts of the country as the charcoal way of cooking because it features use of red-hot coals for cooking fuel. Barbecuing may be done over a simple grill laid over a rock clearance in the garden or camping spot; in a fireplace grill; or on a rotisserie. Rotisseries may be used in or out-of-doors to tempt you to barbecue all around the calendar.

The Smoke-Cooked Meal is usually considered to be one aspect of barbecued cookery because it is done over an open fire. Smoke-cooking is particularly effective if tunneling heat is developed and hickory, bay or green apple sticks are used for fuel, whereas real barbecuing depends upon a charcoal bed for heat. (You can simulate smoked flavor by sprinkling meats with hickory salt, smoke salt or liquid smoke during cooking.)

Whatever your choice for your outdoor cookery, be sure to know local fire ordinances and have a fire permit if required. In the section on hunting and fishing, *page* 295, directions for building several types of fires and putting out fires, also some menu suggestions are listed.

Equipment Needs. For the simplest jaunt you will need: a large basket to carry food, paper plates, cups, spoons, forks, a paper or plastic table-cloth, foil to keep salad perishables fresh and perhaps cooking tools. If the basket is a special picnic basket, all the better, for then it will be lined to keep out dust, sand and moisture. A roll of paper towels will be useful for clean-up.

Your actual cooking tools should include: a heavy frying pan, preferably iron or stainless steel, a folding wire toaster, non-rusting square skewers with sharp points, a long wooden-handled spoon, fork, sharp knife. Steak tongs are convenient for handling roasted potatoes, hot logs and coals, as well as meat. A water pail to carry water is often essential. Canvas collapsible ones are cheap. If you are not sure of the water's source, add purifying tablets according to the directions on the label. Whenever possible carry a jug of water or juice from home. Keep it cold in a commercial container or an insulated cardboard container which costs very little.

Some kind of grill is necessary—a simple homemade one without legs which stretches between two logs or stones, or a portable commercial grill with legs. Some grills made for stony or uneven ground have legs that lock in place. Charcoal grills come in all shapes and sizes.

Menus Easy to Manage. Keep outdoor meals simple. Don't try to cook too many dishes so that you can save plenty of grill space for meat—if you want to have best results. Vegetables, with the exception of corn and potatoes, cool very quickly out-of-doors. For the occasional meal (when you are not camping for several days consecutively) plan to serve your vegetables in salad form—the raw crunchy ones are particularly flavorsome and welcome. A hot soup or beverage, toasted bread and a simple dessert or fruit and crackers and cheese will prove ample fare indeed.

Throughout the book you will find recipes that are easy to prepare and tasty for your outdoor cooking. Some of our favorites are: Hamburgers, *page* 293; Spareribs, *page* 293; Bacon and Eggs, *page* 36; Hashed Browned Potatoes, *page* 123; Griddlecakes, *page* 40; Pig in a Poke, *page* 301, Corned Beef Hash, *page* 282, Roasted Corn, *page* 293.

DO'S AND DON'TS OF OUTDOOR COOKING AND SERVING

1. Allow a charcoal bed of 2 to 3 inches for most grill cooking. An even deeper one is needed for meats that require slow broiling or roasting, such as pork.
2. Allow at least 45 minutes from starting time of fire before beginning to charcoal broil—the coals should be gray-red in color.
3. Plan some "pick-ups" for the waiting period—and let them be part of the meal. Our families like buttered French bread or thin-sliced rye bread and Swiss cheese slices with tomato juice, seasoned with lemon wedges; cabbage wedges with French dressing dunk; popcorn (have a large can of commercially prepared) and blended vegetable juice; hot soup (from the thermos) and an assortment of raw vegetables — cauliflour flowerets, celery and turnip sticks and radishes. Or your own favorites.
4. Choose thick steaks and chops for barbecuing—thin-cuts dry out and get crusty. Make hamburgers thick for the same reason and cook them in wire toaster propped on stones to avoid sticking.

5. Use a meat tenderizer to "condition" less tender cuts of meats, following directions on bottle.

6. Baste chicken, meats and fowl with Barbecue Sauce, *page* 265, to enrich flavor, but do not use it for *every* meat *every* time you do charcoal cooking. (However, it does keep fowl from drying out; also spareribs.)

7. Have some kind of a work table if possible, even when you plan to use trays for serving.

8. Be sure to serve hot foods hot and cold things cold for taste and health. (*See below.*)

9. Make outdoor cooking a cooperative effort—let everyone help.

When you cook the food at home, you may use to carry it anything from a fully equipped picnic hamper, with dishes, cutlery and thermal jars and jugs, to just the casseroles in which you have cooked it. However, an insulated container for hot or cold drinks is always desirable.

When you carry food or drink in thermal carriers, be sure to temper the containers to heat or cold each time before using them. Use ice cubes or water for chilling and keep the containers in the refrigerator while waiting. Hot water will temper them for hot food.

When you carry hot food in a casserole, wrap the casserole first in a number of thicknesses of newspaper, then in a blanket—and tuck it into a basket. The food will keep warm for a good while. Bowls of salad can be protected by oiled silk covers. (Avoid creamed and egg dishes for this type of carrying.)

Many picnickers carry a whole meal in a portable electric roaster or well cooker. The food stays hot while you get to the farthest picnic spot—a good three hours.

Ice cream can be kept firm several hours when packed with dry ice, or with ice and salt. In many cities dry ice can be purchased in small amounts from ice cream companies and caterers.

Gay paper plates and cups today are glazed and grease-resistant. If the paper cups are very thin, better use two—one inside the other—to hold hot liquids. Never bother to carry china or metal dishes if you have not the fitted bag or hamper. Sport shops carry firm handles into which you can slip paper forks and spoons.

Campfire cooking—"away from it all" but close to good food. (See menu suggestions on *pages* 287, 291.)

A picnic at home. Grilled spareribs (*pages* 293, 294), sliced potatoes and onions baked in foil, frozen green beans, toasted French bread—all cooked on the charcoal grill.

When you are afoot, wrap all your food in waxed paper, separately. Make sandwiches of good fillings that will not soak into the bread, nor wilt. Then wrap them in parchment. They can be put into a paper bag, or into a zipper food bag which later can be folded and tucked away in your pocket. Sport shops and household departments carry these very handy zipper bags.

If you are walking, and carrying a drink, use a bottle which you can later throw away, to lighten the burden when you're tired. It's sensible to carry water, or fruit or tomato juice, if you are not sure of water sources where you are to travel. *This holds true of every kind of picnic.* Don't trust springs, streams or even farmers' wells unless you are sure. A rubber, collapsible drinking cup is handy. A lemon, pickle, or tomato will quench the thirst. You can buy lemon powder or lime tablets with which to make refreshing drinks.

Seasoned picnickers and hikers who travel light still find room for a Scout-type saucepan in which to heat water over a small fire. They can then make hot bouillon with bouillon cubes, or hot chocolate with a cake of chocolate, water and a couple of marshmallows. A hot drink can help you over many a rough road. It makes all food taste better.

Need we add that there is a code which true picnickers observe? Leave the picnic site clean. Burn papers, and paper dishes and containers. Soak all ashes with water. Let no brush or forest fire be due to your carelessness. Carry rubbish that cannot be destroyed on the spot back home with you in a paper bag. Remember the next fellow.

For hikers—a collapsible drinking cup and thirst quenchers.

SUGGESTIONS FOR OUTDOOR MEALS

COOKING OUTDOORS

Well-Planned Picnic

Assorted Raw Vegetables, 136
Lamb en Brochette, 292
Potato Salad, 142   Pickles
Bread and Butter Sandwiches
Brownies, 185   Fruit
Hot Chocolate, 35

★

The Barbecue

Grilled Spareribs, 293
Roasted Corn, 293   Coleslaw, 140
Toasted English Muffins, 32
Fresh Fruit   Malted Milk, 205
Drop Cookies, 183

★

Cooked on a Stick or Fork

Frankfurters, 292   or Kebabs, 292
Toasted Buns   Celery
Broiled Canned Pineapple
Toasted Marshmallows
Popcorn   Blended Juice
Doughnuts, 187

JUST EATING OUT-OF-DOORS

Fourth of July Picnic

Veal Loaf, 88   Potato Chips, 123
Rolls   Cabbage and Pineapple Salad
Radishes   Scallions   Pickles
Chocolate Cake, 175   Watermelon
Hot Coffee, 33   Lemonade, 206

★

The Last Day of School

Assorted Raw Vegetables, 136
Tuna Fish Salad, 148
Brown Bread Sandwiches
Date-Nut Sandwiches   Olives
Ice Cream   Cookies
Iced Chocolate, 203

★

De Luxe Picnic

(Carried in electric roaster or thermal jugs)

Fried Chicken, 99
Browned Potatoes, 122   Succotash
Orange Bread Sandwiches, 69
Olives   Pickles
Fruit Salad, 146   Celery
Frosted Cup Cake, 179
Summer Punch, 207

KEBABS

1 (5-pound) leg of lamb, cut in
   1½-inch slices, then in cubes
6 small onions, sliced thick
2 garlic cloves, crushed
⅓ cup olive oil
⅓ cup tarragon vinegar
⅓ cup soy sauce
½ teaspoon ground pepper
2 teaspoons salt

Makes about 20 skewers or 10 average portions.

Arrange lamb cubes and onions in large, shallow pan. Mix remaining ingredients and pour over lamb and onions. Cover and store in refrigerator for at least 6 hours, preferably overnight.

When ready to use, string lamb cubes alternately with onion slices on long skewers.

Broil over coals or rotisserie 15 to 20 minutes or longer. Heat remaining sauce (left from marinating lamb and onions) and spoon over meat when ready to serve.

LAMB-HAM KEBABS

Follow recipe for Kebabs (*see above*), only add 2 slices baked or smoked ham, cut in 1½-inch squares, with lamb and onions.

LAMB EN BROCHETTE

1 pound lamb steak, ½ inch thick,
   cut in 1-inch squares
4 slices canned pineapple, each cut
   in 3 pieces
salt and pepper
smoke salt (optional)

Makes 4 portions.

Arrange, alternately, 4 pieces of meat and 3 of pineapple on each pointed green stick, long fork or skewer. Sprinkle with salt and pepper.

Cook over moderately hot wood coals, turning often to broil all sides. Serve with bread and butter sandwiches, buttered buns, or on toast, as desired.

GRILLED FRANKFURTERS

Impale frankfurter or wiener on green stick or spear. Cook over hot coals for 10 minutes or more, turning frequently. Spread with mustard or ketchup and serve on split and buttered long roll.

SAVORY CAMPFIRE HAMBURGS

1 ½ **pounds round or chuck steak,**
    ground
5 tablespoons butter
celery salt
pepper
Worcestershire sauce
10 tablespoons chopped onion

10 large buns or 20 slices bread,
    buttered

Makes 10 *small hamburgs or sandwiches.*

Shape ground meat into 10 small flat cakes. Sauté in butter in heavy frying pan. While cooking, sprinkle each cake generously with celery salt, pepper and Worcestershire sauce, then with 1 tablespoon chopped onion, pressing seasonings into cakes. Turn to brown both sides.

Serve one between buttered halves of large bun or slices of bread.

ROASTED CORN

On Spear—Remove husks and silk from each ear of corn. Cut off the stem-end to expose the pith of the cob, hollow out a little pith with knife, stick spear far into cob. Cook over hot coals for 15 to 20 minutes, turning frequently. Serve with butter, salt and pepper.

Broiled in Foil—Prepare corn as for kitchen cooking. Brush with butter or margarine and sprinkle with salt and pepper. Wrap each ear in foil. Grill over hot coals about 10 minutes. Serve in foil on each plate. Have salt and pepper and more butter on table.

GRILLED SPARERIBS

2 pounds spareribs, bones cracked
    across middle
salt and pepper
bay leaves

Makes 4 medium portions.

Wipe ribs and cut in serving size. Season with salt and pepper. Lay in wire toaster or on grate over bed of red-gray coals. Broil 45 to 60 minutes. During last 10 minutes of cooking, lay bay leaves on coal and allow its pungent fumes to permeate the meat.

SPARERIBS WITH BARBECUE SAUCE

Follow recipe for Grilled Spareribs (*see above*), only omit bay leaf. Let spareribs stand in a marinade made of ½ cup catsup, ¼ cup vinegar, 2 tablespoons brown sugar, ½ teaspoon salt and 1 teaspoon dry mustard. During broiling period, baste with heated sauce that is left.

FISH IN FOIL

For each serving allow:
1 fillet of sole or other flat fish
1 slice onion
½ bay leaf   1 tomato slice
1 slice lemon
salt and pepper

Makes 1 portion.

Lay fish in center of square of aluminum foil. Top with onion, bay leaf, tomato and lemon. Season with salt and pepper. Bring ends of foil together and make a "drug-store" wrap with double fold. Seal small ends to keep in moisture by folding in toward center of package. Cook on grill about 15 minutes. Turn foil package occasionally during cooking.

CLAM BAKE DINNER

Dig a pit and line it with flat stones; or build a well of stones on top of ground. Then make a hot hardwood fire in pit and keep it burning 4 hours or longer to heat stones. Rake out the smoking wood and put a thick layer of wet seaweeds over the ashes and hot stones. Lay clams, washed free from sand, on top with well-soaked roasting ears of corn (in husks), medium-sized sweet potatoes (wrapped in layers of large, wet leaves), and apples (wrapped first in parchment paper then in wet seaweed). Cover all tightly with a thick layer of seaweed and wet burlap so that no steam escapes. Let steam about 30 minutes. The shells open easily when clams are done. Uncover pit and put clams on individual plates; corn ears and sweet potatoes on large plate, and apples, kept hot in parchment paper, for dessert. Serve with salt, pepper and wedges of lemon, and 1 to 2 tablespoons melted butter in small cups, with one cup for each person. One peck of clams will make about 8 portions; or allow 1 quart per portion.

Fishing and Hunting

There is rest—and a thrill—after a long day's fishing or hunting, in stopping to cook part of the catch or bag before tramping home to a good night's sleep, well earned. Wood smoke in the air and wood smoke's flavor in good, hearty food make a combination hard to beat!

Tools. For a short combination fishing or hunting and cooking trip, a few necessary tools are: a sharp knife, small ax and shovel; a heavy frying pan and reflector oven (if you wish to bake or roast); a saucepan or kettle in which to boil water for the beverage and a water pail (the pail may be of canvas and collapsible); a long cooking fork, spoon and sharp knife; paper or metal plates; paper or enamel cups (aluminum and tin cups get hot and burn); a simple grill, if you wish, on which to rest frying pan and saucepan; matches; paper to start fire if wood is damp (optional but very handy.

Food Supplies. Food supplies will be determined by what you expect to catch or bag and what you wish to eat. They will probably include: some prepared flour for biscuits or flapjacks; a little bacon (bacon makes a good fish stuffing and supplies fat for basting game and greasing skillet); cocoa, or tea or coffee, dried milk; chocolate or candy bars for the sweet bite that camp appetites crave; fruit and raw carrots to munch; salt, pepper, other seasonings, sugar; and perhaps some dehydrated foods. (Dehydrated foods take about one-sixth of the space required for fresh or canned food of the same kind and do not need refrigeration.) Food should be carried in moisture-proof paraffined bags, made especially for the purpose, or in parchment paper with paper bags.

Fire Making

Before you start to build any fire know the fire regulations of the area and secure a fire permit if required. Clean the site thoroughly of dry moss, leaf mold, leaves or grass, or anything inflammable. Do not build the fire against a stump, and be sure that the fire cannot spread up along moss on a tree, or underground in roots or leaf mold.

Kindling and Fuel. Gather your kindling and fuel beforehand. Every part of the country offers its own tinder and fuel, from the grass of the prairies to the pine cones of the north woods.

Standing wood is better for fires than fallen wood. Wood from the ground is apt to be sodden. If you use a fallen tree, choose twigs that have not touched ground. Split wood burns better than round. Green wood burns best in the winter when the sap is down. In wet weather choose twigs from the lower part of a standing tree—and from the under part (though not from the ground) of a fallen tree. A dry squirrel's nest in a hollow limb is good tinder on a wet day.

Starting the Fire and Keeping It Going. A cooking fire should be small. There are a number of ways to start fires—but probably the best foundation is made of three sticks or twigs, about an inch in diameter. With a sharp knife whittle a point at one end of each stick. Then whittle shavings in it away from the point, all the way around and up a short distance. Do not, however, separate the shavings from the center of the stick. Now place each pointed end into the ground—and bring the other three ends together—as if you were making the framework of a wigwam. Place the other twigs, bark, and other tinder around this framework, leaving plenty of draft space. Set a match to the shavings at bottom and watch the flames climb. From then on just feed the fire sufficient wood. Always provide a draft.

Never leave a fire so long as a spark remains. Soak the ashes with water or cover them with damp earth—after every spark has died. Disastrous fires have been caused by careless campers.

The Quick Fire for Quick Cooking. The quick hot fire is made of soft wood. On a short stop it is fine for boiling water for a beverage, and then when the blaze has died down, it leaves ashes just right for frying food. You can either place a folding grill over the fire—or you can place stones around three sides of it—and lay a grill (a legless one) across. Another way is to place two green logs in V shape about the fire, enclosing it. The open space should be toward the wind if the wind is *not* too strong. Pans can rest on the logs and across the fire. Put the larger one at the wide end of the V, the smaller one at the pointed end. If the pans do not stand steadily, with your sharp ax level off the tops of the logs.

The Hardwood Fire for Glowing Coals. A hardwood fire is for longer, slower, roasting, steaming, baking and broiling. It will die down to glowing, roasting hot coals. It is used also for Clam Bakes (*page* 294) and for making Bean-Hole Beans (*page* 301) and for barbecuing.

Reflector Oven Baking. To operate a reflector oven successfully (American Colonial cooks used it to perfection in their kitchens before open fireplaces), a constant flaming fire—preferably hardwood fire—must be maintained. The flames should be as high as the oven and as wide. The oven is set about a foot from the fire, in front of it. To regulate the heat, move the oven back and forth, as you desire to lessen or to raise the temperature. The reflector operates best if there is a high back wall of green logs or stone behind the fire to throw the heat.

Care of Fish and Game

Fish spoils readily and care must be taken to keep it in excellent condition. Game is best when it has had time to hang and bleed.

Keep fish alive in the water in a perforated box. If you cannot do that, kill it immediately after catching. Keep it in the shade and do not let fish touch each other. It is a safe plan to clean the fish before placing it in your basket to carry home. In the basket, place moist ferns or leaves to cushion and cover the fish and keep them apart.

Game of all kinds should have entrails removed at once after the kill. This includes wild birds as well as animals. The skins and feathers are not immediately removed. After being cleaned, game should hang in a cool, shady place. To protect it from insects, hang netting about it. If game must be kept some time before cooking, rub the inside with salt, and add some charcoal as an extra precaution.

DRESSING THE CATCH

Scaling and Cleaning the Fish—Use a blunt or saw-tooth knife for scaling, hold it at an angle and scrape off scales with a swift movement, from tail to head. Turn fish to scale other side. Hold a large fish firmly by the head and a small one by the tail. Fins can be cut off or jerked out by the roots if an incision is first made around each. Smooth fish such as brook trout and mackerel are not scaled. Large fish are slit open from the throat to detach the gills, then down the belly. The gills are then drawn out with the entrails. Tail and head may be left on or cut off. Small fish are opened under the gills just enough to remove entrails. Wash fish under running water, if possible, to remove all slime and weeds. Remove black streak of blood along spine just before cooking, then wipe dry. Bake, broil, fry or boil.

Skinning the Fish—Place undrawn fish on side and make incisions along back fin and jerk it out, then cut down the entire length of the back. Slit skin just below head and around the tail. Beginning at head-end, pull skin downward and outward, loosening skin with fingers and dull knife so as not to tear the flesh. Skin other side. Usually bullheads are skinned, and often perch, pickerel and black bass.

Boning the Fish—Scale or skin, and clean a fish if baked whole. Place fish on side and slit it open to the tail. Begin at tail and with sharp knife cut and scrape the flesh close to the back-bone, at the same time raising the bone with thumb and finger. Turn and repeat on other side. Then lift out back-bone and remove small remaining bones with tweezers or a knife. If scaled, the boned fish can be stuffed and baked whole. For *fillets*, remove flesh on each side in long strip or in several pieces. Bake, broil, fry or boil.

BAKED FISH, ROMANY STYLE

Scale and clean fish but do not remove head or tail. Sprinkle inside with salt and pepper, and insert a strip of bacon. Cover completely with parchment paper, or heavy paper rubbed with bacon or other fat. Then wrap securely in layers of wet paper. Bury the prepared fish in a bed of hot coals and leave it for 15 to 25 minutes, according to size of fish. The outer papers become charred but the inner papers protect the fish.

FISH BAKED IN CLAY

Do not scale or clean fish. Rub soft clay over entire fish. When clay is set, repeated until fish is completely covered with a thick layer of clay. Mud can be used but is not so satisfactory. Leave clay-covered fish near fire for a short time, or until clay is dry, Then bury it in the bed of hot coals and ashes for ½ to 1 ½ hours, according to size of fish and hotness of the fire. Rake out and crack open. The skin adheres to the clay and the entrails are shriveled and easily removed; the flesh separates readily from the bones.

PLANKED FISH, INDIAN STYLE

Use a clean hardwood plank (hickory, oak, or other hardwood); or split a 2-foot-long slab of hardwood in half and use flat side. Board must be wider than the fish. Prop board on end in front of hot coals for 20 to 25 minutes. Scale and clean fish and cut off head. Split down back and remove backbone, if desired. Wipe dry and spread open. Brush both sides with bacon fat and sprinkle with salt and pepper. Tack fish, skin side down, on hot plank, and prop again in front of hot coals. Reverse ends of plank several times to brown evenly, brushing fish each time with bacon fat Allow 20 to 25 minutes, according to intensity of heat. Serve on hot plank with butter, potatoes baked in ashes, and tomato halves, plain or broiled on a stick.

DRESSING GAME FOR COOKING

Skinning, Cleaning and Cutting Up the Rabbit or Squirrel—There is a trick in removing the skin without covering the flesh with hair. You will evolve your own technique with practice. Perhaps a slit down the back, then a vigorous pull with both hands will remove most of the skin in a jiffy. When skinned, slit down the front to remove entrails; heart and liver may be separated and cooked as giblets (*page 99*). Wash inside and outside with acidulated water, using 1 tablespoon vinegar to each cup of water. Rinse and dry. Or wash, then soak in cold, salted water about 1 hour. Rinse and dry. To prepare young rabbits or squirrels for broiling, split down center back and spread open or divide in half. To cut up to fry or fricassee, disjoint legs, split down center back and through breast; cut each half in several pieces.

Picking, Cleaning and Cutting Up Wild Birds—Dry pick warm birds. Plunge cold birds into boiling hot water for 1 to 2 minutes, then remove and pick feathers. If picking is done on paper, the feathers can be rolled up and burned. Singe, draw, wash and cut up as for chicken (*page 95*).

BROILED YOUNG PHEASANT OR SQUIRREL

Pick, singe clean and split pheasant; or skin, clean and split squirrel. Rub with butter or bacon fat and sprinkle with salt and pepper. Place halves, skin side down, on well-greased reflector oven pan. Broil in front of hot fire (*page 297*) for 40 to 60 minutes, or until done, turning pan occasionally to broil meat evenly, and basting with fat to keep meat juicy. Slices of bacon may be put over meat when half done. (Dressing Game for Cooking, *see above*.)

POTATOES BAKED IN ASHES

Rub medium-sized potatoes with soft clay to cover lightly. When clay is set, roll potatoes in clay to cover completely, then dry near heat about 15 minutes. Or wrap clean potatoes securely in several layers of wet leaves, using poplar, maple, basswood or other large leaves. Bury in hot ashes or coals for 40 to 60 minutes. Rake out, break and remove clay covering, or remove leaves, and serve potatoes with butter. Potatoes may be completely buried in hot ashes and baked 30 to 40 minutes; they are likely to be charred on outside and underdone in center if baked too fast.

PIG IN A POKE

Wash and core out the centers of medium-sized potatoes. Put a small link pork sausage or half a frankfurter in each and and close ends with potato. Wrap in several layers of wet leaves and bake in hot ashes about 60 minutes.

RABBIT CASSEROLE

1 young rabbit (3½ lb.), cut in
  pieces
¾ cup flour
1 teaspoon salt
¼ teaspoon pepper
4 tablespoons bacon fat
½ cup hot water
4 tablespoons butter
1½ cups stock or cold water
½ cup cream
salt and pepper
1 tablespoon chopped parsley
2 teaspoons currant or tart jelly

Makes 3 to 4 portions; use 4 rabbits for 16 portions.

Cut up rabbit (*page* 300). Dry and roll pieces in seasoned flour.

Sauté in fat in fryer about 15 minutes, turning to brown all sides. Turn into casserole. Add water to drippings in pan and pour over rabbit.

Bake, covered, in 325° F. (slow) oven about 2 hours, or until tender. Serve from casserole.

Prepare Gravy (*page* 86) from butter, remaining seasoned flour, stock and cream. Season to taste and add parsley and jelly.

BEAN-HOLE BEANS

(See Clam Bake Dinner, *page* 294)

Prepare 2 or 3 times the recipe for Boston Baked Beans (*page* 120). Arrange soaked and cooked beans with other ingredients in large iron kettle with tightly fitting cover.

Place kettle, tightly covered, in hot, stone-lined, large pit, heated for 4 hours by keeping a fire burning in pit.

Rake stones up around kettle, then cover with dirt; no steam must escape. Leave for 6 to 8 hours or longer. Pit can be heated early in morning and beans put in before going out for the day. To open pit, remove dirt and stones and draw out kettle with tongs or hoe. *Serves* 20.

CORN ROASTS

Break off about 1 inch of end of roasting ear and pull out corn silk, then twist husk over open end and fasten. Soak in water about 10 minutes. Bury in hot ashes or coals for 20 to 30 minutes, depending on the heat of the fire.

SPIRAL BREAD ON STICK

Use a 2-foot sweet, green stick such as birch, maple or poplar. Peel and sharpen thicker end, then stick other end into ground, close to a hot bed of smokeless embers to heat thoroughly.

Prepare dough from prepared biscuit mix, following directions on package. Dough should be slightly stiffer than for rolling. Pat about ½ inch thick and cut in 2-inch strips. Remove heated stick, dust with flour and wind dough spirally on hot stick, pressing ends of dough down to hold fast. Thrust stick back into ground near hot coals and bake 12 to 15 minutes, turning stick occasionally to brown evenly. Several sticks can be placed around fire. Remove spiral as soon as done and spread inside with butter. *Two cups biscuit mix make about 8 spirals.*

CAMPFIRE BISCUITS OR CORNBREAD

(Reflector Oven Baking, *page 297*)

1 recipe Baking Powder Biscuits (*page 66*), **or 2 cups prepared biscuit mix; or**
1 recipe Cornbread (*page 65*)

Make biscuits from recipe or prepared biscuit mix; or make cornbread.

Bake in heated reflector oven, turning pan to bake evenly. Time for baking will depend on intensity of heat.

CORN PONE

2 cups cornmeal
1 teaspoon salt
boiling water
2 tablespoons fat, melted

Mix cornmeal and salt, and stir in hot water to make stiff dough. Add fat. Shape in cakes or rolls, 1 inch thick.

Bake on greased hot stones or frying pan, or in reflector oven (*page 297*) for 25 to 30 minutes, or until browned, turning occasionally.

When Special Diets
Are in Order

Appetite is capricious when one is not up to par. But it is true, also, that there is never a time when simple food, attractively served, is more appreciated.

And not the food alone is important. The service of it on tray or table should be attractive. The prettiest doily and napkin, the loveliest silver, the brightest dishes, and a flower, for good measure, all make a picture that helps along the indifferent appetite.

Special Orders. Of course, when a physician is called, he may prescribe a "liquid," "soft or semi-solid," or "light or convalescent" diet. He is not apt, however, to select each dish for you, nor will he tell you how to prepare the food. Foods are listed under the three diets.

SPECIAL DIET LIST

Liquid	*Soft or Semi-Soft*	*Light or Convalescent*
Milk and milk drinks	Liquid diet list	Liquid diet list
Malted milk	Broths with cereals	Soft diet list
Cocoa, chocolate	Refined cereals	Broiled tender beef, lamb
Café au Lait	Vegetable purées	Broiled fish
Coffee, tea	Crisp toast, crackers	Crisp bacon
Broths, beef tea	Milk toast	Roast chicken, beef
Clear soups	Eggs—soft-cooked	Meat or fish soufflés
Strained Cream soups	Scrambled eggs, omelets	Baked potatoes
Eggnog (fruit juices)	Custards, junket	Buttered vegetables
Ices, sherbets (strained)	Creamy rice	Creamed vegetables
Gruels with milk	Simple cream puddings	Fruit soufflés
Gruels with broth	Plain gelatin desserts	Fruits, stewed or baked
Strained fruit juices	Plain ice cream	Simple desserts
Carbonated beverages	Fruit pulps or purées	Sponge and plain cakes

MENU SUGGESTIONS FOR SPECIAL TRAYS

Soft or Semi-solid

Breakfast

Orange Juice
Cooked Cereal   Rich milk
Café au Lait, 34 or Milk

★

Dinner

Chicken Broth with Rice, 305
Poached Egg on Milk Toast, 36
Lemon Gelatin   Thin Cream
Tea, 34 or Cocoa, 35

★

Supper

Cream of Pea Soup, 52
Melba Toast   Butter
Custard Junket, 306
Pineapple Juice

Light

Breakfast

Stewed Prunes
Scrambled Eggs, 37   Buttered Toast
Coffee, 33 or Tea, 34   Milk

★

Dinner

Hot or Jellied Consommé, 80
Roast Beef (lean), 85
Baked Sweet Potato, 122
Vanilla Ice Cream, 159
Cranberry Juice

★

Supper

Chicken Soufflé, 61   Creamed Peas
Buttered Toast   Jelly
Baked Apple, 26   Cream
Iced Chocolate, 203

NOTE: With soft or light diet, serve about 1 cup of one of the following between meals and before retiring, if desired: hot or cold milk or cocoa, fruit juice, or eggnog with fruit juice.

Since one on a liquid diet is served five to seven times a day, and usually only one liquid at a time, no special menus for this type of diet are given. Make each serving refreshing; vary the liquids as much as possible. Remember that broths, beef tea and clear soups, while they have little food value, are stimulating and refreshing. Milk is always nourishing. Serve raw egg in milk, fruit drinks and broth.

Make breakfast in bed for the invalid or convalescent a tempting meal with a tray that holds attractive china, linen, silver and glassware. Perhaps a pot of steaming coffee could be put on the bedside table.

CHICKEN BROTH WITH CEREAL

1 fowl, 3 or 4 pounds
2 quarts water
1 teaspoon salt
cooked rice, barley or tapioca;
    alphabet macaroni or noodles

Makes about 1 quart broth.

Wash and cut up chicken. Cover with cold water and let stand ½ hour. Heat slowly to boiling, skim and simmer, covered, 3 hours or until tender, adding salt after 2 hours of cooking. Strain. Clear (*page* 79).

Serve broth clear or with cooked cereal, adding 1 to 2 tablespoons per serving.

BEEF TEA

½ pound lean round steak, free
    from fat: cut in small pieces,
    chop fine or grind
1 cup cold water
¼ teaspoon salt

Makes about ¾ cup beef tea.

Put prepared meat in fruit jar, add water, cover and let stand ½ hour.

Place jar on rack in pan of cold water. Heat slowly until water reaches 145° F. Keep water at this temperature 2 hours. Do not let temperature go up. Strain; chill.

When cold, remove hardened fat. Season and place jar in cold water, then heat water to 135° F. Serve hot.

CUSTARD JUNKET

½ **junket tablet, unflavored**
2 **teaspoons cold water**
1 **egg yolk**
2 **tablespoons brown sugar, or 1 ½**
   tablespoons granulated sugar
dash of salt   1 cup milk
¼ **teaspoon vanilla**
2 **tablespoons heavy cream,**
   whipped

Makes about 2 portions.

Dissolve crushed junket tablet in water. Beat egg yolk slightly. Stir in sugar, salt and milk. Heat over hot water until just warm (100° F.), stirring constantly. Add vanilla and stir in dissolved junket.

Pour into serving glasses and let stand in warm room until set; then chill quickly. Top with whipped cream.

PLAIN JUNKET

Make like Custard Junket, only omit egg. If flavored junket tablet, or junket powder in package form, is used, follow directions on package. Serve with fresh fruit, whipped cream or Custard Sauce (*page* 162).

INDEX